Policing and the Poetics of Everyday Life

POLICING

and the

POETICS

of

EVERYDAY LIFE

JONATHAN M. WENDER

University of Illinois Press
Urbana and Chicago

© 2008 by Jonathan M. Wender
All rights reserved
Manufactured in the United States of America
C 5 4 3 2 1

∞ This book is printed on acid-free paper.

Library of Congress Cataloging-in-Publication Data
Wender, Jonathan M.
Policing and the poetics of everyday life / Jonathan M. Wender.
p.   c.m.
Includes bibliographical references and index.
ISBN-13 978-0-252-03371-1 (cloth : alk. paper)
ISBN-10 0-252-03371-X (cloth : alk. paper)
1. Police. 2. Interpersonal relations—Philosophy.
3. Law enforcement—Philosophy. I. Title.
HV7921.W46   2008
363.2'301—dc22   2008021745

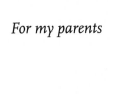

For my parents

CONTENTS

PREFACE

The reader may find it useful to know a few facts about my admittedly improbable background as a "philosopher-cop." Despite its nominal focus on the
interpretation of police-citizen encounters, this book is not an ethnographic
study of policing but an interdisciplinary work of social philosophy that happens to have been written by a fifteen-year police veteran. I served from 1990
to 2005 with the police department in a small, working-class city in the Pacific
Northwest, spending ten years as a police officer and five years as a sergeant.
Except for a two-year stint as my department's training coordinator, I worked
on the street in patrol duty, including assignments as a patrol officer, gang
officer, field-training officer, acting patrol supervisor, and patrol sergeant. For
about half my career, I was also studying for my doctorate, which I earned
in 2004.

Many readers will imagine that a philosopher-cop must have been something
of a fish out of water during his police career; however, the reciprocal supposition may not occur to them that I now find myself no less of an anomaly in the
world of academic criminology and sociology. In fact, although self-consciously
philosophical thinking is rare in bureaucratic policing, it is equally uncommon
in the mainstream social sciences. I mention this not as autobiographical trivia,
but because I think it represents a telling manifestation of an elective affinity
that unites late modernity's predominant approaches to crime. Exploring this
affinity and its ontological foundations represents one of my key objectives in
writing this book. More generally, however, I hope to convince the reader that
the things that strike us as most distantly remote from each other are often
the most intimately connected.

ACKNOWLEDGMENTS

Throughout my police career, I repeatedly witnessed how the nature of human encounter is such that fleeting words and actions could have profound reverberative effects, of which I often would not learn until years after the fact, when someone recounted to me the catalytic influence of a moment on the street that I had long since forgotten. To hear that one has helped to change another human being's life for the better, even on the basis of a brief contact, is both humbling and astonishing, revealing as it does the boundless possibilities and responsibilities that make face-to-face encounters what they are. But it is one thing to have made a difference out of the mere happenstance performance of duty, and another to have done so by affirmatively going beyond the boundaries of its formal dictates. In recognizing their indubitable place in the latter category, it is with delight and enormous gratitude that I acknowledge the colleagues, teachers, friends, and family whose support and inspiration have contributed immeasurably to this book.

As the culmination of a project that began with my efforts as a student to explicate the revelatory power of beauty in everyday life, this book had its informal genesis in conversations and coursework with Ahmad Karimi-Hakkak and Eugene Vance. As teachers and mentors, their encouragement and criticism had an impact far beyond what they likely imagined at the time, when they patiently indulged my unfocused musings on philosophy, poetry, and aesthetics. During the twofold progression of my graduate school and police careers, and my struggle to make sense of their improbable confluence, it was my good fortune to receive guidance and inspiration from Bob Menzies, Tom Kemple, Steve Taubeneck, Ed Hundert, Rob Gordon, Steve Wexler, Jim Risser, Fred Dallmayr, and Richard Quinney. More recently, as this book took shape and moved toward completion, I greatly benefited from convivial and challenging dialogue with Phil Lewin, Gary Backhaus, Marc LaFountain, Fran Waksler, and other colleagues from the Society for Phenomenology and the Human Sciences. Among my colleagues in the world of criminology, special thanks are due to Bruce Arrigo, Keith Hayward, and Jeff Ferrell for their encouragement.

I am deeply grateful to Kerry P. Callahan, formerly of the University of Illinois Press, who, even after leaving UIP, continued to selflessly shepherd my manuscript through the revision process. Since Kerry's departure from UIP, I have been fortunate to work with Joan Catapano, Rebecca Crist, Angela Burton, and Rebecca Schreiber, whose patient reassurance and sage advice have greatly reduced the anxiety that comes with being a rookie author. I am further grateful for constructive suggestions from the two anonymous reviewers who read my manuscript. My sincere appreciation goes to Sheri Fabian for her superb technical job of formatting the manuscript, and even more so for her friendship and moral support.

Confidentiality precludes my naming the police department and community where I served, so I am obligated to thank in anonymity the many colleagues and supervisors whose camaraderie, encouragement, and friendship I will never forget. I am likewise deeply indebted to the people whose stories are recounted in these pages: I hope in at least some measure to have done them justice.

The aesthetic examples that appear in the book are indispensable. I am therefore beholden to the following institutions and publishers for kindly permitting the use of these copyrighted works:

Edouard Manet, *A Bar at the Folies-Bergère*, 1882. Oil on canvas, 96 x 130 cm. The Samuel Courtauld Trust, Courtauld Institute of Art Gallery, London. Reproduced by permission.

Paul Klee, *Senecio (Baldgreis)*, 1922, 181 (accession no. 1569). Oil on canvas, mounted on cardboard, original yellow-edged frame, 40.5 x 38 cm. Kunstmuseum Basel. Photo credit: Kunstmuseum Basel, Martin Bühler. Reproduced by permission.

"The Panther," from *The New Poems* (1907), by Rainer Maria Rilke, bilingual edition translated by Edward Snow. Translation copyright 1984 by Edward Snow. Reprinted by permission of North Point Press, a division of Farrar, Straus and Giroux, LLC.

"Notes Toward a Supreme Fiction," "Study of Two Pears," "The Poems of Our Climate," "A High Toned Old Christian Woman" copyright 1954 by Wallace Stevens and renewed 1982 by Holly Stevens. "An Ordinary Evening in New Haven" from *The Collected Poems of Wallace Stevens*, by Wallace Stevens, copyright 1954 by Wallace Stevens and renewed 1982 by Holly Stevens. Used by permission of Alfred A. Knopf, a division of Random House, Inc. United Kingdom rights by permission of Faber and Faber Ltd.

My parents, Stephen and Harriet Wender, my sister Regina, and my brother Andrew deserve the closing words of these acknowledgments: their unconditional love is a sustaining force.

INTRODUCTION

The Bureaucratic Paradox

The world and reason are not problematical. We may say, if we
wish, that they are mysterious, but their mystery defines them:
there can be no question of dispelling it by some "solution,"
it is on the hither side of all solutions.

—Maurice Merleau-Ponty,
Phenomenology of Perception, 1962

MOMENTS FROM THE STREET

- Police arrest two teenage brothers after an all-night spree of breaking into cars. When an officer telephones their mother to arrange for
her to pick them up at the police station, she tells him, "I'll take the
younger one, but I don't want the older one back."
- A domestic violence suspect, who has just severely beaten his girlfriend, exclaims to the arresting officer, "I don't understand, I just
kept hitting the bitch, and hitting her, but she wouldn't die!"
- Police respond after someone fires a shotgun at close range through
the living room window of a house, barely missing a young man sitting on the sofa watching television. The man refuses to cooperate
with officers; and his mother is threatened with arrest when she tries
to keep them from entering her house to investigate the shooting.
- A woman calls police after her nine-year-old son throws a tantrum
and smashes several holes in her bedroom door with a hammer.
- At the scene of a sudden infant death, the father finally succeeds in

convincing his grief-stricken wife to hand him the body of their son. The man takes the dead baby and gives him to officers and an investigator from the medical examiner's office. "Take care of my son," says the man. At the same moment, a call is dispatched for an ambulance to respond to an imminent childbirth.

- After invoking his right to silence and declining to be interviewed, a man arrested for selling crack cocaine engages an officer in a casual conversation. "You're a cop, I'm a drug dealer," remarks the man. "You did your job better tonight than I did mine."

THE BUREAUCRATIC PARADOX

At root, modern police work involves armed bureaucrats encountering their fellow human beings in various states of crisis and predicament. These crises and predicaments range from relatively minor situations, such as petty thefts and noisy neighbors, to the overwhelming gravity of violently disintegrating relationships and unforeseen death. In the course of ordinary routine, police officers bear witness to life's transformative moments, as well as to the mundane woes that perennially irritate the human spirit, at times with such intensity that its passions spontaneously surge forth. The police spend their days conversing with people about everything from whether or not they still love their spouses, to why they have attempted suicide. So it is that the defining qualities of the human condition at its best and worst—love, hate, redemption, betrayal, jealousy, revenge, forgiveness, greed, sacrifice, hope—all unfold in the remarkable sequence of events that constitutes a patrol shift. To the bureaucratic eye, these events appear as specific problems with a determinate and univocal official significance. Imagined otherwise, they may be regarded as *moments of poetry*—lived creations of meaning in which human beings struggle to make sense of the mystery of their own existence, and the existence of others.

To describe police-citizen encounters as moments of poetry is to invoke an ontological notion of the poetic that both transcends and grounds its usual literary meaning. I call this notion ontological because it treats poetry first and foremost as an elemental aspect of human existence, of which poetic language in the ordinary sense of verse is only one particular manifestation. Applied within the specific context of policing, an ontological notion of the poetic offers a unique vantage point for locating the existential horizon within which this decidedly momentous form of social praxis occurs.

At first glance, it might seem altogether improbable, bizarre, or perhaps even ridiculous to juxtapose policing and poetry. The reader may indeed wonder with justifiable skepticism what could remotely be poetic about the mundane vicissitudes of street-level policing. To avoid any possible misunderstanding, let me stress from the outset that my approach has nothing whatsoever to do with sentimentalizing police-citizen encounters, or with aestheticizing the profound tragedies by which they are all too frequently occasioned. Quite the contrary, by engaging them as moments of lived poetry, and contextualizing them in relation to the ontological foundations of the human condition, police-citizen encounters cease to be reducible to abstract "problems" or "data" and challenge us to face the full depth and mystery of predicaments we might otherwise blithely regard as "solvable." I must also emphasize that my attempt to demonstrate the poetic structure of social praxis is not meant to hold forth poetry as a practical or ethical corrective for dealing with the sociopolitical limitations and defects of modern policing. Rather, by drawing on an ontological concept of the poetic to elucidate police-citizen encounters, my aim is to show how the existential stance of human beings is such that poetry, understood as the lived creation of meaning, is always already present even in the most ordinary moments of social praxis. Poetry as I treat it here is thus neither an ornament for softening the hard facade of modern bureaucracy nor a specific "method" of praxis or communication. Simply put, we cannot elect to choose or reject poetry: it is part of our very being.

To the extent that every intentional human activity involves the creation of meaning (*poiesis*), it constitutes a form of poetry.[1] The mere recognition of one's own presence—"here I am!"—is a poetic act. In making this claim, I am drawing especially on Martin Heidegger's essay, "Poetically Man Dwells" (1971). Pointing to its etymological origins in the Greek *poiesis* (making or creation), Heidegger argues that poetry in its literary form is only a subsidiary manifestation of the elemental form of poetry intrinsic to human existence (1971:214–15). For Heidegger, this elemental poetry creates the possibility and condition of dwelling, because it is only the human capacity to create meaning that makes "dwelling" what it actually is: a presence to oneself and others that is irreducible to the passive occupation of space (215). Poetry regarded in this way emerges as an inseparable dimension of all thinking and praxis. Every "moment" intentionally experienced *as such* is poetic in nature: it is created by a determination of significance that marks it off from the otherwise undifferentiated flow of time.[2] What applies to a fleeting moment applies to all intentional human activity. Accordingly, any kind of praxis—scientific, governmental, administrative, or otherwise—is apprehensible in its ontological structure as a form of poetic creation.

By applying this notion of the poetic to police-citizen encounters, my immediate aim in this book is to engage *policing as poetry*. My broader objective in undertaking this analysis is to bring the voice of the phenomenological tradition in philosophy and aesthetics to a topic that has traditionally been viewed almost exclusively as the province of mainstream social scientific and bureaucratic discourse. In doing so, I hope to occasion a moment of philosophical self-reflection among social scientific and bureaucratic practitioners, who might otherwise give little heed to the ontological presuppositions that animate their commonsense thought and actions. Such an engagement with the ontological foundations of everyday praxis helps make it possible to "imagine otherwise," and thereby create approaches to human predicaments that would view them in their primordial fullness, before they are reductively translated into "problems" or "data." I further hope that this book will illustrate how philosophical and aesthetic reflection, far from standing at a distant removed from the concerns of everyday life, is inseparable from them.

Police-citizen encounters give stark testimony to the often-tragic consequences of the modern, bureaucratic *problematization of human being*. Few other kinds of social interaction so vividly illustrate the disparity between the profundity of human predicaments and the shallowness of bureaucratic responses to them. To encounter someone as a "problem" depends on processes of reification and abstraction that efface human presence and translate it into an entity available for scientific analysis and methodical control. So it is that modernity's bold claim to have substituted "objectivity and neutrality" for avowedly moral praxis withers before the gaze of the troubled faces encountered by the police. Given the momentousness and intractability of the plights they face, the police are often ill equipped and ill suited to resolve or address them in any meaningful way. Rather, the police give transient palliation by way of bureaucratic resolutions imperfectly crafted through the reification of human beings and their predicaments into finite "problems." To do more would ultimately demand relinquishing their bureaucratic mandate. Police officers thus constantly find themselves acting within circumstances informed by what I call the "bureaucratic paradox." The bureaucratic paradox may be summarized as follows: though it is their official role as bureaucratic agents that first brings them into the presence of their fellow human beings, that role is precisely what often must be transcended in order truly to ameliorate the given predicaments at hand. Traced to its roots in the ontological structure of human encounter, the bureaucratic paradox is more than a political or ethical phenomenon emerging out of the inherently tragic exercise of juridical and administrative power (compare Weber, 1946:77–128, and Muir, 1977). Rather, it is a manifestation of the existential conditions that frame social praxis and determine the horizon within which such power is always exercised. As I will argue in these pages, the tragic politics of bureaucratic policing ultimately derives from a clash of ontologies that unfolds on the street.

LOCATING THE HORIZON OF BUREAUCRATIC PRAXIS

The preceding characterization of police work and the bureaucratic paradox derives from my professional experience in policing and my philosophical re-flections upon it. Although I have written this book in the hope that it might offer the reader something more than a poignant autobiography, I cannot deny that it is the outcome of the improbable personal situation of one whose interdisciplinary academic interests, which broadly center on phenomenologi-cal philosophy, happened to have developed in tandem with fifteen years of police service. Given my particular concern with the relation between ontol-ogy and everyday life, I continually saw in events on the street evidence of the inseparability of theory and practice. It became ever more apparent to me that the crises and predicaments to which I responded as a police officer were ul-timately manifestations of sociohistorical dynamics rooted in the ontological foundations of modernity.

In this unusual situation as a "philosopher-cop," I have consistently returned to a pair of reflections on the nature of street-level policing. The first is that police-citizen encounters, however else they become formally translated into bureaucratic problems, occur foremost and abidingly as the unfolding of on-tology in everyday life. As I have already suggested, this unfolding is a poetic process—a creation of meaning that may be described as "ontology in action." The second reflection is that insofar as it is structurally disengaged from the ontological foundations of police-citizen encounters, mainstream social scien-tific research on policing remains largely cut off from the profundity of what actually happens on the street. Even more consequentially, given the elective affinity that weds modern social science to bureaucracy, this disengagement both reflects and intensifies the growing isolation of administrative praxis from the vicissitudes of social life. Withal, the disengagement of modern bu-reaucracy and mainstream social science from the existential roots of human predicaments is traceable to their shared ontology.

One of the defining characteristics of this ontology is its meticulously cultivated attempt to eschew and disavow theoretical speculation, as if such an attempt were not itself inherently theoretical (see Nietzsche, 1974 and 1994). In mainstream social science, this approach is exemplified by the claimed reduction of theory to an instrument of experimental hypothesis—a necessary heuristic for empirical research, but something otherwise to be avoided as "impractical" (see Sherman, 2005). Little wonder, then, that in a field such as mainstream criminology, the role of philosophical reflection "has withered into veritable nonexistence" (Arrigo and Williams, 2006:2). This is not at all to say that criminology or any other branch of social science lacks a philosophical dimension. Far from it, in their shared naïve presumption to have disengaged from "impractical" philosophical speculation, mainstream social science and bureaucracy exemplify what Niklas Luhmann characterizes as the inability of modern society to admit the tautological and paradoxical nature of its self-descriptions (1990:127).

Given its inseparable relation to bureaucratic praxis, the case of criminology demands specific attention. The attempt to grapple with the crisis of philosophical self-reflection in criminology is not without precedent: for my purposes, the most significant such effort is Herman Bianchi's *Position and Subject Matter of Criminology* (1956).[3] Written as his doctoral dissertation, this book marks a little-known but crucial philosophical engagement with the theoretical foundations of criminology, strongly influenced by phenomenology and existentialism, and their related streams in philosophical anthropology. Far more renowned for his work on penal abolition and restorative justice, Bianchi is largely overlooked for his stark prediction of the intellectual future of criminology: "If criminology were to dispense with philosophical foundations it would cause its own euthanasia. Building up the general theory of criminology implies the fundamental critique and accurate examination of its concepts" (1956:4). Appealing to Bianchi's ideas as evidence of the contemporary relevance of philosophy for criminological inquiry may seem pointlessly impractical or anachronistic. Today, more than fifty years later, criminology has expanded into a massive enterprise that is intertwined with governance and social administration, to say nothing of the cultural, political, and psychological self-reflections of modernity. Yet, this burgeoning influence belies the scandalous reality that criminology's intellectual legitimacy is in a deepening state of crisis (compare Braithwaite, 2000:48). The same situation holds true in bureaucratic praxis, which is to be expected given its shared ontological foundations with mainstream social science. Like mainstream social science, bureaucracy is haunted by what Alasdair

MacIntyre calls "unrecognized theoretical ghosts" (1977:217), which are all the more powerful for their remaining unacknowledged and uncriticized.[4]

THE ZOLLIKON SEMINARS:
ONTOLOGY IN DIALOGUE WITH PRAXIS

Bianchi's philosophical critique of criminology assigns a decisive role to phenomenology in general, and to the work of Heidegger in particular. Bianchi was especially interested in Heidegger's philosophical anthropology and his closely related critiques of the disciplinary self-conceptions of psychology and psychiatry (1956:62).[5] Heidegger subsequently elaborated these critiques and discussed them directly with psychologists and psychiatrists in the forum of the Zollikon Seminars, which marked his most sustained effort to engage scientific and clinical practitioners in a philosophical dialogue about the ontological foundations of their work.

Each year from 1959 to 1969, Heidegger conducted a series of seminars with several dozen psychiatrists and psychotherapists in Zollikon, Switzerland, at the home of his close friend and colleague, Medard Boss. The Zollikon Seminars, as they came to be called, had their genesis in correspondence between Boss and Heidegger, which Boss initiated in 1947 as he labored to make sense of Heidegger's *Being and Time* (see Heidegger, 2001:xv–xxi). Trained and educated as a clinical psychiatrist, Boss struggled to comprehend Heidegger's radical critique of modern thinking about the nature of human being (*Dasein*).[6] For Heidegger, it is the theoretical notion of human being as abstract *subjectivity* that enables individual human beings to be approached as *objects* practically amenable to scientific, diagnostic, and therapeutic processes. Reading *Being and Time* and corresponding with Heidegger forced Boss to reflect on the grounding principles of modern scientific thinking and its allied forms of praxis, which together had long assumed the status of commonsense truth— seen as requiring methodological refinement, but otherwise regarded as the apodictic basis for understanding human beings and their actions.

The Zollikon Seminars centered on Heidegger's attempt to challenge clinical practitioners in psychology and psychiatry to systematically unveil and question the ontological foundations of their disciplines. In his introduction to the compiled seminar protocols, Boss observes how, for clinicians and scientists confronted with ways of thinking so utterly different from their own, Heidegger's questions and arguments generated confusion, if not even shock and outrage (Heidegger, 2001:xviii). Conversations at the seminars were frequently punctuated by long silences; and Boss even went so far as to compare a number of Heidegger's remarks to the attempt by a Martian visiting Earth to communicate with humans (Heidegger, 2001:xviii). Heidegger himself also grew frustrated at times, at one point opening a seminar by bluntly declaring the previous day's meeting to have been "rather a failure" (2001:17).

The conversational dynamics of the Zollikon Seminars, to say nothing of the substance of Heidegger's actual critiques, suggest the extent to which modern scientific praxis rests on a vast and complex foundation of ontological principles, the presence and influence of which its orthodox practitioners remain unaware, and any critique of which is met with the most strident skepticism and resistance (Heidegger, 2001:94). During one of the seminars, Heidegger minced no words in describing this situation: "science is dogmatic to an almost unbelievable degree everywhere, i.e., it operates with preconceptions and prejudices [which have] not been reflected upon. There is the highest need for doctors who *think* and who do not wish to leave the field entirely to scientific technicians" (2001:103, emphasis original).

It is with this admonition in mind that Heidegger and Boss jointly sought to challenge clinicians to reflect on the foundational ontology of modern psychiatric medical science, and to grasp how that ontology creates the very possibility of clinical praxis, by determining beforehand that human being is of such a nature that it can be "subjected" to scientific analysis and treatment (Heidegger, 2001:137–40).

Whatever the intellectual and emotional frustrations of the Zollikon Seminars for all participants, the seminars' longevity (abbreviated only by Heidegger's deteriorating health) and persistent striving for mutual understanding attest to the fruitfulness of the underlying project (Heidegger, 2001:xviii–xix). In keeping with this spirit of hopefulness that animated the Zollikon Seminars, I focus here on police-citizen encounters as an initial way of engaging bureaucratic practitioners and social scientists in a similar kind of dialogue on the ontological foundations of everyday praxis.

A PHENOMENOLOGICAL AESTHETICS OF ENCOUNTER

The underlying theory and approach of this book form the basis for a phenomenological aesthetics of encounter, which applies the kind of critical philosophical reflection exemplified in the Zollikon Seminars within a different (though intrinsically related) practical context. Using this interpretive framework, I juxtapose narrative summaries of police-citizen encounters, drawn from my professional experience in policing, with aesthetic representations of social encounter taken from a variety of artistic and literary genres, including paintings, novels, poetry, drama, and short stories. Out of this juxtaposition, I develop a phenomenological critique, which draws on the unique disclosive aspects of aesthetic experience to reveal some of what is effaced when human presence is reduced to the methodical encountering of a "problem." This critique, in turn, represents part of my wider interest in fostering the development of a *metacriminology* that would combine interpretive approaches from philosophy (especially phenomenology and hermeneutics), critical theory, and the humanities to create a counterpoise to the prevailing reductionism of mainstream social scientific research.[7]

In applying a phenomenological aesthetics to the interpretation of police-citizen encounters, I seek to engage aspects of human presence that elude the analytic logic and ken of bureaucratic praxis and mainstream social science. With this idea in mind, a phenomenological aesthetics of encounter may be understood as functioning prismatically, through a refraction of the seeming transparency of everyday social praxis into the constitutive elements of its ontological "spectrum." It derives from phenomenology an analytic perspective aimed at restoring to the apprehension of everyday moments their "original transcendence and strangeness" (Merleau-Ponty, 1964b:97). Just as the prismatic refraction of light reveals its otherwise unseen order, beauty, and harmony, correspondingly, what follows here is an attempt to look anew at episodes from everyday life in a way that might occasion similar astonishment.

In revealing their ontological foundations, the prismatic view of police-citizen encounters afforded by a phenomenological aesthetics of encounter enables them to be critically engaged as concrete instances of the *problematization of human being*. As I will argue below, the problematization of human being is the guiding ontological principle that informs bureaucratic and mainstream social scientific praxis. I trace its roots to the *distinction between intersubjectivity and co-presence,* which marks the divide between two radically diverging conceptions of the nature of human being. By *intersubjectivity,* I mean the uniquely modern conception of encounter as the meeting of atomistic "egos," or individual "subjects," who are understood to exist in a state of isolation from one another. The notion of *co-presence,* by contrast, regards the notion of the "subject" as historically contingent, rather than ontologically absolute, and seeks to engage the irreducible holism of human existence that perdures and transcends its hypostasization as "subjectivity," "a problem," and so forth. From the standpoint of such a phenomenological description of human being, "intersubjectivity" cannot be accepted on its own terms, as the supposed objective basis of encounter, but rather must be seen as the product of modernity's particular conception of human existence as "subjectivity." This conflict between the notions of human encounter as a moment of intersubjectivity, as opposed to a moment of co-presence, is the analytic focus of all that follows here.

By critically engaging this fundamental conflict, I seek to demonstrate how bureaucratic praxis in police-citizen encounters enacts an ontology of intersubjectivity, and to show how this ontology constitutes the basis for its elective affinity with social science, especially mainstream criminology. In bureaucracy and reductionist social science alike, the ontology of intersubjectivity provides the theoretical basis for the problematization of human being, which stands as the unacknowledged yet indispensable prerequisite for applying administrative and scientific technique to the analysis and organization of social action. Just as the social scientist abstracts "facts" and "data" from human circumstances conceived as "research problems," the police officer similarly reduces encounters with fellow human beings to particular "problems," in order to render them amenable to bureaucratic resolution. Crucially, the social scientist and police officer alike typically undertake their respective work with little or no recognition of the ontological presuppositions grounding their praxis. This crisis of reflection, brought about through an ingrained abdication of theory, as well as a deep faith in instrumental reason and its presumed objectivity and neutrality, compounds all other attempts to gauge the implications of bureaucratic and social scientific action.

At this point, the affinity between a phenomenological aesthetics of encounter and Heidegger's critique of praxis in the Zollikon Seminars should be fairly apparent: in both cases, praxis is understood as an enactment of ontology. This affinity has a further dimension: like the Zollikon Seminars, my approach of a phenomenological aesthetics of encounter is fundamentally distinct from most qualitative social scientific research. Rather than following the particular methodological tenets of such research, a phenomenological aesthetics of encounter seeks to bring an avowedly philosophical voice to criminological inquiry in order to show what such inquiry commonly takes for granted, even when it imagines itself to be proceeding in accordance with the highest degree of "rigor."[8] By "bracketing" the notion of method and suspending its commonsense self-conception, a phenomenological critique can effectively illuminate the fundamental relation of method to the existential context of everyday life.[9] With this notion in mind, I undertake a phenomenological analysis that treats method in terms of the concept of *approach*. From this standpoint, I argue that "method" in the human sciences and bureaucratic praxis alike essentially involves the *interpretation of proximity*. Following the implications of this argument, I frame the interpretive processes used in this book in terms of the idea of "approach," rather than "method." As the experience of the Zollikon Seminars suggests, an endeavor of this kind, which sets out to question the most elemental underpinnings of commonsense thought, will undoubtedly be regarded with skepticism by a number of readers, who are accustomed to more straightforward and pragmatic treatments of "method." That is a good thing; and, indeed, perhaps the relative worth of my argument might be gauged in some measure by the degree of discomfiture it arouses.

STRUCTURE AND ARRANGEMENT OF THE BOOK

I have arranged this book into two divisions. In the first division, I lay the theoretical and practical foundations for a phenomenological aesthetics of encounter. I begin chapter 1 with an abbreviated overview of phenomenology, which should be especially helpful for readers who have little or no familiarity with phenomenological philosophy. Following a discussion of the nature of modern bureaucratic praxis, I devote most of the chapter's remainder to an elaboration of the problematization of human being, and its relation to the pivotal distinction that I make between co-presence and intersubjectivity. In chapter 2, I critique some of the major sociological and criminological approaches that have already been taken to the study of police-citizen encounters. I am especially concerned in this discussion with showing how the praxis of bureaucratic policing stands in dialectical relation to academic research that makes policing the "object" of scientific analysis. Chapter 3 opens with a phenomenological critique of the traditional social scientific concept of "method," on the basis of which I justify my rethinking of method as a question of *approach*. From here, I turn my attention to elaborating the structure of a phenomenological aesthetics of encounter, including a brief consideration of the truth value of aesthetic experience.

In the second division, I apply a phenomenological aesthetics of encounter to the interpretation of representative episodes from each of five different types of police-citizen encounters. These include domestic violence, contacts with juveniles, drug-related situations, instances of mental and emotional crisis, and death. I discuss each type of encounter in a separate chapter (chapters 4–8) and pair it with a corresponding interpretation grounded in one of five aesthetic genres, including paintings, novels, poetry, drama, and short stories.

In the concluding chapter, I draw on a phenomenological aesthetics of encounter as a catalyst for rethinking the economy of response and responsibility in bureaucratic praxis, and thus for creating the incipient possibility of "imagining otherwise." If the reader comes away with even a slightly heightened capacity to do so, I shall have achieved at least some of what I have set out to accomplish.

DIVISION I

ONE

Approaching Human Beings as Problems

You see a sad, hard but determined gaze—an eye peers out,
like a lone explorer at the North Pole (perhaps so as not to peer
in? or peer back? . . .). Here there is snow, here life is silenced;
the last crows heard here are called "what for?," "in vain,"
"nada"—here nothing flourishes or grows any more. . . .

—Friedrich Nietzsche,
On the Genealogy of Morality, 1994

THE FACE OF THE ASCETIC IDEAL

A police officer who read Nietzsche's words might be forgiven for thinking that they were written to describe the hopeless gazes encountered every day on patrol duty. In fact, Nietzsche is describing modern varieties of the "ascetic ideal" and their nihilistic renunciation of purpose and meaning in human existence. Having stripped life of any inherent value, the modern ascetic ideal proceeds without a hint of irony to locate human dignity precisely in "this laboriously won *self-contempt*" (Nietzsche, 1994:122, emphasis in original).

The ready applicability of Nietzsche's description to the practical context of police-citizen encounters is indicative of something more fundamental than emotional appeal or stylistic felicity. Indeed, his words suggest how the speculative foundations of modernity play a determinative role in ordering the self-reflections of everyday life, no less than they inform philosophical reflections on the structure and meaning of history. Perhaps, then, in consideration of the notion that modern man's "*piercing* sensation of his nothingness" (Nietzsche, 1994:122, emphasis in original) is the creation of ontological reflections born of the ascetic ideal, it will seem neither strange nor farfetched that I would venture to approach police-citizen encounters as manifestations of the grounding ontological principles that inform the social praxis of modernity.

To acknowledge the inseparability of theory and praxis is to recognize that the *practical* ways in which bureaucratic institutions approach human beings as problems ultimately derive from the *theoretical* notion of human existence as *subjectivity*. The notion that human existence is properly comprehensible in terms of subjectivity realizes its practical implications in the conceptualization of encounters as moments of *intersubjectivity*, as opposed to what I call *co-presence*. Regarded as moments of intersubjectivity, human encounters are interpreted as discrete events of intersection between atomistic, isolated "subjects." By contrast, to understand encounters in terms of co-presence is to acknowledge that by virtue of the mode of their existence, human beings are always already meaningfully present to one another. It is the ontological notion of human beings as abstract "subjects" that enables their practical reification as "objects," which may be approached, analyzed, and manipulated in ways deemed effective for attaining the intended purposes of modern praxis. .

A BRIEF OVERVIEW OF PHENOMENOLOGY

I do not pretend that what follows in this section constitutes an adequate account of phenomenological philosophy. It is meant only to introduce readers who may have minimal familiarity with phenomenology to those of its ideas that bear most directly on my interpretive approach of a phenomenological aesthetics of encounter.[1] The overview should also be of interest to readers with a firmer grounding in phenomenology, who may find it of value in getting a clearer sense of where I situate the project of a phenomenological aesthetics of encounter within the phenomenological tradition at large.

An initial step toward understanding phenomenology may be taken by regarding phenomenological philosophy as a radical way of thinking that seeks to restore our awareness of the strangeness and mystery of seemingly uncomplicated thoughts and actions (see Merleau-Ponty, 1964b:92–98). The word "radical" should be construed here with respect to its etymological derivation, and considered accordingly as a returning to the roots of thought. For phenomenology, these roots mark the ontological interpenetration of human experience and the world in which it is situated. Phenomenology considers how any form of thought, prior to being consciously formalized into the particular tenets and axioms of a discipline or discourse, always already finds itself grounded in what phenomenologists call the "lifeworld" (*Lebenswelt*).[2] Taking this condition of thought as its irreducible and determinant horizon, phenomenology seeks to make explicit and thematic the constitutive principles of everyday life, principles that are ordinarily elided within experience and subsumed as unproblematic and pre-given. By disrupting our notion of the transparency of the ordinary, phenomenology effectively transforms unconsidered common sense into critical awareness.

Phenomenology is therefore most accurately regarded not as one more intellectual discipline or method among others, but rather as a more elemental attempt to reflect radically on the very possibility and origin of ideas such as "discipline" and "method." This difference between phenomenology's analytic focus and the focus of many of the internal self-critiques of science and other forms of praxis is one that frequently leads to confusion (see Heidegger, 1996:8–9, and Gadamer, 1989). As a way of thinking that seeks to understand human activity with continuous reference to the ontological nexus uniting thought and human being, phenomenology questions what the internal reflections of all disciplines apodictically presume as the basis for their particular kinds of thought and action (see Heidegger, 1982a:3 and 2001:131–32). This does not necessarily mean that phenomenology seeks to refute these apodictic assumptions and axioms; rather, phenomenological reflection aims at demonstrating the power of such grounding principles by illuminating their role as the unconsidered foundations upon which any given form of interpretation or praxis is contingent (see Merleau-Ponty, 1964b:97–98).

This process of reflection begins by taking up the task of interpreting the stance of human beings in their everyday existence within the "natural attitude" (Husserl, 1982:53–55), which remains all but completely disengaged from conscious or critical attention to its foundations:

"Daily practical living is naïve. It is immersion in the already-given world, whether it be experiencing, or thinking, or valuing, or acting. Meanwhile all those *productive intentional functions* of experiencing, because of which physical things are simply there, go on anonymously" (Husserl, 1960:152–53, emphasis added). By "productive intentional functions," Husserl means those processes of consciousness through which the world comes to be structured as meaningful. The term "intentional" refers to the fact that consciousness is always conscious *of* something. To think of a given entity, or to be conscious of it, involves the directing (intending) of the mind toward the object of its attention (Husserl, 1982:64). Intentionality provides a conceptual basis for understanding how all thought is necessarily directed to or "intended" toward a given entity.[3] Explained phenomenologically, the simplest act of paying attention to something, or heeding it, is a process that makes experience meaningful within consciousness. This suggests one of the decisive reasons why intentionality is inseparable from the poetic aspect of human existence.

That experience attains any significance or meaning whatsoever demonstrates the intentional qualities of the mind. This is not at all to argue that there is no substantive reality existing apart from human consciousness. Rather, to say, as Husserl does, that physical things are simply "there" because of the experiencing mind means that it is only the coexistence of world and consciousness that enables entities to exist *as things*, or even to be "there" at all.[4] The world could not be experienced as such without the intentional processes that constitute it in this way. This kind of theoretical attentiveness to the ontological conditions of understanding is manifestly remote from the preoccupations of everyday life; yet, precisely because these conditions pass unnoticed, they assert themselves all the more powerfully. Phenomenology will make this general claim in one form or another, whether in the context of metaphysics, history, or reflections on the nature of crime.

From a phenomenological standpoint, every kind of interpretation constitutes a mode of comportment toward that which has already been meaningfully experienced in the course of human existence. Here, phenomenology makes a decisive connection between the nature of understanding and the nature of human being. For phenomenology, human being is, as such, significant to itself. Simply put, we know that we exist. We continually ponder our existence, its potentialities, contingencies, and what we discover fairly early on will be its unavoidable terminus in death. Our own existence is also at the same time inextricably tied to the existence of others, whom we know intuitively and immediately to be in the same situation in which we find ourselves.

Human existence is of such a nature that it always has an awareness of its own "here and now" (Heidegger, 1996:10). The simple exclamation, "here I am!" illustrates the uncanny ability for ontological reflection, which distinguishes human being from the mode of existence of objects and things. A being that speaks its own name, engages the fact of its own existence, and the temporal presence of that existence, is *eo ipso* a being like no other. This is expressed in Heidegger's naming of human being as *Da-sein:* unlike the mode of being of other entities, human existence is not merely passive being

(*Sein*), but "there-being"—*Da* + *Sein*—being that always already finds itself meaningfully engaged with its own existence. Understood as *Da-sein*, human being is that kind of being who lives in and through the interpretation of its own self-awareness: "Da-sein always understands itself in terms of its existence, in terms of its possibility to be itself or not be itself. Da-sein has either chosen these possibilities itself, stumbled upon them, or in each instance already grown up in them" (Heidegger, 1996:10). The stance of human beings toward their own existence gives that existence a *momentous* quality, which comes about through the ascription of meaning and significance to the flow of time. To speak of a "moment" is only possible for a kind of being that engages the mystery of its own existence and locates that existence in time.

Given the self-interpreting mode of human existence, it follows for all phenomenological investigations that the analysis of human activity necessarily occurs as the "interpretation of interpretations" (see Zaner, 1978). Human being has a (self) defining *hermeneutic quality*—its ontic mode of existence is informed by its ontological stance of having always already *interpreted* itself and its world (see Heidegger, 1996:108–10). For phenomenology, this hermeneutic quality of human being is its decisive characteristic; indeed, *the approach proper to the phenomenological investigation of human being is hermeneutics* (Heidegger, 1996:33).

Heidegger's idea finds its best-known elaboration in the work of his student, Hans-Georg Gadamer. Gadamer's magnum opus, *Truth and Method* (1989), presents an extended critique on the possibility of valid interpretation in the human sciences (*Geisteswissenschaften*). Gadamer seeks to understand how the scientific concept of objectivity became the basis for judging the validity of interpretations of human action, and how that concept is irresolvably at odds with the hermeneutic structure of understanding. He argues: "Hence the human sciences are connected to modes of experience that lie outside science: with the experiences of philosophy, of art, and of history itself. These are all modes of experience in which a truth is communicated that cannot be verified by the methodological means proper to science" (1989:xxii). "Naïve faith in scientific method" (Gadamer, 1989:301) fuels the desire to apply the methodological structure of natural science to human beings in ways that are intended to find a ground of certainty beyond the effects of historical consciousness. As a corrective to this naïve faith, Gadamer posits the notion of *historically effected consciousness* (*wirkungsgeschictliches Bewußtsein*), which characterizes the hermeneutic nature of understanding as a participatory event. So conceived, the interpreting mind and what it seeks to understand are in a state of coexistence, whereby prejudgment is an inescapable condition of interpretation, not necessarily as a form of prejudice in its limited, pejorative connotation, but rather as an expression of the historicity of human being (Gadamer, 1989:301–11).

Like Heidegger before him, Gadamer shows that any epistemological investigation of the possibility of valid interpretation must begin by understanding the ontological conditions within which all human activity is grounded. Whether those conditions are expressed in terms such as Heidegger's notion of "being-in-the-world" (*in-der-Welt-sein*), Gadamer's "historically effected consciousness," or otherwise, such as Merleau-Ponty's idea of "incarnated spirit" (*esprit incarné*), phenomenology as a whole challenges the modern, post-Cartesian vision of the isolated ego or subject standing over against the world.[5] Accordingly, one of phenomenology's defining tasks is to restore attentiveness to the elemental primacy of lived experience, as opposed to the formalized, self-reflective experiences of the "subject," which, upon phenomenological investigation, emerges in its historical nature as the uniquely modern hypostatization of human existence.

In order to show what thought and action take for granted, phenomenology engages in a process of "bracketing," "parenthesizing," or suspension, which Husserl called the phenomenological *epoché*.[6] The *epoché* functions as a critical device that makes it possible to acknowledge the indubitable reality of a given phenomenon, while simultaneously making explicit all that we take for granted in the act of being conscious of it. For Husserl, the *epoché* is not a disaffirmation of reality but rather what he described (1982:58–59) as a *change in value*, by means of which reality is wholly *affirmed* through the explicit and thematic treatment of what is ordinarily taken for granted, without reflective or critical attention. Husserl cautions against conflating the *epoché* with the kind of methodological demands typical of positivism, which seek in vain to dispense with theoretical notions seen as undercutting the possibility of objective research (1982:62). The *epoché*, then, is "*a certain refraining from judgment which is compatible with the unshaken conviction of truth*" (Husserl, 1982:59–60, emphasis original).

What does the *epoché* offer in terms of an actual interpretive vantage point for the analysis of everyday social action and its underlying meanings? Applying the *epoché* as a means of reflecting on a given form of praxis, such as police-citizen encounters, involves suspending or "bracketing" the commonsense foundations of the bureaucratic comportment. This act of suspension does not necessarily entail the wholesale rejection of bureaucratic policing. At the same time, however, such a suspension reveals the contingency of bureaucratic praxis upon a set of ontological principles that would otherwise remain hidden from view. Functioning as it does, the *epoché* thus raises the possibility that a given form of praxis—here, policing—could be other than it is. Any phenomenologically oriented critique, including the present one, will argue that such reflection is a necessary prelude to practical reform and meaningful change.

A phenomenological critique of bureaucratic police praxis thus requires setting aside the "natural attitude" within which police-citizen encounters are understood as bureaucratic events, such that this attitude and all that it entails are *"put out of action"* (Husserl, 1982:61, italics original). Following Husserl's argument, this means we must now exclude from common sense what has been "placed in brackets." Under these circumstances, a phenomenological inquiry will ask, *"what if we suspend and thereby no longer take for granted the possibility that human beings can be encountered meaningfully and authentically as problems?"* By submitting bureaucratic praxis to the phenomenological *epoché*, the question of its nature emerges as one of articulating the nature and meaning of human presence.

THE NATURE OF MODERN BUREAUCRATIC PRAXIS

Critical analyses of modernity have long recognized the essential affinity between scientific and bureaucratic praxis, and their common derivation from an ontology that regards human beings as abstract "subjects" and calculable "objects." Over time, bureaucracy evolved in dialectical and reciprocal relation to social statistics and positivistic social science, a process exemplified forcefully by the ascendance of mainstream criminology and juridical administration.[7] With respect to the particular case of criminology, Russell Hogg (1998:150–51) observes: "[t]he entire history of modern criminological knowledge is unthinkable outside the institutional configurations of modern government—the production of statistics on a massive scale, the knowledge of individuals, particular social strata, urban habitats, and so on." Whatever its particular institutional setting, modern bureaucracy extends the logic of instrumental rationality, calculation, and science to the realm of social administration. Long before Foucault developed his genealogical analysis of the disciplinary production of various forms of the modern "subject," Marx, Nietzsche, Weber, the theorists of the Frankfurt School, and others had all, in varying ways, explored the epistemic nexus linking modern administration, social science, and the self-conception of modernity.[8] For my immediate purposes, Weber's careful study of bureaucracy in *Economy and Society* (esp. 1978:956–1005) provides the foundational analysis for interpreting the relation between bureaucratic praxis and broader social dynamics of rationalization and modernization.[9] I am especially interested in the congruence between the Weberian analysis of bureaucracy and the thought of Nietzsche and Foucault.

Weber argued that the theoretical reconceptualization and practical reconfiguration of modern society renders it amenable to scientific analysis, as well as to bureaucratic control: "The development of modern forms of organization in all fields is nothing less than identical with the development and continual spread of bureaucratic administration. . . . *The whole pattern of everyday life is cut to fit this framework*" (Weber, 1978:223, emphasis added). The administrative enactment of the theoretical principles of rationalization effectively creates a self-fulfilling prophecy, in which instrumental rationality claims vindication by continually transforming society in ways that make it ever more accessible as a domain for increasingly intricate and farther-reaching forms of control and manipulation.[10] Weber explained that the role of bureaucracy in the totalizing rationalization of society is accomplished by deploying the calculative power of science in the ordering of human affairs: "Bureaucratic administration means fundamentally *domination through knowledge*" (1978:225, emphasis added). By transforming scientific speculation into the practical grounds for social administration, bureaucracy reifies normative questions as abstract "problems," and reduces consciously ethical reasoning into scientific analysis that purports to evaluate social predicaments according to other than moral criteria.[11]

According to Weber, bureaucracy does this through the institutionalization of modes of praxis designed to function in an objective and calculable way, "without regard for persons," and according to the principle of *sine ira ac studio* (without anger or passion) (1978:975).[12] As such, says Weber, "[b]ureaucracy develops the more perfectly, the more it is 'dehumanized,' the more completely it succeeds in eliminating from official business love, hatred, and all purely personal, irrational, and emotional elements which escape calculation" (1978:975). Just as efficient exchange relations serve the predetermined ends of a rational, money-based market economy, it is the same with bureaucratic encounters, which serve a similar instrumental function by circumscribing ethico-political praxis as detached, calculable transactions aimed at the predictable enactment of administrative order. It is therefore no coincidence that the dehumanization intrinsic to the bureaucratic relationship essentially mirrors the abstract impersonality of the market relationship, which, as Weber describes it, is exclusively focused on the commodity and assiduously maintains that focus through a calculated exclusion of all intimacy, spontaneity, or regard for the other (1954:192 and 1978:975; see also Simmel, 1990).

The relation that Weber establishes between power and knowledge anticipates much of Foucault's thought, all the more so because of the common ground shared by Weber and Nietzsche. If Weber recognized the nexus between epistemology and politics, Foucault saw the ontological and creative dimensions of power, whether political, juridical, scientific, or otherwise: "Discipline 'makes' individuals; it is the specific technique of a power that regards individuals both as objects and as instruments of its exercise" (1977:170).[13]

Foucault's work provides a strong basis for incorporating a Weberian theory of bureaucracy within the broader framework of phenomenological critiques of human being as subjectivity. In particular, Foucault's historical genealogy of the subject and his critique of bio-power enable the Weberian analysis of modern bureaucracy to be contextualized in direct relation to phenomenological ontology.[14] Where Foucault formulates a genealogical critique of the discursive creation of the objects of praxis—what I would call a "poetics of power"—Heidegger and Merleau-Ponty (among others) offer ways of situating this poetics with respect to phenomenological investigations of the existential conditions of human being. In Merleau-Ponty's words (1974:95, 1951:50), "Every science secretes [*sècréte*] an ontology; every ontology anticipates a body of knowledge [*savoir*]" (compare Foucault, 1970:318–28). Merleau-Ponty's statement calls attention to the decisive poetic quality of scientific thinking and the practices it dialectically generates and perpetuates. Yet, the fateful limitation of social science—its structurally ingrained abnegation of ontology—rests on an attempt to disengage from this formula.

It will be apparent to anyone familiar with the work of Foucault, Merleau-Ponty, and kindred philosophers that when I speak of a "body of knowledge," I mean this in two distinct but ultimately inseparable ways. Here is a decisive point of confluence between Foucault and Heidegger—the notion of a body of knowledge theoretically and practically inseparable from the history of the human being as subject, and from all notions of what, for my purposes, may be identified in all respects as the "subject of criminology."

The role of policing in this context is particularly decisive, because it exemplifies the bureaucratic reaction to social crises engendered and perpetuated by modernity, which demand resolution (or at least control) through the imposition of administrative regulation needed to fill the vacuum left by the disappearance of an organic normative order (compare Habermas, 1975:130–43). With modernity's claimed disseverance of reason from morality, society imagines that it has ceased to function according to an avowed moral imperative (Bauman, 1990:29). Rather, orderliness and efficiency supplant ethical standards with what purport to be forms of objective, neutral praxis: "Modern society is a setting in which an orderly conduct of life is possible without recourse to the innate human capacity of moral regulation" (Bauman, 1990:29). In fact, this results in praxis that is not truly amoral so much as it is cryptically moral, as well as all the more inauthentic for its lack of a conscious grasp of its actual nature.

By way of a mundane example, the late modern police officer trying to resolve a dispute between feuding neighbors will commonly appeal less to a sense of mutual ethical recognition than to the presumed self-interest of the involved parties: "Look, you need to turn down your stereo, because your neighbor is entitled to some peace and quiet." The officer making this statement is not weighing competing moral claims; instead, he or she is merely regulating social relations between atomistic individuals, who often share nothing beyond a common faith in the pursuit of individual self-interest.[15] No one knows or even cares if the aggrieved neighbor *deserves* peace and quiet: it is simply the furtherance of social efficiency and order that dictates an *entitlement* to them.

Even in a situation as simple as the loud stereo complaint, the responding officer has effectively transformed an ethical dilemma into a bureaucratic problem, and thereby demonstrated an eminently practical knowledge of what Habermas means in arguing that late modern society is devoid of binding normative structures intersubjectively communicated (1975:131). Working in this environment, where the mandate of bureaucratic efficiency is often regarded as a sufficient end in itself, the officer abstracts a manageable problem out of a complex organic setting, and "handles the situation" by reducing the neighbors to fungible entities that become mere objects for the application of power. The preceding hypothetical episode further reveals the unacknowledged moral precepts of instrumental rational praxis, against the self-conceived notion that it does not have any: this is the presumption of neutrality and objectivity intrinsic to bureaucratic praxis and mainstream social science. If the mathematization of physical space enabled the rise of natural science, the same may be said to have occurred with "social space." In both cases, what Husserl calls the "superficialization of meaning" (*Sinnesveräusserlichung*) occurs in an acute and monumentally powerful way.[16]

THE PROBLEMATIZATION OF HUMAN BEING

Just as scientific investigation delimits the world in terms that render it theoretically comprehensible as a totality of analyzable objects, and thus practically available to experimental method and technology, bureaucracy depends upon an implicit belief in the possibility of problematizing human being. Placed in historical and philosophical context, this idea is altogether extraordinary, for it is assuredly neither natural nor intuitive to regard another person as "being a problem." To understand this state of affairs, we must ask how it happens that in the moment of encountering another human being, we might literally think of him or her as a problem. Addressing this question from a phenomenological standpoint requires considering how bureaucratic praxis enacts a specific ontological notion of what it means to exist in the presence of another human being. It is a notion that radically assigns determinative significance to the presence of the other, insofar as he or she may be bounded and reified as an isolable "problem." A crucial distinction emerges here between human presence regarded holistically, as opposed to its reductive isolation. That we are able to distinguish between the problematization of human being and the existentially greater presence of which it is a shadow or cipher indicates the reality that human presence is of such a nature that it always resists, eludes, and transcends attempts at its reification and abstraction.

According to Alfred Schutz (1962), encounters become coherent through the typification of what is already beforehand present to consciousness. In everyday experience, and prior to any processes of formal analysis, typification renders meaningful what Schutz (1962:75, 79) calls "prepredicative" thought. Language typifies the lifeworld, making the flow of experience significant by naming things, both in general as well as specific terms: this is a flower, that is a rose; this is a criminal, that is a burglar (Schutz, 1962:59–60 and 1970:116–22). Hence, with respect to human encounter, there is no possible mode of existence that would place us in the pure, undifferentiated presence of another person, or even ourselves.

Following the logic of instrumental rationality, modern bureaucratic praxis typifies human beings in ways that reduce to happenstance or outright irrelevance any aspects of their presence that exceed the specific criteria judged meaningful for the accomplishment of the given ends at hand. This suggests why Weber believed modern bureaucracy to be the most rational and predictable form of social administration, and thus the form of administration best suited for a capitalist civil society and its foundations in abstract market relations. For Weber (1954:193), the logic of market relations depends on a kind of "absolute depersonalization," which ensures their continued rationality. The extension of this logic to the entire range of possible social action carries with it this same spirit of depersonalization, along with all of its consequences. Drawing on Schutz (1962, 1971), it becomes possible to understand the problematization of human being as an instance of typification. Whether it occurs as the bureaucratic problematization of human being by the police or takes place in another context, "typification is essentially an abstracting of meaning from the *occasion of designation*" (Natanson, 1986:45, emphasis added). That is, how the flux of experience becomes delimited and interpreted is a function of the way in which one construes the "problem at hand."

The bureaucratic engagement of human presence as an isolable, abstract entity is fundamentally related to the ontological precepts guiding the scientific delimitation of the natural world. Heidegger's characterization of the underlying logic of modern science suggests what this entails: "Modern science's way of representing pursues and entraps nature as a calculable coherence of forces. Modern physics is not experimental physics because it applies apparatus to the questioning of nature. The reverse is true. Because physics, indeed already as pure theory, sets up nature to exhibit itself as a coherence of forces calculable in advance, it orders its experiments precisely for the purpose of asking whether and how nature reports itself when set up in this way" (1993:326).[17] Bureaucratic problematization follows the same practical logic, because it derives from the same grounding ontology. In experimental physical science and bureaucratic policing alike, praxis derives its operational approach not from the holistic presence of the respective "objects" of its manipulations, but rather from what that presence is pragmatically taken to be. Heidegger's argument in the preceding passage suggests how for modern science, what "really matters"—in the fullest sense of conflating the whole of existence with mathematized *corpo*reality—is only that which can be made available for being *put* or *placed* into *frameworks* amenable to scientific analysis. The effective manipulability of the world in the grasp of such praxis is powerfully reinforced by the fivefold repetition in the German text of differing forms of the verb *stellen,* which means to put, arrange, position, or place.

Social scientific and bureaucratic praxis extend the ontology of natural science to the realm of human being. As a result, human being becomes meaningfully "available" as an object of investigation, prediction, analysis, and control: "Contemporary psychology, sociology, and the 'behavioral sciences,' which manipulate man as if by remote control [*ferngesteuert*], belong to the Galilean-Newtonian conception of nature. The human being is also [understood as] a spatiotemporal point of mass in motion" (2001:154). The significance of the scientific objectification of human being becomes more apparent if we consider it in light of the German *Gegenstand,* which means "object" or "thing." In its literal expression of the relationship of "standing-against" (*Gegen + stand*), *Gegenstand* points to the grounding ontological premise central to objectification. Scientific method and its allied forms of praxis share a common faith in their ability to isolate and stand over-against the objects of their attention.

I have thus far repeatedly observed how scientific and bureaucratic praxis approach, encounter, and conceptualize human beings *as* one thing or another—as objects, problems, data, and so forth. My emphasis on the word "as" owes much to Heidegger's identification of its interrelated ontological and epistemological significance, with respect to which he explicates the "as-structure" (*Als-Struktur*) of understanding (1996:139).[18] The "as-structure" specific to the problematization of human being is the means by which it *translates* that being into a form that becomes *approachable* in a certain manner. From a phenomenological standpoint, the decisive element of any such act of "seeing-this-as-that" depends on there being a prior interpretive relation to the existential whole ("this"), which I then interpret "as that." Hence, understanding a fellow human being as a problem, or as an object, is only possible on the basis of typifying a more elemental or essential human presence.

The "as-structure" of bureaucratic policing represents the totality of the analytic and practical methods that purport to engage human beings "as problems," for which "solutions" may be enacted through appropriate instrumental-rational action. This demands that human presence be delimited and reduced to a fungible, manipulable object or thing. Berger and Luckmann's description of reification (*Verdinglichung*) offers a useful means of understanding this process of delimitation and reduction (Berger and Luckmann, 1966:89–92). Their analysis treats reification primarily as a "modality of man's objectification of the human world" (1966:89). At its extreme, when reification is enacted upon human presence itself, the result is a transformation of identity. In this way, the other person merely becomes for me *"nothing but"* that into which he is typified (Berger and Luckmann, 1966:91, italics original). Even more than this, in a manifestation of what Maurice Natanson (1986:64–66) calls the "doubling effect" of typification, the act of constructing oneself as an "outside observer" effectively walls off one's presence to the other person, thereby attenuating (or at least transforming) the nature of the encounter. This describes, of course, the detached clinical or bureaucratic stance (see Schutz and Luckmann, 1989:94–97).

THE HUMAN BEING AS SUBJECT

For modernity, the subject is held to be the indubitable and absolute foundation (*fundamentum inconcussum*) of human existence (see Heidegger, 2001:117). From the standpoint of modern thought, all of the particular qualities of human being—vitality, consciousness, rationality, and so forth—are regarded as predicates of an abstract entity defined as the "subject." This idea may be simplified by following Heidegger's comparison (1982a:125–29) of the ontological principle of human subjectivity to the grammatical and logical concepts of the subject. We know that in a sentence, the "subject" is that to which the predicate refers; it is that "about which" the predicates speak. The identity of the subject becomes a function of its predicates. Apart from the context of a particular sentence, the grammatical subject is devoid of meaning and content: it is merely the substratum of predication. Likewise, the human being as subject lacks any intrinsic ontological valence, and thus becomes the abstract, contentless substratum or "repository" of various predicates (Heidegger, 1982a:127 and 2001:117–18).

The problematization of human being represents only one particular configuration of subjectivity; examples of some of its other especially consequential instantiations include the *ego cogito* of Cartesianism, the self-interested "individual" of liberalism and political economy, the tabula rasa of Locke's empiricist epistemology, the Freudian ego, and so forth (compare Heidegger, 1996:19). Together, these examples represent an interrelated set of configurations of subjectivity, all of them defining moments in the development of modernity. In Heidegger's words, "[t]hat period we call modern . . . is defined by the fact that man becomes the center and measure of all beings. Man is the *subjectum*, that which lies at the bottom of all beings, that is, in modern terms, at the bottom of all objectification and representation" (1982b:28).[19] For Heidegger, the idea of human being as subjectivity reflects the fateful reification of consciousness as something objectively present to itself (1996). To understand Heidegger's point, it is necessary to note the traditional philosophical meaning of "subject" as "substratum." As I previously noted, this meaning endures in the grammatical and logical concepts of the "subject" as the topic of a sentence or syllogism.

Descartes located the indubitable substratum of human being in its existence as *res cogitans*—a "thinking thing"—and thereby effectively established the presence of consciousness as the reified object of its own attention: *cogito, ergo sum*. By virtue of their self-conception as "subjects," modern human beings reflexively stand over against themselves and the world. In this way, human being's consciousness of itself as subject becomes the object of its speculative reflections. As Heidegger explains this, "[t]he subjectivity of the subject is therefore synonymous with self-consciousness" (1982a:152, see also p. 157). The ego as thinking thing stands over against itself as subject to object; and its subjectivity lies precisely in its ability rationally to grasp its own "contents." Thus, in the modern age, the human being as subject becomes the object of its own forms of praxis and speculation.[20] Modernity reconfigures lived experience in all of its sociohistorical and existential modalities into "themes" and "problems" shaped by varying forms of subjectivity. The self-reflexive constitution of human existence as abstract subjectivity or "selfhood" becomes dialectically interrelated to the rationalization and reification of the lifeworld into "worldviews," "cultures," "institutions," and so forth (Habermas, 1984:157–85 and 212–42). In other words, whether at the personal, interpersonal, or world-historical level, the experience of modernity, or, more precisely, the consciousness of "being modern," is grounded in the experience of one's own existence and the existence of others as "subjectivity."

For modernity, following its Cartesian legacy, the thinking ego is subjectively given to itself as the factual object of its own consciousness. However, this leads to an ontologically grounded self-alienation and self-estrangement, because human being self-conceived as "subject" has already lost sight of its own constant, vital self-transcendence (compare Hegel, 1977). Human being is always more than it can say or predicate of itself, or than others can say predicate of it. Human being cannot be objectively present; its more authentic reality is its self-constancy (*Selbständigkeit*), on the basis of which it is reducible neither to substance nor to subject (Heidegger, 1996:281). It is nothing less than mystery (Marcel, 2001).

CO-PRESENCE VERSUS INTERSUBJECTIVITY

The corollary to modernity's view of individual human beings as "subjects" is the conception of encounters between "subjects" as moments of *intersubjectivity*. As I use it in this book, intersubjectivity describes any one of an array of reductionist notions of human interaction, all of which ultimately regard encounters as engagements between atomistic "subjects" or "egos." In radical contrast to intersubjectivity, I understand human encounters in terms of the idea of *co-presence*, which I argue offers the grounds for a more holistic approach to the actual existential foundations of interaction. A phenomenological interpretation of encounters rooted in the idea of co-presence thus enables critical attention to be focused on the very aspects of human presence that would otherwise remain ignored.

The heart of the distinction between intersubjectivity and co-presence rests on the principle that human presence is irreducibly different from the mode of presence of all other entities.[21] The "here" or "there" of a human being is never equivalent to the "here" or "there" of a rock, a tree, or a chair. This is because human presence *resists* all reduction to what Heidegger calls "thingliness" (*Dinglichkeit*) or objectivity (1996:43). Heidegger speaks of human existence as "Ek-sistence" or "ek-stasis"—a standing out or standing forth (*Hinaus-stehen*): "Since ancient times, inanimate things have been represented as being in space and time. But the human being exists in an entirely different way in space and time than things insofar as he, as a human being, is spatial and temporal *himself*. When I translate 'ek-sists' as 'standing out into,' I say this in opposition to Descartes and against his idea of a *res cogitans* [thinking thing] in the sense of immanence" (2001:218).[22] Things "are," but it is only humans who ultimately "exist" in the fullest sense of the word.

Whether the praxis in question is clinical medicine or bureaucratic policing, formal encounters in which human beings are approached and treated as "subjects" reduces interaction to a "concerned handling of objects" (Heidegger, 2001:215; see also Schutz, 1962:21). The kind of thinking that can transcend reification, and restore the keen attunement to what Richard Zaner calls "vivid presence" (1981:229), stands to benefit from phenomenological reflection that "brackets" the unquestioned foundations of praxis, and reveals what is taken for granted in the problematization of human being. As I have suggested here, at least part of what such reflection reveals is how the notion of intersubjectivity accepts *a priori* a conception of the subject or self as the definitive mode of human existence, such that the ego stands over against others, who exist as an "alter ego" (Natanson, 1970:31). By contrasting this attenuated conception of human encounter with the notion of co-presence, phenomenology suggests, however, that my interlocutor is not foremost and primordially present to me as another "subject."

GENERAL PHENOMENOLOGICAL REFLECTIONS
ON HUMAN ENCOUNTER

To "encounter" another human being has a range of nuanced definitions. The term varyingly means a face-to-face meeting, an unexpected or chance meeting, a meeting of momentary or fleeting duration, or an adversarial or hostile interaction. "Encounter" derives from the Latin *incontra,* a word combining the notions of "in" and "against." *Incontra* provides a glimpse of the ontological foundation of human co-presence in its uniting grammatically and semantically what is already united existentially in the lived actuality of encounters. As with the word *incontra* itself, being with another is always a unity of "in" and "against." To know that I am with another human being means recognizing that I am in the presence of another ("an other"), over against whose existence I grasp my own. To describe the meeting of two human beings as an "encounter," or to use the verb "encounter," thus brings to light the intuitive and fundamental understanding of co-presence as being in the presence of another, which is necessarily the *recognition* of the other as someone other than myself. The concept of "recognition" gives a further indication of the ontological foundations of human encounter, and of their immediate relevance for ordinary praxis. "Recognition" is just that—a "re-cognizing"—a thinking through again or acknowledging of that in the presence of which (or whom) I find myself. For the police officer, social scientist, or anyone else, recognizing another human presence is thus a particular interpretation or thematizing of what occurs within the existential horizon of co-presence.

The most fleeting encounter between two human beings unfolds with inestimable complexity, and by its nature eludes analytic containment. One human being stands before another, gazes meet, and voices are heard: most simply, a presence is felt and known. At its most essential level, then, any human encounter proceeds from the absolute awareness of an irreducible human presence (Schutz, 1971:24). Regardless of what I know or do not know in specific about the other person, and apart from our particular social relation, I am certain that what stands before me is another human being, with whom I am together present at a discrete point in time and space (Schutz, 1971:21–24).[23] I know that I am alive and self-aware, and know that the actuality of this situation is not equivalent to my consciousness of it: that is, as a human being, I have the uncanny ability to stand over against myself and the world, and to render meaningful my own existence as well as the existence of other people and entities (see Schutz, 1962:152 and 1997:102). Moreover, whenever I find myself in the presence of other people, I assume that they experience themselves and the world in the same way. Whatever significance my interlocutor or I may ascribe to the moment, in the intertwining of our reciprocal self-awareness, each of us accepts without conscious reflection that the other exists as he or she does: it is this indubitable fact in which all human encounters are grounded.

Schutz defines this awareness of a fellow human presence as the *Thou-orientation* (*Du-Einstellung*) (1971:24, 1997:163). He is careful to note that the Thou-orientation does not result from a specific evaluative judgment; instead, it is what he calls the "prepredicative" awareness of another human being *as such* (Schutz, 1971:24 and 1997:164). All other acts of interpretation and interaction proceed from this ontological basis of existential communion. It follows that any formal interpretation or ascription of meaning to specific human actions occurs within the historical situation of everyday life that forms our existential horizon. It is for this precise reason that the Thou-orientation is an ideal concept, which never actually occurs in "pure form," because we can only experience another human being in the particularity of specific circumstances (Schutz, 1971:24). Rather, actual experience occurs only from specific intentional stances.

In this lived reality of everyday experience, the participants are simultaneously both within and beyond the moment, speaking of it, and mindful of "being-here." To exist as a human being means constantly to interpret the moments of that existence, both consciously and unconsciously. This may be thought of as the *momentous quality of ordinary life:* to divide the passage of time into "moments" suggests the dual character of each event as both "momentary" and "momentous"—transitory, yet consequential. We interpret an event's significance, and in doing so, imbue it with ever-transforming meanings. This is the difference between mere sensation, which occurs in any sentient creature, and conscious experience: "no particular thought reaches through to the core of our thought in general, nor is any thought conceivable without another possible thought as a witness to it" (Merleau-Ponty, 1962:400).[24] As we continuously bear witness in this way to our own lived experiences, and in so doing perpetually interpret their meaning, we judge what seems most significant within the immediacy of a particular moment, according to the intent we have in mind. Our intended purpose determines how the flux of experience is made relevant (Schutz, 1970:111–12; see also 1962:3–5). This seems clear enough; yet, it still fails to explain the matter in full.

Social scientific and bureaucratic praxis, which may both be regarded as the manipulation of "social objects," depend on configuring the world into an ensemble of such objects. Schutz calls this process of configuration the "construction of objects by thought" (Schutz and Luckmann, 1989:231), and describes how it is achieved by taking one's existential "situation" and transforming it into a "problem" through the radical exclusion of anything that is judged irrelevant for achieving the pre-chosen end. The resulting decision of relevancy "determines the level of scientific research in the broadest sense, that is, the abstractions, generalizations, formalizations, idealizations, in short, the constructs required and admissible for solving the problem (*indeed even the conditions under which it can be considered solved*)" (Schutz and Luckmann, 1989:232, emphasis added). The applicability of Schutz's argument to interpreting police-citizen encounters should be self-evident. By clearly demonstrating how the determination of relevancy occurs on the basis of the hermeneutic-circular (*not* tautological) relationship between the interpreter and the interpreted (the "subject" or "object"), Schutz points to the same conditions of understanding that prevail in the kinds of bureaucratic encounters constituting the setting of police praxis.

On the one hand, the scientific attitude of the researcher, and its analogue in the "neutral, impartial" bureaucratic stance, each operate by seeking to exclude or circumscribe the ineluctable fact of the interpreter's own presence, except insofar as it is narrowly relevant in methodological or operational terms. On the other hand, however, that exclusion is possible because an affirmation has been made that only certain elements of the encounter are practically relevant. If, then, as Schutz argues, a specifically identified problem is "the 'locus' of all possible constructs relevant to its solution" (Schutz and Luckmann, 1989:232), and thereby becomes the sole basis for determining the structure of relevance (1989:233), it becomes very easy to become so fixated on "solving the problem" that the broader horizon framing such practical thinking recedes from view.

In a related observation that is readily applicable to the interpretation of policing praxis, Marcel (2001:127) notes that the decision to be a "mere spectator" depends on first recognizing a greater reality and deeper level of engagement, and then affirmatively prescinding from it. For example, the police officer arriving at the scene of a call has already made a range of commitments relating to the performance of official duty, and also relating to "emotional self-preservation" as this idea is generally conceived within police culture. Sociological reflection turned back upon the social sciences themselves reveals similar practices in the constant admonition to researchers that they "distance" themselves from "their subjects" in order to adopt a "neutral" or "objective" stance. Whatever its good intentions, such thinking proceeds from the misguided assumption that human presence can be reduced to a manageable, instrumental capacity: "This is why the spectator, also, betrays his own nature when he chooses to regard himself as a mere recording apparatus; and it is enough, indeed, for him to reflect for a second on the emotion which a spectacle is capable of arousing in him, for the image of himself as a mere apparatus, with which he was satisfied at first, to be at once shattered" (Marcel, 2001:127). Reading Marcel, it becomes more apparent that formal practices customarily treated as "problems of method" are more elementally understandable in phenomenological terms as reflections of the condition of existential proximity.

TWO

The Common Roots of Bureaucratic Policing and Mainstream Social Science

The supreme achievement would be: to grasp that
everything factual is already theory.

—Johann Wolfgang von Goethe,
Maximen und Reflexionen: A Selection, 1986

INTRODUCTION: HORIZONS OF THE QUESTION

At the level of everyday praxis, the work of mainstream social scientists and bureaucratic police officers proceeds according to the shared, unreflected notion that whatever their complexity, human interactions are ultimately "manageable" through the methodical operations of praxis. Just as social scientists must abstract "facts" and "data" from the totality of lived circumstances in order to translate them into "research problems," police officers must similarly reduce encounters with other human beings to particular "problems," which admit of bureaucratic resolution. In this respect, the comportment of police officers toward the people they encounter bears an essential similarity to the intuitive comportment of social science researchers toward the "subjects" of their research. Put another way, the ontological roots of bureaucratic and mainstream social scientific praxis are inseparably set in the same ground.

Most social scientific analyses of police-citizen interactions are based on field research, which is primarily conducted in the form of participant observation, often supplemented by various kinds of interviews, surveys, or questionnaires. There is little disagreement that participant observation and its ancillary methods of research are fraught with the difficulties intrinsic to translating field observations into purportedly "objective" data. A great deal has been said about these and other related methodological questions, and need not be revisited here. Instead, I would like to reframe such pragmatic and technical questions of methodology in order to show how they may be construed otherwise, as illustrations of the extent to which, whatever their vast differences (both obvious and not so obvious), mainstream social scientific research and bureaucratic policing share common ontological presuppositions. This commonality at the level of grounding first principles carries through undiminished to their respective practical approaches to human interaction.

The social scientific observation, categorization, and analysis of the actions of the police rest on processes of judgment, translation, and interpretation, which are fundamentally akin to the analytic practices employed by police officers in their encounters with the public. As with all sociological research, the analysis of police-citizen encounters involves a complex hermeneutic rooted in the act of interpreting a fellow human being's acts of interpretation. This hermeneutic is substantially influenced by the dialectical interaction of academic social science and police praxis, through which the conclusions that criminological researchers reach about their "subjects" become the ground for reflexive institutional changes among the police themselves (compare Wilson, 2000). Often by official invitation, and motivated by a complex array of sociopolitical and organizational considerations, these changes themselves become the "object" of subsequent study, as the police "make themselves subject" to scientific investigation.

I have arranged this chapter according to the following broad categories of social scientific literature on policing: ethnographic, ideological/pragmatic, and phenomenological. With that said, my aim is not to provide a comprehensive summary of research on policing but rather to refine the basis for arguing that there is an elective affinity between bureaucratic and mainstream social scientific praxis. Readers familiar with the literature on police research will therefore find that many classic studies go unmentioned here. For similar reasons, readers without this background knowledge should not be misled into thinking that what follows here constitutes an adequate literature review.

ETHNOGRAPHIC STUDIES

Ethnographic and participant observation studies represent the most common type of research on police-citizen encounters, and were especially prolific during the 1960s and 1970s. Several of the hallmark police ethnographies focus directly on police-citizen encounters, while others engage the topic as an element within broader analyses of the organizational culture of policing and the "police personality."

Perhaps more than any single work, Michael Banton's comparative study (1964) of policing in the United States and Scotland stands as the inaugural moment in the "golden age" of police research. Unlike studies limited to the analysis of deviant or excessive police behavior (e.g., Westley, 1970, and Skolnick, 1966), Banton directed his "occupational sociology" toward the working practices of the police operating under fairly innocuous circumstances (1964:xii). While acknowledging that police-citizen encounters always have a coercive dimension, Banton argues that the outcome of contacts is actually determined by both parties, and cannot be understood solely in terms of the formal exercise of power. From this standpoint, one of Banton's major conclusions is that effective policing, whether in the United States, Scotland, or elsewhere, hinges on officers' abilities to cope skillfully with a vast and unpredictable range of encounters, many of them highly charged. He argues that this ability develops *unconsciously* from experience (1964:178), a point that he supports by juxtaposing veteran officers' manifest deftness at handling complex situations with their inability to explain how they actually do so (1964:178; see also Skolnick, 1966:244).

This kind of apparently intuitive resourcefulness and practical creativity also figure prominently in Egon Bittner's poignant ethnographies of police-citizen encounters (1967a, 1970, 1974), which he grounds in his conception of policing as a "mechanism for the distribution of non-negotiably coercive force" (1970, reprinted in 1990:131). Bittner pays close attention to the ways in which police-citizen encounters are shaped by officers' attempts to seek and maintain dominance and control of situations (1990:26). He shows as well how the public draws on this coercive power to serve its own ends by enlisting the police in the resolution of troublesome predicaments and conflicts, in a move he terms "calling the cops" (1990:36).

Bittner's ethnography of the policing of skid row (1967a, reprinted 1990:30–62) describes how "keeping the peace" demands the pragmatic application of legal mandates, not with the overt goal of "enforcing the law" but rather as a means of dealing with the complex exigencies of particular situations. Although the coercive power of the officer is omnipresent, it is deployed selectively as warranted by specific circumstances. Indeed, while emphasizing the subtext of power beneath all police-citizen transactions, Bittner convincingly explains how, in the skid row setting, these transactions are nonetheless carried out with respect to intricate networks of personal acquaintance and a nuanced familiarity with the neighborhood.

Bittner highlights officers' awareness that effective interaction in an anomic social environment is determined by their ability to function across a broad "spectrum of affiliations" (1990:44). The nature of these affiliations is reflected in everyday encounters: where officers perceive common sociopolitical interests with their interlocutors—as they do, for example, in their affiliations with business owners—a formal, abstract relationship tends to prevail, while interactions with the marginalized residents of a skid row neighborhood are often characterized by an element of familiarity and intimacy (1990:43–47). The suggestion thus emerges from Bittner's work that the more tenuous the social connection between officer and citizen, the more crucial it becomes to cultivate the interaction at a fundamental level of mutual recognition. Bittner's observation represents a preliminary foray into a realm of interaction central to modern sociality: literally faced with people with whom one has nothing in common—not even the most basic shared notions of tradition or custom—the remaining alternatives are either to seek out existential commonality or else turn to an effacing abstraction (see Bauman, 1990).

A similar dilemma emerges out of Donald Black and Albert Reiss's observational study of police behavior and its formative attitudes (1967). Black and Reiss trace the underlying logic of police-public interactions to the participants' mutual (but often conflicting) desire to control and order social situations. They argue that the relative degree of control that people can assert in encounters with the police is largely a function of status, and of having the capacity to subvert the means of police action.[1] During encounters with the public, officers enact their legal mandate with varying levels of responsiveness, a process that can formally recognize citizenship without acknowledging humanity (Black and Reiss, 1967:26). Using detailed assessments of encounters between officers and the public, Black and Reiss tabulate officers' methods and styles of interaction, giving particular attention to any apparent signs of demonstrated prejudice. A key point to emerge from their research is the "paradox of civility"—the fact that civility may be construed on the street as disrespect (1967:57). What an officer might sincerely intend as a professional, detached manner can be perceived as cold indifference. On the other hand, an officer might regard a citizen's relaxed attitude as civil but insufficiently deferential. In my own experience, this is most commonly apparent in the umbrage that many officers take at being called "cops."

Black and Reiss's paradox of civility reveals a methodological and ethical problem shared by policing and social scientific research. It is a problem that stems in large measure from the attempt by one's interlocutors to find the "real" motive for contact and inquiry. People are often highly suspicious of

police officers who try to strike up conversations, which are frequently perceived (often correctly) as thinly veiled "fishing expeditions" for information or
intelligence.[2] Yet, just as officers' casual conversations with citizens frequently
have ulterior investigative motives, field researchers' similar conversations
with police officers are likewise oriented toward the attainment of a predetermined, instrumental end, namely the acquisition of "valid data." Along these
lines, Black and Reiss note that the idle conversation between academic observers and the police officers with whom they are working "easily translates
into a somewhat unique research medium—'conversational interviewing'"
(1967:132).[3] They go on to comment: "[s]ince often a good deal of camaraderie
developed between the observers and the officers, such attitude data [i.e. personal sentiments revealed in casual conversation] often are particularly 'rich'
in quality and content" (Black and Reiss, 1967:132). Recalling Bittner's notion
(1990:26) that legal coercion quietly hovers above even the most outwardly
innocuous police-citizen encounters, it is fair to conclude in light of Black and
Reiss's comment that the interpretive powers of social science are similarly
deployed, constituting the police officer as an object for analysis, manipulation, and control. Indeed, whatever the difference of magnitude between their
potential negative consequences, "informant" relationships in social science
and policing arguably present a common set of ethical quandaries centering
on staged efforts at friendship and confidence (compare Lieberman, 2007).

Another similarity between policing and social science emerges in the practical delineation of situations as "calls" or "runs." A key example is a study by
Reiss (1971a:xi), in which he adopts an operational, positivistic definition of
police-citizen encounters as quantitatively isolable interactions that are subject
to *systematic social observation*. He identifies roles, behavior, and decisions as
the fundamental dimensions of each encounter.[4] Like the police officer who
must thematically delimit the predicament of a fellow human being according
to the legal and administrative parameters of a bureaucratic organization, the
social scientist operates under an analogous mandate.

IDEOLOGICAL AND PRAGMATIC RESEARCH

James Q. Wilson's analysis of institutional "styles" of policing in his *Varieties of Police Behavior: The Management of Law and Order in Eight Communities*
(1968) endures as a classic study of police praxis. The appearance of the word
"management" in the book's title bespeaks Wilson's theoretical perspective:
he proceeds on the assumption that police work is directed at the effective and

efficient solving of "problems at hand" (1968:2). From this standpoint, Wilson analyzes police-citizen encounters as instances of the discretionary exercise of legal authority aimed at the maintenance of order. According to Wilson, order maintenance largely occurs through the exercise of police discretion in situations centering on transgressions such as simple (misdemeanor) assault, disorderly conduct, vandalism, and public drinking, which occupy a substantial part of police officers' time and represent the vast majority of arrests (1968:5–7 and 17–20). Officers dealing with these and related predicaments find themselves working in an environment marked by turmoil, passion, and antagonism, all of which are compounded by the fact that the best the police can usually do is to document information, or offer temporary palliation.

Wilson correctly perceives the emotional disparity between the impassioned states of the people involved in a given situation and the detached indifference of the officers who respond to resolve it. This disparity creates a perpetual and irresolvable dilemma: if officers display an attitude of detachment and suspicion born of routinizing crisis and hearing a constant flurry of lies, they invite public anger and resentment; and dropping their impersonal facade of bureaucracy amounts to an acknowledgment—if only implicit—that legal authority cannot suffice to resolve many situations (1968:24; see also Banton, 1964). All of this is inestimably complicated by the violence and hostility intrinsic to the enforcement of social order, not the least source of which is the friction occurring in the tense interactions between the police and the kinds of people whom they target for attention.

Wilson identifies three general "styles" ("watchman," "legalistic," and "service") representing the different ways in which various police agencies handle the task of law enforcement and order maintenance. At the operational level of police-citizen encounters, officers' actions in all three styles are directed by considerations of utility and cost-benefit analysis, rather than by legal or moral factors (Wilson, 1968:83). Operationalizing an agency's particular organizational style at the street level demands the proper "managing" of officers in ways that ensure efficient performance consistent with predetermined goals, so that the officers, in turn, can go forth and predictably "manage" public problems, disorder, and social conflict. Wilson's explanation of this dynamic exemplifies the close interrelation between sociological research on policing and normative recommendations for policing praxis. By problematizing police-citizen interactions in terms of institutional concerns about liability, ethics, and public image, social science becomes a key factor in shaping organizational self-conceptions and the forms of administrative action arising out of them.

This phenomenon finds another powerful example in the work of Goldstein (1977), who assesses ways of "controlling and reviewing" interactions between the police and the public. Goldstein's ideas have long been viewed as de rigueur for advocates of community policing, "problem-oriented policing," and other such theories, which typically share a conception of the police as "delivering a product" (safety, law and order, and so forth) to the "public," and imagine further that they do so in a rational, bureaucratic fashion (see Manning, 1977:208–17). For theorists of police management such as Goldstein, police-citizen interactions are unstructured moments requiring close administrative supervision to minimize risk (1977:167–79). According to this line of thought, police conduct requires managerial "control," "identification," and "correction"—words from a lexicon used elsewhere to characterize ways in which people on the street are handled and disciplined by the police. Goldstein's remedy for abusive conduct by police toward the public is a projection of authority that is "calm, unemotional, and somewhat detached" (1977:172). He argues that the ideal organizational structure for effectuating this kind of stance is the "professional model" (e.g., Vollmer), which epitomizes central, apolitical control aimed at bringing about efficient, predetermined ends (1977:2).

A similar view exists in various psychological studies that seek to influence and reform police praxis by developing scientific bases for "behavioral self-management" (Wilson and Braithwaite, 1995:22). Wilson and Braithwaite note the prevalence of authoritarianism among police behavioral traits, and attempt to analyze how police behavior during interactions with the public may be predicted on the basis of officers' personality traits, considered together with training, background, socialization, and other variables (1995:18–23).[5] They argue for the application of research psychology to explain the behavior of police and citizens during their interactions, and present evidence indicating (to no great surprise) that officers with strong communications skills can usually keep hostility to a minimum.

Wilson and Braithwaite contend that once police officers have a purportedly scientific, objective basis for understanding their own behavior, as well as that of the public whom they encounter, they gain a predictable means of "managing" encounters in order to minimize risk. They conclude that shaping and controlling officers' behavior is a "critical tool in effective risk management" (1995:22). Among other measures, Wilson and Braithwaite advocate training programs to heighten officers' critical awareness of their own behavioral traits, in particular how they are shaped by environmental pressures born of the group dynamics of police culture. Herz (2001) evaluated one such program, a curriculum intended to give officers de-escalation skills to improve the outcome of their encounters with juveniles. Such thinking again exemplifies the calculated development and application of a sense of reflexivity mediated through the interpretive perspectives of psychological and social scientific analysis.

EXISTING PHENOMENOLOGICAL RESEARCH

The voice of phenomenology, let alone phenomenological philosophy, has been and remains a faint one in research of policing. Despite occasional consideration of its potential value for criminological inquiry (e.g., Downes and Rock, 2003:202–24, and Holdaway, 1989:60–61) and its more systematic integration within other fields of social science, there has been little conscious application of phenomenology to criminology in general, or to the study of policing in particular. To the limited extent that phenomenology has a presence in criminological research, it is primarily in the subsidiary form of ethnomethodology (especially Garfinkel), symbolic interactionism, and various qualitative studies in the sociology of deviancy (notably Cicourel, 1968; Matza, 1969; Douglas, 1970; Sudnow, 1972; and Rock, 1973).

There are a number of fairly clear reasons for the paucity of phenomenological criminology. Often dismissed as a form of radical subjectivism that either relativizes or completely abandons all claims to truth (Taylor, Walton, and Young, 1973; Gellner, 1975; Quinney, 1975; and compare Downes and Rock, 2003:215–24), phenomenology has traditionally been regarded with more suspicion than favor in a field that traces its roots to positivistic social science and empiricism and frequently has little patience for theorizing (see Downes and Rock, 2003, and Holdaway, 1989:60–61). In an elaboration of these critiques, phenomenology has also been faulted by radical criminologists for abdicating normative questions through an ostensible isolation of meaning from its sociopolitical context (Taylor, Walton, and Young, 1973:279–80). To be fair, there is plenty of phenomenological social science deserving of this kind of criticism; however, it is erroneous to claim that phenomenology categorically yields flawed research.

There is a small body of research in the sociology of deviance that explicitly uses phenomenological concepts to explain police behavior. Most noteworthy is Paul Rock's study (1973), which draws on Schutz's (and Husserl's) principle of the suspension (*epoché*) of the natural attitude to explain the systematic use of distrust by police officers as well as offenders to interpret their everyday surroundings. This "existential commitment to deviancy" (1973:76) explains the suspicious comportment of officers widely discussed in police ethnographies, and takes a major step toward treating such practical activity as a function of the enactment of ontology. Similarly, Simon Holdaway's research on British policing (1989:63–65 and 1980) uses participant observation, and acknowledges a debt to Schutz and to Berger and Luckmann. More recently, Patricia Paperman (2003) uses phenomenology in a very general sense to explain how police officers on the Paris Metro manage the concepts of visibility and invisibility in their encounters.

From a phenomenological standpoint separate from ethnomethodology and the sociology of deviancy, Peter Manning (1977) uses a dramaturgical metaphor to explain the processes of symbolization that occur in police-citizen interactions. Manning regards the police first and foremost as "dramatic actors" (1977:17), whose "grammar of social interaction" provides them with the means of interpreting the situations in which they find themselves. Locating himself in the tradition of Burke (1935 and 1945) and Goffman, Manning seeks to read the social control activities of the police as symbolic rituals that assume meaning and significance through the interpretive practices of the involved actors.[6]

In a later study (1988), Manning explores symbolic communication in his analysis of telephone calls received at police dispatch centers. He shows how the symbolic processes used to interpret and code calls for police service determine their meaning and relevance. Manning's study examines the institutional practices through which the nuances of communication become "mere organizational products" (1988:6). Manning concludes with a statement on the limits of social scientific language, which, he says, "is not poetic or aesthetic but merely a language for expressing and elevating contradictions. In the end, when the sun shifts, splays against the carpet, and radiates in the room, words fail to capture its warmth and logic cannot 'restore' human attachment, which, like the sun, regularly fades, dips, and perhaps rises again" (1988:266–67). Manning's words strongly echo the phenomenological critique of reductionist thought that unquestioningly transforms human experience into administratively meaningful data.

WHAT REMAINS UNCONSIDERED

In his cultural history of twentieth-century American policing, Christopher Wilson (2000) argues that much of the canonical research on the police is framed by wider dynamics of political rhetoric and storytelling that escape notice in the customary self-descriptions of mainstream social science. For Wilson, the academic focus since the 1960s on police-citizen encounters as the defining aspect of the policing function both accepts and reinforces as a fait accompli a distinct neoliberal vision of civic order. Wilson argues that the relationship that developed between the "blue knights" of policing and the "brown jackets" of academia yielded analyses that contributed to the decisive reshaping of the subjects of social scientific attention: "Police science had yoked itself to the language of human relations, and imagined that routinized, bureaucratic work was the best way to anticipate public disorder. Under the progressive-sounding banner of efficiency and actuarialism, the procedural approach aspired to make policing into a predictive, rather than merely reactive enterprise" (Wilson, 2000:94). Wilson convincingly demonstrates how police institutions reflexively responded to the social scientists who came to study them *in situ*. However, the process goes further: indeed, social science practices have evolved to accommodate the institutional expectations of police agencies that open themselves to academic scrutiny (compare Leo, 1996, and Musheno, 1997). Like the patient who volunteers to participate in a medical study, police departments want some tangible benefit in return for their time, effort, and discomfort.

From my standpoint, this relationship between social scientific research and policing needs to be viewed at a more elemental level, within the context of the ontological affinity between bureaucracy and social science. For example, prior to the advent of the "golden age" of police ethnography, David Matza already recognized that in applying classificatory schemata to observed phenomena, police officers confront a methodological problem that "is similar in almost every respect to that faced by sociologists."[7] Bittner (1980:91) likewise considers how patrol officers' cultivation of "area knowledge" is based on a "good ethnographic grasp" developed through modes of inquiry that bear a marked similarity to social science field research (1990:174–77). Another example of this phenomenon appears in Richard Ericson's study of patrol operations, one element of which classified crime victims according to a variety of criteria, including "socio-economic standing," which, according to Ericson (1982:102), was determined by researchers' judgments made on the basis of factors such as dress, speech, type of car driven, and/or place of residence. Here once again, with no apparent awareness of its underlying irony, social scientific research enacts the same logic as the object of its critical attention. Finally, Holdaway (1989:55–56) goes so far as to argue that intense sociological scrutiny of the police has often used them as a "testing ground," less out of concern for the police themselves than for their convenient availability as research subjects.

In fact, the present-day affinity between bureaucratic and social scientific methods finds early anticipation in narratives such as Edgar Allan Poe's short story "The Man of the Crowd" (1840), which explores the quotidian uses of typification in the everyday settings of urban modernity, and reveals how the nascent logic of positivism quickly became an intrinsic element of social administration and the dialectics of modern self-identity. Poe would likely not be surprised that today, the police are increasingly heedful of calls from social scientists to adopt the methods as well as the conclusions of scientific research in order to become more "modern," "professional," "scientific," "rational," or "efficient." Trojanowicz and Dixon (1974:xi) exemplify these sentiments with their admonition that the successful, modern police officer "must become a social scientist." In such arguments, the focus remains on reforming policing and improving its level of technical efficiency and predictability, by grounding police praxis in what Bittner terms a "resolutely calculating approach" (1990:179). Paradoxically, a call like Bittner's for emotional calm and rational efficiency in the discharge of police duties is at odds with poignant ethnographic descriptions that express shock and dismay at the apparent indifference, or even dark humor, with which officers go about their work. Descriptions of this sort highlight the irresolvable dilemmas and underlying moral tensions at issue in the process of struggling to balance professional detachment with compassion and an entire spectrum of emotional, intellectual, and spiritual responses.

For example, the common observation (e.g., Herbert, 1997:84–85) that officers sometimes appear unaffected by scenes of horrific tragedy does not always consider the pressure of public expectations that the police be detached and composed, not merely with respect to the immediate situation at hand but even more so for the next call to which they must respond. A demonstrably traumatized or emotionally distraught officer will not inspire public confidence, which suggests that the penchant for "laughing at death" is not necessarily explicable as a demonstration of machismo. We are thus left to wonder: to what extent does facing crisis and tragedy require delimiting one's human presence out of a supposed imperative to be "detached"; and conversely, how does such an act of suspension emerge out of a prior recognition of a greater manifold reality, the very bracketing of which from practical consideration subverts the possibility of meaningful action?

Paul Weiss (1975) highlights this struggle to balance professional and holistic presence, which is in no way unique to police officers (see Goffman, 1961). Its intensity, however, is certainly more pronounced in the context of a vocational milieu such as policing. Even while discharging their duties behind the partial anonymity of the uniform, officers must

> be sensitive to *what other beings are* and make a kind of sympathetic *reaching to the presence of other individuals.* [The police officer] functions therefore as a being who takes a kind of *distance* at the same time that he has some kind of *grasp. He must understand what it is for another being to be over against him.* Now this is ultimately a question of human sensitivity. There are people who have no or very little understanding of what the feelings of others are. They are intelligent, they are fair-minded, they are industrious, they believe in the right, but what they cannot sense is how others feel. The first function then of a policeman *as an individual* is to quicken the sense of what others are feeling. (Weiss, 1975:28, emphasis added)

With this argument, Weiss goes beyond the usual bromidic recommendations for the grafting of ethics, patience, or politeness onto what nonetheless remains, in the end, a bureaucratic, instrumental-rational process. At the same time, it remains altogether unclear how idealistic visions such as Weiss's might ever become normalized in bureaucratic praxis. The tragic reality is that they likely cannot, which Weiss seems to tacitly acknowledge in speaking of the police officer "as an individual." To routinize the human qualities of which Weiss speaks would be, in fact, to transmute them into something other than what they authentically are—a responsive poetics unavailable to bureaucratic praxis because of their ontological irreconcilability.

This aporia is suggested in the headlong clash between the sort of intricate schema that Weiss lays out and what Bittner calls the intrinsic "crudeness" of police work. As Bittner explains it, this crudeness stems from the bureaucratic handling of "subtle human conflicts and profound legal and moral questions, without being allowed to give the subtleties and profundities anywhere near the consideration they deserve" (1990:97). Yet hope remains; for the ability to perceive the inadequacy of reductive praxis derives from a more elemental comportment that is antecedent to it, and constitutes its unconsidered horizon. By understanding the irreducible co-presence of human beings to one another, and its role as the ontological foundation of any encounter, that horizon may be brought to light.

THREE

The Approach of a Phenomenological Aesthetics of Encounter

Any genuine method is grounded in the appropriate preview
of the fundamental constitution of the "object" or area of
objects to be disclosed. Any genuine reflection on method,
which is to be distinguished from empty discussions of
technology, thus at the same time tells us something about
the kind of being of the being in question.

—Martin Heidegger,
Being and Time, 1996

Art, then, is an increase of life, a sort of competition
of surprises that stimulates our consciousness and keeps
it from becoming somnolent.

—Gaston Bachelard,
The Poetics of Space, 1994

CONTEXTUALIZING AND TRANSCENDING
THE QUESTION OF METHOD

Whatever the context in which it is posed, the question of method always reflects a prior concern with the given object of its attention. For example, when
criminologists or police officers seek the best methods for preventing homicides, their search is motivated by the indubitable fact that they are already
engaged with the existential reality of murder. The question of method is the
question of determining how to get "closest" to the problem, or "to the heart
of the matter." This existential relation underlying the formal structuring of
method suggests how the notion of method may be clarified using a *phenom-*

enology of approach. A metaphor such as "getting to the heart of the matter" illustrates how the notion of approach is already implicit within our common-sense notions of method. In fact, the question, "what is your method?" may be reformulated as, "what is your method for approaching this problem?" or "in what way do you approach this subject?" Questions such as these indicate how, at a level of thought prior to formal analytic reflection, we seem to have an intuitive idea that "method" involves coming near to someone or something. To find the "best method" for undertaking a given task or inquiry means determining how one ought to approach it; hence when we speak of the "best method," we often refer metaphorically to the best or easiest "way" to arrive at a given end. Literally speaking, to approach something is to draw near to it, or to come into proximity with it. Furthermore, the idea of approach is not confined to physical proximity: in an abstract or figurative sense, to approach something is to be concerned with it or to engage it from a certain intentional stance. The question of method may therefore be understood in terms of how we interpret relations or states of proximity.

As soon as I decide to approach a person or thing, whether in response to an immediate presence or at a remove through theoretical reflection, my decision and its accompanying processes of cognition create a particular comportment—an intentional stance. Approaching is a coming near *to* someone or something: this is evident in the etymological derivation of the word "approach" from the Latin *adpropiāre,* which combines *ad* (to) and *prope* (near).[1] As I showed in the previous paragraph using the example of homicide, this intentional dynamic of approach is existentially grounded in the hermeneutic phenomenon, because the act of drawing near is possible only on the basis of an existing relation of foreknowledge and anticipation. Applying a phenomenology of approach to the notion of method thus reveals how, beyond its usual self-conception, method occurs as a hermeneutic process in which the "subject" or "object" is known beforehand in elemental ways that the formal precepts of method rarely acknowledge.

In order to focus attention on this phenomenological reconception of method, I have deliberately used here the term "approach" where "method" might be more customary. The distinction between "method" and "approach" is especially significant for understanding the notion of method shared by bureaucratic and social scientific praxis. The police officer, in determining how to "manage" human encounters as problems, continually deals with intuitive, preconceived notions of space and proximity, not only in a legal and administrative sense but also in tactical terms. This occurs most notably with respect to assessing and reacting to the potential physical threats posed by the close presence of another human being. To inquire phenomenologically into the bureaucratic approach, and to do so in the particular context of understanding police-citizen encounters, means asking: how does a police officer, as such, approach another human being, in the most elemental sense of establishing a state of proximity, and then interpret that other human being's presence as meaningful? The same question could be posed in order to understand how the social scientist "approaches" human beings as "subjects" of research or "objects" of analysis. Just as the police officer reads human presence for manifestations of crime, disorder, and transgression, so the researcher approaches human presence as an abstract repository or substratum of data or "observable behavior and phenomena."

TOWARD A PHENOMENOLOGICAL
AESTHETICS OF ENCOUNTER

How do we face the ineffable mystery of human presence and render it into the "facts and circumstances" demanded by various practical ends? To answer this question, we need to discern the ontological conditions that frame the translation of presence into "facts," and provide the basis for assessing the extent to which those facts bear an authentic relation to what they are supposed to represent. For example, as Heidegger explains in the Zollikon Seminars (2001:81–85), the competent clinician or therapist realizes that corporeal phenomena such as tears, blushing, and other such manifestations of inner emotion cannot be interpreted "objectively," except in a pointlessly superficial manner that wrests them from their existential context. To measure the tears of a crying person or to quantify the blood flow in the face of someone who is blushing is to reify grief, shame, or other emotions into "facts," which are meaningless precisely because of their reduction to "objectivity" (see Heidegger, 2001:81–82).

In bureaucratic policing, the representation of emotional phenomena in officers' reports has an underlying logic fundamentally similar to the clinical attempt to objectify manifestations of emotion. Science by its very nature demands the kind of univocal answers that secure the possibility of calculability and prediction (Heidegger, 2001:137). This demand obtains with equal force in social scientific analysis and in the administrative functions of modern bureaucracy. For the clinical practitioners with whom Heidegger conducted the Zollikon Seminars, therapeutic diagnosis and treatment depend on psychiatrists' abilities to create and maintain a certain comportment toward their patients, which allows behavior and utterances to be read as symptoms of mental disease, defect, or disorder. For the police officer responding to or "handling" calls for service, the same is true: immensely complex human predicaments must be pared down to administratively treatable "problems" or judicially remediable crimes or violations of law.

This "paring down" is more precisely understandable as a process of abstraction. "Abstraction" denotes a drawing away or separation (Latin *abs* + *trahere*). In scientific terms, abstraction is the drawing away from an entity of that aspect deemed to represent its decisive nature. This abstraction then becomes the singular significance (*Eindeutigkeit*), on the basis of which praxis judges the entity in question to be practically knowable and meaningful (see Heidegger, 2001:137). Modern science is grounded in the abstract representation of nature as an object or mathematically calculable array of spatiotemporal processes knowable through experimental method, and manipulable through the application of technology.[2] The definitive belief of science in univocal meaning (*Eindeutigkeit*) grounds the logic of scientific method: "But this belief is justified only if one believes in the dogma that [everything in] the world is completely calculable and that the calculable world is the [only] true reality. This conception is pushing us toward uncanny developments—already looming now—in which one no longer asks who and how the human being is. Instead he [the human being] is conceived of beforehand from the background of the technical manipulability of the world" (Heidegger, 2001:141). Heidegger identifies a profound crisis, which is central to any critical analysis of encounter: scientific and clinical practitioners have ceased addressing themselves to human beings as such, and have thereby effectively disengaged from what is ultimately most real about human beings and their predicaments.

To make this crisis more tangible, and place it in the context of street-level police encounters, consider the following episode:

> Lise is fourteen years old, and is confined to a wheelchair because she is paraplegic. She lives alone with her mother. In private conversation, Lise often reveals a dark and violent personality. She speaks of having a passionate desire to burn down her house, and imagines aloud the pleasure she would take in watching futile efforts to extinguish the flames. She talks of wanting to torture young children, and of "loving evil." Her words often seem to reflect a frightening indifference toward other people: Lise can talk in the same breath about torture and her favorite snack foods, eliding one topic into the other with a bored, blasé attitude.

Lise's anger also manifests itself in the kind of self-destructive behavior common among deeply anguished teenagers. On one occasion, she intentionally slammed one of her fingers in her bedroom door with such force that the tip turned black, and bled from beneath the nail. An account of this incident notes how Lise stared at the blood in fixated fury and muttered to herself. Yet, despite such displays of rage, Lise often demonstrates with equal force an affectionate side, and expresses a yearning for unconditional love. Her mother is at a loss over how to deal with her, and has turned for help to a physician, as well as to a close family friend, who knew Lise when she was a little girl, and is now a cleric.

Lise's seemingly nihilistic outlook, vituperative expressions of hatred, and acts of self-mutilation exemplify the kinds of phenomena that are commonly read as "warning signs" or "risk factors" by teachers, parents, police officers, social workers, and counselors in the struggle to prevent school violence, teenage suicide, and other such tragedies. Lise, however, is not someone whom I encountered on the street. In fact, readers familiar with Dostoyevsky may recognize her as a character from *The Brothers Karamazov*.[3]

In an obvious sense, Lise is a "fictional" character; thus, it might be said that her story is not literally or historically "true." Yet, in other respects, Lise's story is much more than an engaging fictional characterization. Dostoyevsky's narrative gives voice to an essential truth that remains muffled, if not wholly muted, within the kinds of reductionist analyses that dominate social scientific and bureaucratic praxis. His description of Lise illuminates the despair, existential anguish, and loneliness of a teenage girl, and expresses her inner turmoil with a force and poignancy that remain fundamentally beyond the reach of praxis that might serve as a basis for "diagnosing" children like Lise, and categorizing their behavior according to one pathology or another (compare Heidegger, 2001:136–43). Even more than this, Dostoyevsky's description of Lise is *true* not so much because of what it says about her in particular but rather for how her character assumes a universal significance, a significance even greater for its revealing how she knows herself through encounters with others, and vice versa (compare Dufrenne, 1973:527). Alyosha Karamazov tells Lise, "there's something spiteful and at the same time innocent about you" (Dostoyevsky, 1958:681). With these words, the moral tension of social interaction begins to emerge in its ontological "thickness" and "primitive density" (Marcel, 2001:45). For the nature of Lise's personality is not comprehensible merely by objectively noting her grinding teeth, her "flashing eyes," the nature of her dreams, or her histrionics. In each of these instances, the significance of what might otherwise be reducible to clinical symptoms or to transgressive behavior of one kind or another emerges instead as a poetic struggle to create meaning.

THE POETIC ASPECT OF ORDINARY LIFE

To develop further a point that I made in the introduction, I imagine that a number of readers will have been struck by the seemingly incongruous juxtaposition in this book's title of poetics and policing. What can one possibly have to do with the other? My reply to this question begins with Gaston Bachelard's remark that "every human activity wishes to speak" (1990:283). Like Heidegger, Bachelard regarded poetry as an elemental force of human imagination that transcends its usual literary meaning. For Bachelard, poetry must be understood phenomenologically as the creation of meaning intrinsic to imagination and its linguistic self-expression. To say that "every human activity wishes to speak" refers to the idea that poetry does not *represent* so much as it *creates*. Poetry in this sense occurs as the continuous reaching forth of imagination, and the enactment through language of the "spiritual mobility" (*mobilité spirituelle*) that interweaves mundane human existence with transcendence (Bachelard, 1990:8–13). The functioning of poetic language as Bachelard understands it echoes Merleau-Ponty's characterization of speech as "the surplus of our existence over natural being" (1962:197; compare Ricoeur, 1991:171–74).

To understand more clearly what this means, it is helpful to continue following Bachelard and others in searching out a more fundamental notion of the poetic. Nowhere, perhaps, has such a notion been more succinctly achieved than in a line from one of Friedrich Hölderlin's late poems, "In Lovely Blueness" (*In lieblicher Bläue*): . . . poetically man dwells . . .[4] Less known in their own right than as the title and subject of an essay by Heidegger (1971), these three words point to the origins of poetry in the existential constitution of human being. To exist as a human being is perpetually to struggle to seek, find, and *create* meaning in response to the mysterious fact of one's own existence. Of course, the "fact" of my existence is never merely that: the singular realization of my own existence forever eludes its own grasp (compare Marcel, 2001:167–68). This struggle is the existential horizon against and within which every human encounter occurs.

With the word "create," we arrive at the etymological origins of the word "poetry" in the Greek *poiesis*, meaning "creation," which, in turn, derives from *poiein*, to make, do, or create. Poetry taken in its strictly literary sense is thus only a particular cultural manifestation of a much more fundamental sense of the poetic, which is rooted in the existential nature of human being itself (see Bachelard, 1990). This more fundamental sense defines the "constitutive role" of the poetic as the most basic means by which we take the measure of the world, not mathematically but in terms of meaningfully responding to the awareness of our own existence that makes us what we are (Heidegger, 1971a:xiv–xvii). It is in this existential character of human being, as a kind of being that is defined by the perennial search for meaning, that we see the central place of the poetic in shaping the comportment of ordinary life. Furthermore, to speak of a poetic quality of human being is to recognize it as a universally shared and essential aspect of personal existence that antecedes any kind of particular poetic "skill," which might be more accidental. Understood in this way, the idea of the poetic assumes a crucial role in any kind of phenomenological inquiry into human action, the present one included. In more specific terms, *attempting to disclose the ontological foundations of ordinary moments such as police-citizen encounters requires the ability to reveal their poetic dimension.*

Phenomenology takes as its point of departure this "momentousness" of human experience, where the term is understood in the dual sense of both temporality and significance. Formal, technical observation can reveal the "fact of the matter," but not much else. Suppose, for example, that a police officer or researcher enters a house and notices someone drinking tea and eating a cookie. How little will be noticed about this fact in a way that discloses the "surplus of existence!" Phenomenology, on the other hand, seeks to understand the inner truth expressed in an event such as Proust's smelling the aroma of the *madeleine*.[5] A phenomenological investigation of this moment would try to understand the intermingling of time, memory, emotion, and smell, which are elicited by the "objective fact" that dipping a cookie into lime tea emits a certain aroma that stimulates the olfactory sense and conjures up recollections of childhood. From the standpoint of a phenomenological aesthetics of encounter, the episode of the *madeleine* illustrates a universal kind of ordinary experience, and a concomitant universal ability to poeticize it. Though Proust's account of the *madeleine* reveals the poetics of human self-identity at work in the rarefied context of literary reflection, the spontaneous pouring forth of meaning and memory is equally at work in crises on the street.

Consider the apparently simple question, "what should I do?" that police officers hear every day, often under desperate circumstances. Viewed in phenomenological terms as the search for the right word, thought, or action, the question is indubitably *poetic*. It manifests the human desire to create meaning in the face of the condition of perennially existing ahead of oneself. Restored to its "original strangeness" (Merleau-Ponty, 1964b:97), this utterance might come to be seen as a fulfillment of the desire to give coherence to the present moment. Coherence might be quite easy to attain when the question, "what should I do?" is asked in relation to an innocuous matter, such as how to re-solve a civil dispute with a next-door neighbor. When, on the other hand, it is asked by someone in a moment of utter despair, torment, or crisis, as when it was posed to me by a man who had just found the body of his son-in-law after he had committed suicide with a shotgun, the question is astonishingly force-ful in its instantaneous disruption of bureaucratic problematization (*compare* Marcel, 2001:45).

APPLYING A PHENOMENOLOGICAL AESTHETICS OF ENCOUNTER

The application of a phenomenological aesthetics of encounter involves the integration of three core components:

1. A general phenomenological critique of the problematization of human being that occurs under the regime of the late modern conception of "method" and its allied forms of bureaucratic and social scientific praxis.
2. The phenomenological analysis of police-citizen encounters drawn from my professional experience in policing.
3. The phenomenological interpretation of aesthetic representations of human encounter drawn from five genres, including paintings, novels, poetry, drama, and short stories.

With the investigation of method reframed as an inquiry into the phenomenol-ogy of proximity, it becomes possible to see police-citizen encounters in a new light, which illuminates their elemental poetic quality. This perspective, in turn, enables the ontological distinction between intersubjectivity and co-presence (see chapter 1) to be engaged with respect to its practical implications, as they unfold in actual instances of the problematization of human being.

I present these instances in the form of case studies drawn from my fifteen years of police service in a small working-class city in the Pacific Northwest region of the United States. The case studies consist of narratives of encounters I had with members of the public within a wide variety of contexts, which, in the aggregate, represent some of the typical kinds of interactions experienced in police patrol work. The encounters range from casual social contacts, in which no crime occurred, to high-risk, emergency situations involving dangerous felonies or violent crises.

I have written the case studies using narrative and expository approaches intended to summarize the general "facts and circumstances" of each particular encounter, as they were deemed bureaucratically meaningful at the time of its original occurrence. Simultaneously, I approach these bureaucratic interpretations anew using phenomenological analyses that attempt to understand police methods for "managing" encounters as an immediate function of officers' enactment of the problematization of human being. In their style, the case study narratives bear some similarities to various kinds of ethnographic writing. I hasten to add, however, that the methodological precepts of ethnography have been less influential in my structuring of the narratives than have the analytic precepts of phenomenological philosophy and social theory.[6] This is particularly so with respect to my analysis of the underlying ontological significance of events surrounding the encounters.

In formulating and explicating the narratives, I have paid special attention to interdisciplinary dialogues long ago inaugurated among ethnography, literary criticism, aesthetics, and philosophy. Aptly summarized in terms of Geertz's notion of "blurred genres" (1980), these conversations have fostered the radical rethinking of social scientific orthodoxy and orthopraxy. Ideas such as "blurred genres" have contributed to the opening of a critical space for the interspersion of literary/artistic and social scientific analysis, in particular by challenging hallmark modern notions of "objectivity," "fiction," and conceptions of truth wedded to Cartesian and other epistemological paradigms beholden to the ideals of "accurate representation" or "correspondence" (e.g., see Webster, 1982, and Crapanzano, 1992). It is further worth noting how Geertz's description of fieldwork as "fiction" (1980) bears immediately on my use of the idea of the poetic, insofar as Geertz invokes a sense of fiction that regards it not as lies or falsehood but rather as *fictio*—"something made" (Webster, 1982:102; Geertz, 1980).

All of the information in the case study narratives derives from my direct encounters with the public, which occurred while I was conducting official police duties. The structure and setting of these encounters varied widely, from intimate, personal conversations in a living room to police station interrogations and violent fights on the street. None of the other participants in the encounters (aside from a number of my colleagues) was aware that I had any formal academic interest in my work experiences. I have protected the confidentiality of all of the people involved in the various encounters, even where a particular incident has otherwise become a matter of legally accessible public record, or the topic of media attention. The names in the case study narratives have all been changed; however, in every other respect, I have not altered any facts or details. The people involved in the encounters represent a broad demographic spectrum in terms of race, ethnicity, gender, age, social class, and other such customary social scientific categories. In fact, specific affiliations such as these are peripheral concerns for an analysis that aims at engaging universal aspects of encounter.[7]

My police service began in 1990 and continued through the writing of the original manuscript out of which this book developed. I spent almost my entire career "on the street," assigned primarily to uniformed patrol duty, first as an officer and later as a sergeant. Given the fifteen-year span of my tenure in policing, some of the case study narratives reflect the fortuitous advantage of a longitudinal perspective. Thus, I am sometimes in a position to comment on repeated encounters with the same person that were separated by a decade, or even longer. The longitudinal dimension of this study has also undoubtedly influenced my own interpretive stance: the professional evolution from anxious, wide-eyed rookie to staid, veteran sergeant must have shaded my interpretation of events and circumstances in ways that might elude me, yet be more apparent to the reader.

By now it should also be fairly evident that I make no claim to present an analysis that is "neutral" or "disinterested." More to the point, this is precisely the kind of chimerical stance that I regard as a reflection of the attenuated self-conception of praxis undertaken with a dogmatic adherence to faith in "method as technique." To this extent, my position with respect to the incidents recounted in the book is rather unconventional. During my entire police career, I was consciously aware of simultaneously occupying two roles—fulfilling an official duty as armed bureaucrat while perpetually stepping back in an intellectual capacity to reflect on the manifest strangeness of my own position as a "philosopher-cop." Given the personal and intellectual predilections with which I came to policing, I always tried to maintain and refine a phenomenological basis for developing insights into my work as a police officer. From the earliest stages of my career, I regarded the street as an *in vivo* setting within which to bear witness to the poetics of everyday life. The more time I spent on the street, the more dissatisfied I became with most of the analyses and descriptions of policing offered by mainstream social science. In developing a phenomenological aesthetics of encounter, I have sought to find a way to reveal the astonishing, complex, and tragic creation of meaning that I saw on the street, but which largely seemed to escape the attention of mainstream social scientific and bureaucratic thinking. By appealing to aesthetic form as a corrective or counterpoise to the reductionist interpretations of mainstream social science and bureaucracy, I have tried to develop a rigorous approach that draws on the truth value of aesthetic form to produce an exercise in what Bachelard calls "direct ontology" (1994:xvi).

To solidify this nexus between everyday social action and aesthetic form, I use the book's analytic chapters to juxtapose my case study narratives of police-citizen encounters with aesthetic representations of encounter. Each of these chapters is structured around a different type of police-citizen encounter and paired with examples of human encounter drawn from five different aesthetic genres, including paintings, poetry, novels, drama, and short stories. I intend for the aesthetic examples to serve as phenomenological counterpoints to the conventional bureaucratic interpretations that were applied to each of the incidents in question at the time of its original occurrence.

My choice of the aesthetic examples is shaped by what I regard as their disclosive and cognitive value as illustrations of the ontological foundations and poetic dimension of human encounter. I make no claim to expertise as an art or literary critic. For this reason, my selection of the works included here has been guided by established critical interpretation, and not merely by my limited judgment that they offer apposite phenomenological insight into the foundations of human encounter. To the extent that the works I have chosen are inherently open to a wide range of critical interpretations, I have good reason to anticipate that on any one of numerous grounds, objections will be raised to some of my choices, or at least to the ways in which I have interpreted them. Whatever the variance of critical opinion, which will undoubtedly reveal presently unseen flaws and errors, the validity of my general argument does not depend on whether or not one concurs with my particular interpretation of a given work. However, my argument *does* depend on the notion that aesthetic experience reveals something real and true.

THE DISCLOSIVE CAPACITY OF
AESTHETIC EXPERIENCE

To accept the potential interpretive validity of a phenomenological aesthetics of encounter requires believing that aesthetic experience stands in meaningful ontological relation to the world, and thus has a truth-value. In turn, this notion is itself contingent upon an understanding of aesthetic experience that regards it as irreducible to simple emotional affect or subjective taste. That such an understanding runs contrary to the dominant currents of modern, post-Kantian aesthetics goes without saying. The modern mind tends to view skeptically the idea that aesthetic experience has any actual truth-value. This attitude originates in the aesthetic philosophy of the Enlightenment, and its general redefining of aesthetic experience as a matter of epistemology and psychology rather than metaphysics. According to this redefinition, aesthetic experience ceases to be construed as an expression of an ontological unity of human beings and the world, and instead becomes reduced to a function of the subjective evaluation of certain kinds of sensory experience. Even where, as in the Kantian *sensus communis,* some effort is made to avoid collapsing the epistemological subjectivity of aesthetic experience and judgment into absolute relativism, the disseveration of aesthetics from ontology nonetheless endures (compare Gadamer, 1989:42–44). As Ernst Cassirer points out (1951:297–311), this transformation in the understanding of the nature of aesthetic experience is historically inseparable from the advent of scientific method. Without digressing into a lengthy discussion of modern aesthetics, it is important to appreciate the significance of Cassirer's argument, which lies in the recognition that modern science and modern aesthetics stand as common responses to the reimagining of nature as a domain of phenomena accessible to inductive, empirical investigation (compare Merleau-Ponty, 1996).

Perhaps the strongest sustained challenge to the subjectivization of aesthetic experience has come from phenomenology: to name Bachelard, Bakhtin, Gadamer, Heidegger, Ingarden, Marcel, Merleau-Ponty, Ricoeur, and Sartre is to suggest the range and depth of phenomenology's ongoing concern with aesthetic experience as a form of truth (see Ihde, 1977:147–52, and Kaelin, 1970). Though it would be a gross oversimplification to collapse the vast differences among these philosophers, their notions of aesthetic experience nonetheless share the broad view that it is irreducible to mere representation. Fritz Kaufmann aptly summarizes this phenomenological perspective: "A work of art does not substitute, but institutes an original awareness of existence on the whole; it does not so much reproduce and represent as produce and present a total experience" (1966:147). As Kaufmann suggests, the value of aesthetic experience rests on its ability to disclose what simple representational experience cannot accomplish. Put another way, aesthetic experience occasions what Maurice Natanson calls "an epiphany of the familiar" (1974:169). In this crucial respect, aesthetic experience and phenomenology share common ground in their starting from everyday experience as a source of transcendental reflection (Kaufmann, 1966:146). This affinity suggests how aesthetic experience can challenge the naïveté of unreflected scientific and technical thinking by showing that what goal-oriented praxis takes for granted as "real" is a methodologically created abstraction from a more fundamental reality, which aesthetic experience can effectively disclose and make present to consciousness.

Building on Heidegger's rethinking of truth as disclosure (*aletheia*), rather than as the hypothesized correspondence of an isolated "object" to its "subjective" representation (re-presentation) in consciousness, Gadamer argues in *Truth and Method* (1989:134–44) that aesthetics must likewise go beyond the naïve idea of the picture as mere presentation (*Darstellung*). For Gadamer, again in accord with Heidegger, the truth unique to aesthetic experience does not lie in the potential of a given work to represent with accuracy, but instead rests within the inseparable ontological relation between world and image, which is all but overlooked in modern aesthetics. Works of art exist for Gadamer not so much as "things" but as events, which represent the coming to presence of the world in aesthetic form (Gadamer, 1989:134–44; Heidegger, 1971a:44–50).

What is immediately decisive here for my purposes is Gadamer's articulation of a concept of aesthetic form that focuses on a noninstrumental relation between an "original" and a "copy." Whether this ontological relation between original and copy is expressed as a hermeneutic event or placed in a political context (e.g., Benjamin), it is clear that such thinking about aesthetics engages a nexus between ethics and ontology that is lost when the question of truth is framed merely as a question of method or epistemology. Here, *tout court,* is the value that aesthetic experience can offer as a critical counterpoint to the limited self-reflections that typically occur in mainstream social scientific and bureaucratic praxis.

The preceding claim can be elucidated by considering how even in the most "accurate" or "realistic" depictions that occur in a medium such as photography, what is ultimately valued is not the technical ability to produce faithful representations but the uncanny disclosure of what lies beyond the "factual presence" of the subject of the photograph. Photography creates a supplement, and is in this sense poetic. We need only think of photojournalistic works or documentary photography, which often attain a moral, aesthetic, and spiritual significance far beyond that which the photographer imagined in the technical process of taking the picture. Although we speak of the ability of photography to "capture" a moment, it is more accurate to say of the best photographs that while they are meaningful at one level as "objective representations," they may be more fundamentally understood as forms of aesthetic creation that disclose truth by way of a solicitude that lets things be.[8]

Preliminarily, it may be said that aesthetic modes of knowing diverge from technical and mainstream scientific knowledge in the dependence of the former on a comportment toward its subject that demands a kind of *solicitude*. This distinction is one that Heidegger considers in great detail in order to establish the radical difference between the self-disclosure of being and its "enframing" through reductive forms of understanding and praxis (see Heidegger, 1971a and 1993). Aesthetic experience is thus nothing like the disinterestedness of Kantian philosophy; rather, it pays attention to a specific "object" in a way that always knows the impossibility of reducing it to mere factual presence. Moreover, the truth or meaning of an accurate depiction does not lie in its realistic quality but in its illumination of what lies behind the apparently simple presence of things (see Dufrenne, 1973:527). This formulation closely mirrors Paul Klee's characterization of his painting as "a striving to emphasize the essential character of the accidental" (1968:185), or Cézanne's view of his task as an artist: "What I am trying to translate to you is more mysterious; it is entwined in the very roots of being, in the impalpable sources of sensations."[9]

Mikel Dufrenne presents a similar idea of the relation between aesthetic experience and subjectivity in his magnum opus, *The Phenomenology of Aesthetic Experience:* "The subjectivity of the aesthetic world is not a defect, because the singular (insofar as it is the human) is here universal" (1973:507). It might be objected in response to Dufrenne (as well as Klee and Cézanne) that the move from singularity to universality ever remains the province of individual judgment, and in no way bears a meaningful relation to the "real," whatever might be meant by this term. At least from Dufrenne's perspective, this objection itself has already ceded to scientific understanding a monopoly on intelligible understanding of the real (1973:508). The truth of art, however, does not consist in its constituting an adequate representation of a world already given. Such a claim effectively reduces aesthetic creation to a narrow, technical skill aimed wholly at "realism"—a *method,* in fact, that abdicates its theoretical stance vis-à-vis the real (see Dufrenne, 1973:516).

In making this argument, Dufrenne helps to show how aesthetic experience contextualizes our notion of the real by transcending its conflation with modern notions of "objectivity" (1973:529). Particularly in an age where the cosmos has been reduced to the mathematized lifeworld, art serves as a form of recollection. Insofar as this mathematization has been visited as well upon the social world, the task of a phenomenological aesthetics and critical projects alike becomes all the more urgent. If, as Dufrenne remarks (1973:528), "the reality of the real is a presence which I encounter and to which I submit," aesthetic experience can open possibilities for thought and reflection by making human presence meaningful in ways that evoke the fullness of its existential significance, a fullness that is lost under the regime of pure method. As Gabriel Marcel similarly argues, aesthetic truth holds the possibility of making explicit the human relation to transcendence (2001:45).

This point may be understood more clearly by recalling my earlier discussion of the poetic aspect of ordinary existence. Poetic thinking appeals to a reality beyond its self-consciously known expressive limits, strains to give that reality meaning, and, yet, does not purport to capture it as an abstract entity. Art retains a reverence for the order it depicts and discloses. Aesthetic creation remains ever aware of the fallibility of its own gesture, not as a failure or imperfection of method to be resolved at some future date but as an ontological reality. In this realization of its fallibility, aesthetic creation reveals its ethical engagement with the tragic: in its greatest moments of exaltation and exhilaration, there is always a presence of finitude and melancholy, which carries over to aesthetic experience, imparting to it that uncanny affective quality united with an intuition of wholeness.

Gadamer notes that art history and art criticism never claim to duplicate in their analyses the aesthetic experience of the work of art itself, which is recognized as unique unto itself. Rather, the work of art "asserts itself against all attempts to rationalize it away" (1989:xxiii). Gadamer argues that it is the same in the case of understanding in the human sciences. Here, he discerns a fateful moment in the history of the human sciences, and shows its direct relation to the subjectivization of aesthetic judgment. Art "cannot be defined as an object of an aesthetic consciousness because, on the contrary, the aesthetic attitude is more than it knows of itself" (1989:116). For Gadamer, the wider relevance of aesthetic experience is the way in which it depends on more than mere passive response to perception. It is the performative response of the spectator that creates the experience of tragedy, whether in classical drama or in the experience of human presence on the street. If Gadamer is correct in saying of the experience of dramatic tragedy that "[t]ragic pensiveness flows from the self-knowledge that the spectator acquires" (1988:133), we can readily see how the intentional stance of which he speaks assumes eminently greater ethical gravity in the realm of social praxis.

The disclosive capacity of aesthetic experience to produce a recognition and recollection—a rethinking that gathers up (*recolligere*) the familiar world in a new way—thus holds critical value for interpreting the sort of praxis like bureaucracy, which of necessity does not have the contemplative stance of art. Still, the creation of social order viewed as a poetic process reminds us of the common thread of tragedy running through creative activity of any kind, be it art or politics. As Weber argues in "Politics as a Vocation," we struggle in vain to imagine that the necessary exercise of power can ever transcend the ethical paradoxes that imbue the political with tragedy. Yet the ethical struggle in justly exercising power is to maintain an authentic mindfulness of this state of affairs, a task that demands a reflective stance beyond the passive performance of duty. This is the context within which a phenomenological aesthetics, and approaches like it, might bring to light some of the ontological foundation of the sorts of praxis like bureaucratic policing, which are constantly threatened by the logic of efficiency and routinization and all that it portends.

DIVISION II

FOUR

Domestic Violence Encounters: The Eye of the Painter and the Eye of the Police

Art lets truth originate.

—Martin Heidegger,
"The Origin of the Work of Art," 1936

INTRODUCTION

The police response to domestic violence calls provides an especially vivid illustration of how bureaucratic praxis resolves face-to-face encounters into manageable problems. Perhaps more than any other common type of call for police service, domestic violence situations exemplify the awkwardness of introducing armed bureaucrats into the midst of hostile intimate relationships. The intense emotion, discomfiture, and outright animosity of domestic conflicts assume even wider ramifications when the police become involved. However we might try to explain this dynamic—psychologically, sociologically, legally, or otherwise—the introduction of police officers into these situations fundamentally alters the ways in which domestic disputes unfold, often *unpredictably* and *uncontrollably*. This is a fact that police officers are taught very early in their careers, when they are cautioned about the intensity of domestic violence situations, and the unique set of tactical dangers, investigative challenges, and socioethical conundrums presented by responding to them.

To speak as a police officer of the "unpredictable" or "uncontrollable" aspects of domestic violence situations is to allude to the practical manifestation of two of the grounding ontological concepts of bureaucratic problematization.

Within the context of street-level encounters, officers use the notions of "unpredictability" and "uncontrollability" to interpret resistance to the exercise of their authority. Placed in a more elemental context, however, these notions may be read as descriptions of the indecipherability of human presence in the face of problematization. Following this line of analysis, unpredictability and uncontrollability emerge as forms of ontological resistance, which are irreducible to legal acts of resistance against bureaucratic authority, such as refusing to answer investigative questions, or physically resisting arrest. Within the unfolding dynamics of encounter, the first sign of resistance is met in the gaze of the person, who stands before a police officer as the would-be object of bureaucratic praxis.

Using a phenomenological aesthetics of encounter, it is possible to explain how the gaze of a fellow human being is recast through bureaucratic praxis into the "facing of a problem." I will present such an explanation here by focusing on two narratives of domestic violence incidents, and analyzing each of them using painted representations of the human gaze. The first narrative recounts an incident in which I contacted the victim of a domestic violence assault under relatively stable circumstances, after her assailant had fled the scene. I will explicate this encounter using Edouard Manet's *A Bar at the Folies-Bergère* (Figure 4.1). The second narrative describes a far more volatile situation, involving the police response to a brutal fight between a father and his adult son. My interpretation of this incident draws on Paul Klee's *Senecio* (Figure 4.2). In both instances, a phenomenologically oriented attentiveness to what these paintings reveal about the nature of encounter, and especially to the role that the gaze plays in it, will show how the notions of controllability and predictability occur as decisive elements of the discordant bureaucratic response to human presence.

ENCOUNTER #4-1: MELISSA

On a busy Saturday night, two other officers and I responded to a report of a domestic violence assault. The dispatcher advised us that the female victim dialed 911 after having been choked by her ex-boyfriend, who had since fled. When I arrived at the scene, the woman, "Melissa," was standing in the driveway in bare feet, crying, and holding her three-year-old son. Melissa is twenty-two years old. She told me that she and her ex-boyfriend, "Richard," the father of her son, dated for the past seven years, and had broken up several months earlier.

Richard had spent the day with the little boy, who lived with Melissa most of the time. When Richard brought him home to Melissa, a heated argu-

ment ensued. Melissa said that she and Richard "got into it." As she tried to explain what happened, she repeatedly interjected the unsolicited comment, "it's my fault; I hit him first." After evading my investigative questions about the incident and protesting several times that she did not want to file a report and see Richard go to jail, Melissa disclosed that he had thrown her to the floor and choked her so hard that she had momentarily lost consciousness. "I thought I was going to die," she told me.

Melissa had red marks on her neck and throat and fresh bruises on her arms, all of which were consistent with her story. She said that her neck was numb on one side, but she refused to let me call an ambulance to evaluate her injuries. I suggested to Melissa that she really ought to be seen by a doctor. I also told her that information from a medical examination could help to prosecute Richard. Melissa finally agreed to allow her grandmother, who lived nearby, to give her a ride to the emergency room. I drove Melissa to her grandmother's house.

While we waited for her grandmother, I began completing my department's standard domestic violence report. This entailed interviewing Melissa, obtaining a written statement from her, photographing her injuries, and documenting them on a schematic diagram. I also asked Melissa to sign a release that would allow the police department to obtain copies of medical records related to the treatment of her injuries. When I finished, I gave her a "victim information sheet." This form lists the case number for the incident, provides information on community resources for victims of domestic violence, and explains the process for obtaining a protection order, which would prohibit Richard from contacting her, either directly or indirectly. I explained to Melissa that a domestic violence investigator would contact her for further follow-up, as well as to assist her with court paperwork, child custody arrangements, and other matters that might arise.

I asked Melissa where she thought Richard might have gone. She was very reluctant to tell me anything. Melissa's grandmother arrived to pick her up, and our encounter came to an end. I told the dispatcher to broadcast information notifying other officers in the area that there was probable cause to arrest Richard for domestic violence assault. I then advised that I was clear of the call, and went back into service.

FACING A PROBLEM

As bureaucratically situated "expert observers," police officers are taught to process and record *what they see* with the aim of accomplishing the predetermined objectives of law enforcement. Expressed in Weberian terms, the police are engaged in an instrumental-rational (*zweckrational*) task, one that is "determined by expectations as to the behavior of objects in the environment and of other human beings; these expectations are used as 'conditions' or 'means' for the attainment of the actor's own rationally pursued and calculated ends" (Weber, 1978:24). Applying this description to my encounter with Melissa, my colleagues and I discharged our bureaucratic duty by enacting a set of presuppositions that allowed us to approach her situation in terms of the formal task of finding and solving a problem and then efficiently "clearing the call." This depended on our interpreting the encounter using various legal and operational notions about "domestic violence." The actual process of interpretation occurred through our adopting a specific practical *stance* toward Melissa, with respect to which her presence could be approached as something meaningfully subject to problematization.

"Stance" refers literally to how one stands before or faces another human being. For police officers to encounter human beings as problems, or for them to encounter the predicaments of their fellow human beings as "calls" or "incidents," requires taking a specific stance that enables the abstractive circumscription of meaning with respect to the accomplishing of predetermined bureaucratic tasks. Stance thus constitutes the basis for one's approach to the intentional awareness of another presence. Stance and gaze are fundamentally interrelated aspects of most face-to-face encounters.

Police officers not only maintain a constant, passive eye for suspicion, but even more essentially, through the effective managing and training of their gazes, they also actively seek out and detect suspicion on the basis of interpreting encounters with others (see Rubinstein, 1973:220–23, and Sacks, 1972).[1] Officers learn to watch people, and to study them with a conscious awareness that their doing so arouses disruption, fear, consternation, and curiosity. The simple fact of an officer's passively "being there" can evoke a powerful response. Beyond its role as a means of surveillance, the officer's gaze serves as a key element in the dialectic of encounter, through which response and counter response create and justify opportunities for formal intervention of various kinds.

One common example of this phenomenon may be observed in the responses of drivers sitting next to a police car at a traffic light. Experienced officers know that the law-abiding citizen will often cast a fleeting, curious, or even friendly glance at the officer, however briefly or surreptitiously. On the other hand, a criminal will frequently try to "make himself invisible," taking almost too much trouble to "look innocent" by gazing intently forward with a practiced indifference that conveys precisely the opposite meaning of its superficial appearance. Officers in many police circles refer to this phenomenon as "giving the look," or simply, "the look." If an officer stops someone who manifests this gaze, and ends up making an arrest, the vindicated judgment of suspicion is often reported to a colleague as follows: "I just *had* to stop him; he gave me the look." Of course, more-sophisticated lawbreakers are aware of the phenomenon of "the look" and act accordingly to confuse officers' expectations. This leaves officers in the position of having to judge the underlying intentions behind smiles and waves. This kind of dynamic can occur with equal intensity in contacts with victims of crimes, such as Melissa.

However it manifests itself, the gaze of the officer examines, scrutinizes, and judges, looking for evidence, truth, and falsehood. The police officer is a watchful stranger, who by legal and social mandate enters into the lives of other strangers, often in moments of profound crisis.[2] The mere presence of a police officer necessarily changes the dynamics of an encounter, a reality that finds practical acknowledgment in the designation of "officer presence" as the starting point for most police agencies' use of force continua.[3] Police officers learn to develop and carefully project their "presence," a key aspect of which is the gaze. The old adage that "the eyes are the windows to the soul" has been repeated many times over to rookie officers, as they are taught the importance of watching people's eyes for signs of danger and deceit. As those who enact and enforce order within a given social space, police officers learn to become highly specialized versions of what Michel de Certeau (1984:93) calls "practitioners of the city" and *Wandersmänner*. The stance of the practitioner directs action toward the "imaginary totalizations produced by the eye" (Certeau, 1984:93).

THE EYE OF THE PAINTER
AND THE EYE OF THE POLICE

Edouard Manet's *A Bar at the Folies-Bergère* (1882) is renowned for its striking treatment of the human gaze. It offers an especially apt vantage point from which to consider the role of the gaze in my encounter with Melissa, as well as for undertaking a wider phenomenological analysis of the gaze as a manifestation of co-presence. *A Bar at the Folies-Bergère* disrupts the presumed relationship between the eye and the world by drawing viewers into its depicted scene, and demanding that they consider their relationship to the image on the canvas. In this crucial respect, *A Bar at the Folies-Bergère* directly engages the event of representation by foregrounding the relation of the "subject" of the work of art to the eye and presence of the viewer.

The aesthetic, moral, and philosophical significance of *A Bar at the Folies-Bergère* consists in its revealing and questioning what underlies the everyday act of standing over against another human being, as "subject" to "object," or outsider to spectacle. Interpreted in this way, *A Bar at the Folies-Bergère* lends insight toward achieving an understanding of the grounding concepts and dynamics of the problematization of human being in police-citizen encounters.[4] That insight derives largely from Manet's masterful depiction of the irreducible experience of human co-presence.

The center of *A Bar at the Folies-Bergère* is the barmaid. She stands facing the viewer, her palms pressed against a marble countertop spread with a wealth of offerings—liqueurs, champagne, beer, oranges, and flowers. Everything that we know of the broader context of the picture appears in the form of a mirror image, reflected in the huge mirror behind the bar and the barmaid. Looking at the mirror's reflection, the viewer indirectly sees the bustling activity of the crowded Folies-Bergère, which the barmaid sees directly as she looks about from her vantage point.

What is most conspicuously visible in the mirror, however, is not the crowd but the reflection of the barmaid's back, and the reflection of a man who, according to the placement of his image, should be standing at the bar facing her. But he is not. It seems that he should be standing precisely where the viewer of the painting also stands, although the configuration of the mirror image simultaneously suggests that the man must be standing off to the right. This seeming incongruity has been the focus of extensive debate and painstaking analysis, and is widely read as more than a compositional flaw.[5]

Although the reflection in the mirror and the woman standing at the bar are clearly meant to be the same person, differences between the "real" woman and her mirror image suggest an intended symbolic dissonance between the two (see Clark, 1984, and Collins, 1996). The woman in the image leans forward, as if engaging in conversation with the man standing before her. However, the "actual" woman appears detached, aloof, and even wistful or melancholic. This ambiguity is literally reflected and made visible in the mirror, by leaving the position of the spectator unclear (Armstrong, 1996:58). Indeed, many critics suggest that the man in the mirror is meant to be the universal observer or viewer of the painting.[6]

FIGURE 4.1. Edouard Manet (1832–83), *A Bar at the Folies-Bergère*, 1882. Oil on canvas, 96 x 130 cm. The Samuel Courtauld Trust, Courtauld Institute of Art Gallery, London.

Perhaps the only aspect of *A Bar at the Folies-Bergère* to receive as much criti-cal scrutiny as the mirror reflection is the barmaid's gaze. Her gaze has been read as "both weary and absent" (Cachin, 1995:124); "distant and melancholy" (Flam, 1996:164); beautiful, but "strangely lusterless, her eyes clouded with fatigue or boredom" (Bataille, 1955:99); "detached" (Clark, 1984:254; Boime, 1996:56); and a "blank stare" (Armstrong, 1996:26). The viewer could well imagine that Manet had in mind the words of his close friend Baudelaire when he painted the barmaid's face: "Dullness is frequently an ornament of beauty. It is to this that we owe it if eyes are sad and translucent like blackish swamps or if their gaze has the oily inertness of tropical seas" (quoted in Benjamin, 1968:190). Whatever the range of their descriptions, most analysts of the paint-ing comment on the inexpressive and indecipherable look on the barmaid's face, summarized aptly by Ross in her characterization of the barmaid as "the psychological and compositional focus of a scene in which she is not wholly a participant" (1982:9).[7] The powerful effect of the barmaid's gaze is heightened by the fact that there is no angle from which it meets the gaze of the viewer.

Expressed in terms of the idea of approach, no matter how one tries to draw near to the canvas, the barmaid's gaze—and thus her presence—remain enig-matic. Such a reading accords closely with the experience of the crime victim, who merely becomes the pliant "object" of bureaucratic operations. Manet's painting shows the tensions and forms of resistance inherent to this kind of modern social interaction, in which, as Zygmunt Bauman (1990:24–25) puts it, people are "morally distant yet physically close." However, as Manet's painting suggests, human presence resists the transformation of proximity into abstrac-tion. Mauner (1975:161) similarly notes how "we *submit* to the strangeness of the gaze of the central and static barmaid" (emphasis added). This submis-sion is instinctive, reciprocal, and instantaneous: the barmaid's gaze almost involuntarily engages our own.[8] Standing out in front of the ephemeral reality reflected in the mirror, the barmaid's presence seems to demand a response. To look at her is to intuit immediately the existential reality behind theoretical articulations of human encounter such as the face-to-face (Levinas, 1979), the I-Thou relation (Buber, 1958), or answerability (Bakhtin, 1990). Each of these ideas expresses what I characterized earlier (see chapter 1) as the ecstatic nature of human being—the way that human beings "stand forth" into the world, ab-solutely otherwise than as objectively present things, such as the bottles or fruit sitting on the bar. It is no far reach to say that the bureaucrat, exemplified by the detached, efficient police officer, and the blasé urban denizen, exemplified by the *flâneur* depicted in *A Bar at the Folies-Bergère*, act out common variations of the same distinctly modern notion of encounter, in which the fullness of the face-to-face moment becomes transmuted into abstract "intersubjectivity." The *flâneur,* who refined the ability to gaze upon the human spectacle of modern life in a meticulously enacted regime of self-isolation and self-management, thus bears a close affinity to the police officer.

When I arrived at the "scene of the call" involving the assault against Melissa, I quickly set about the task of *typifying* her and other "relevant parties" (her son and Richard) in accordance with the need to determine "what happened" (see Schutz, 1971). As this process unfolded, the situation itself became reified as a *possession* that "belonged" to me as the primary investigating officer. Officers are conscious of this quality of their encounters; hence they will say of a call, "I've got this one," or "this one's yours." Officers assisting at a scene will frequently relay information to the primary investigating officer using similar possessive terms. Pointing out the various people present, or handing over a slip of paper with names written on it, officers will tell their colleagues, "OK, that's your victim over there, there's your suspect," and so forth.

Quickly placed into the role of being "my" victim, Melissa's presence immediately assumed practical significance as an evidentiary object, as I sought out marks, words, impressions, and images, which could be transformed into the "facts and circumstances" of a police report. The gaze of the police officer must remain focused but detached, so that the investigation can progress unimpeded by the "imponderability of personal relationships" (Simmel, 1971:327). The eye of the officer seeks confirmation of its suspicions in the victim's utterances: what is "the story?" The "story," at least initially, is one that officers try to elicit as quickly and efficiently as possible with a view toward attaining their ends. In my encounter with Melissa, it was imperative for me to determine if there was probable cause to arrest Richard. The urgency of this process is often determined by tactical considerations more so than by legal ones. Knowing that Richard had fled from the scene in his car, the officer who had responded to assist me was now driving around the area looking for him. He needed information about Richard's appearance, whether or not he was armed, if there was a legal reason to detain or arrest him, and so forth.

Rapidly eliciting legal and tactical information from a victim is a very delicate process. The momentum of bureaucratic praxis can overtake a situation, subsuming the actual occasion for the summoning of police assistance within the operational needs of the officers. Emotionally and spiritually drained victims, to say nothing of those who are physically injured, must be pressed persistently but gently (at least one hopes) for "the story." This process raises a decisive ethical question that will recur throughout this book: how can one listen effectively and patiently, in a way that does not reduce compassion to a superficial anodyne?

As I interviewed Melissa, I had to consciously watch her, looking and listening for information that would fit logically into the categories on the officer observation sheet, which I would complete as part of an official domestic violence report. The dynamic in this process bears a marked similarity to structured interviews undertaken for social research. Amid reassuring glances and expressions of understanding and patience, I sought the elements of probable cause, which would build the legal case against Richard: "OK, Melissa, can you tell me what happened tonight?" She hesitated. I tried a different approach. "How long had you guys been going out?" "More than seven years, he was my first boyfriend." Melissa went on to provide a lengthy, emotional account of her involvement with Richard. She choked back tears several times. "How many times has he hit you before?" I asked, hoping to elicit information about a history of domestic violence. "Nothing like tonight," she replied, "we just used to get into it a lot." "Get into it?" "You know, a lot of yelling and stuff, maybe some grabbing and shoving, but it was never like tonight." As I spoke with Melissa, I sensed that her mind was shifting back and forth between engaging my questions and the questions she seemed to be asking herself internally in an effort to comprehend Richard's actions. As she answered my questions, she paused occasionally, as if an answer she gave me might have a bearing on her internal dialogue.

As my encounter with Melissa illustrates, the police officer's natural attitude accepts *a priori* the possibility for the meaningful interpretation and representation of human predicaments on the basis of their problematization in administrative and juridical terms. This is the horizon framing interactions in which officers "deal with" or "respond to" these predicaments, both as lived moments bringing human beings face to face with each other, and as "matters of fact" in the form of encounters between an agent of the state and a citizen. Like the calculatedly detached and nonchalant *flâneur* in Manet's painting, the police officer as bureaucrat presumes an ability to stand over against another human being as a disinterested or neutral observer, look at him or her as "being there" in the form of one problem or another, and then walk away, both literally and figuratively. It is the moral and existential basis of this presumption that is so forcefully challenged by *A Bar at the Folies-Bergère*. To be sure, the police officer is potentially capable of genuine sympathy and compassion no less than the *flâneur* was capable of kindness and gentility. However, such responses can only emerge as the reply to an awareness of human presence that exceeds its conceptualization for the instrumental rational ends of bureaucratic praxis. It is this same irreducible awareness that makes it possible for the viewer of *A Bar at the Folies-Bergère* to identify the barmaid as the compositional and existential center of the painting.

INVOCATION AND RESPONSE

Art historians and critics have speculated widely on the notion of "response" in *A Bar at the Folies-Bergère*, offering a range of ideas about what is being said (or left unsaid) in the encounter between the barmaid and *flâneur*. To respond to someone in a conversation means, of course, to offer an answer or reply; however, in police work, its connotation is radically different. The everyday discourse of policing speaks of "responding" to calls, problems, or situations, though not of "responding to people." Another common variation is the notion of "answering" calls for service. In the case of both words, "respond" and "answer" lose the ethical significance assumed in face-to-face conversation, creating an absence that signifies the translation of existential complexity into a bureaucratic problem or object. Under the sway of such thinking, the administrative interpretation of an event becomes conflated with the event itself.

When I "responded to a domestic" and identified Melissa as the victim of an assault, her role in an administratively delimited encounter was *to be* the victim of a crime. Face to face with her, I followed legally and socially sanctioned rituals that permitted me to enter abruptly into the life of a complete stranger. I went on to ask her a range of personal questions, sat in her living room, photographed her, walked through her house, and so on, all with a view toward constructing an officially meaningful account of a particular moment in her life, to the practical exclusion of that life's more elemental nature. From the standpoint of the criminal justice system, presumably in concert with society at large, the ideal result of this account would be the amelioration of Melissa's suffering and the imposition of legal sanctions against her ex-boyfriend, Richard, in the hope that such punishment might deter him from committing future assaults, or, if nothing else, at least visit upon him some consequences for his actions. Considered in terms of a socially recognized need to aid crime victims, there is nothing inherently wrong with this. However, what *is* both wrong and avoidable is to fail to recognize the fatal inadequacy of the official comportment on the basis of which such aid is rendered.

One manifestation of this inadequacy is observable in the phenomenon of the "uncooperative victim." These are instances in which the victim of a crime resists participating in the rituals necessary for the documentation and prosecution of an offense. Melissa was, at least initially, an "uncooperative victim" to the extent that for some time she persistently hesitated to provide a complete account of the incident, and would not disclose Richard's whereabouts. The immense range of possible motives for this response (for Melissa, perhaps fear of Richard, or lingering affection for him) is not of immediate relevance here; rather, the more pressing point is to illustrate how the "objective reality" or factual understanding officially assigned to the predicament of another human being becomes its sovereign truth, eclipsing the person's own lived experience. The person involved in a domestic violence incident, who does not act according to a bureaucratically expected role, becomes a force that militates against efforts by the police at control and prediction. As this process unfolds, the encounter becomes for the officer a process of overcoming resistance in order to contain and problematize the situation.

This is not simply a question of unsympathetic attitudes or ideologically motivated disinterest. Indeed, to officers' great frustration and dismay, "uncooperative" victims are often present when there is the sincerest desire to help someone who is regarded as truly deserving of assistance. It is not uncommon under such circumstances for compassion to turn quickly into impatience, annoyance, or outright disgust, as a result of which the victim, on whose behalf the investigation is presumably conducted, comes to be experienced as stupid, selfish, and wasting the valuable time of the police.[9] Indeed, being "uncooperative" during a given encounter will often be taken by officers to lower one's potential moral legitimacy as a victim in subsequent contacts. In more extreme instances, victims who are obviously lying, and especially those who have been previously arrested or contacted by the police as suspects in other crimes, may, for example, be labeled privately by officers as "vuspects"—people whose perceived lack of virtue means that their legitimacy as "real" victims is effectively nil.[10] This phenomenon exemplifies what Edward Tiryakian (1973:200–205) describes as the shift in consciousness that accompanies a change in moral value. Some of the tensions intrinsic to such a shift are evident in the next encounter.

Encounter #4-2: Isaac and Henry

While working as a shift supervisor on a New Year's Eve, I heard two of the officers on my squad get dispatched to a disturbance at an address well known for the chronically violent behavior of the family living there. The dispatcher said that the 911 operator who took the call could hear loud yelling in the background, and believed there to be some kind of fight occurring. The dispatcher also advised that the address was flagged as an "officer safety" hazard, because one of the residents, "Isaac," had a history of violent assaults against police officers. An "officer safety" flag usually mandates that at least three officers respond to the call, so I told the dispatcher that I would be heading there, in addition to my two colleagues who were already en route.

By the time I arrived, the other two officers had preceded me into the house. I heard one of them ask the dispatcher to "close the air," that is, restrict radio traffic in order to ensure unimpeded communication until the situation was safely under control. I knew that the officer's request meant that he and the second officer were probably involved in some kind of physical altercation. As I quickly approached the house, Isaac's girlfriend, Bonny, beckoned from just inside the open front door, and hurriedly ushered me past a rather unfriendly dog, along a path of overturned furniture and large blood spatters. Bonny directed me to the second floor of a detached two-story garage located behind the house and said, "they're upstairs."

I went upstairs and found the other two officers handcuffing a prone Isaac. They told me they had found Isaac and his father, Henry, lying on the floor, locked together in a spastic, emotional embrace that seemed to be hovering indiscernibly between combat and affection. Knowing Isaac's propensity for unpredictable violence, the officers had separated him from his father. Isaac was not struggling with the officers; however, he was extremely agitated. As the other two officers turned Isaac onto his back in order to stand him up, I spoke to him, reminding him that we knew each other, and asked for his cooperation in trying to calm down. Isaac acknowledged me by name, and seemed surprised that I had perhaps doubted for a moment that I knew who I was. Isaac and Henry had both obviously been severely beaten. Blood poured uncontrollably from Henry's nose and mouth as he held his hands to his face. Isaac complained of broken ribs. His face and shirtless torso were covered with cuts and abrasions. Henry and Isaac denied they had been fighting with each other, and blamed a third party, "Frank," who was now gone. "He's driving a black Toyota truck," shouted Isaac, "look what he did to my father! Go get him!" Isaac's angry yelling dissolved into hysterical sobs.

Henry was incoherent, his drunken stupor made all the worse by the punishing assault he had sustained. He could barely stand up, and had difficulty telling the difference between the police officers and the fire department personnel whom I had called to evaluate his injuries. Henry's eyes moved about slowly and warily. He refused to be treated by the aid crew, and refused to talk about the events that had caused his injuries. Even in his intoxicated, wounded state, I treated him cautiously, knowing he could lash out with little warning. As I helped him to his feet, he gripped my hand powerfully, and an unfriendly smile momentarily replaced the look of confused delirium, drunkenness, and pain.

What little information we could gather strongly indicated to my colleagues and me that Isaac had obviously assaulted his father. However, our "gut feelings" and intuitions did not equate to the legal standard of probable cause; and thus, we had no grounds on which to make an arrest. Frustrated by the unwillingness of Henry and Bonny to give an accurate account of the assault, I told the other officers at the scene that I "really wanted PC" [probable cause] to arrest Isaac for felony domestic violence assault. All of us were aware that Isaac had recently been released from prison and had been involved in another violent assault at a nearby nightclub several weeks earlier, in which he had hurled cue balls across a crowded room, striking and injuring several people. We shared the strong opinion that he needed to be "taken off the street" sooner rather than later.

As matters stood, this was not to happen, at least not immediately. After pleading and cajoling for several minutes, I finally convinced Henry to go to the emergency room for treatment and X-rays. Not least of all my persistence was motivated by the hope that the discovery of fractures might provide evidence for the subsequent filing of felony domestic violence assault charges against Isaac. As Henry stumbled toward the front door escorted by the fire department aid crew, he abruptly threw himself at Isaac, who was sitting handcuffed in a large armchair, and began sobbing. Isaac also started to cry. Isaac again protested that the police should "get Frank" for assaulting his father. Henry fell conspicuously silent, and followed the firefighters and Bonny outside to the waiting ambulance. I spoke with Bonny, and asked her if she thought she would be safe with Isaac at the house. She expressed no concerns. Isaac was released from his handcuffs. My colleagues and I left, knowing well that upon his father's return, the situation would almost surely rekindle. At the end of my shift, when I briefed the sergeant who was relieving me, I told him to expect further problems from Isaac.

Several hours later, Henry returned home after being discharged from the emergency room, and Isaac assaulted him again. Isaac then stole Henry's pickup truck and wrecked it a short distance from home. He was arrested and booked into jail.

THE APPEARANCE OF TURMOIL

As a call for police service, the incident between Isaac and Henry was obviously far less "manageable" than the assault against Melissa. Both in tactical as well as investigative terms, it epitomized the uncontrollability and unpredictability that are characteristic of many domestic violence incidents. From the standpoint of the exercise of bureaucratic problematization, Melissa's case had been

FIGURE 4.2. Paul Klee, (1879–1940), *Senecio* (*Baldgreis*), 1922, 181 (accession nr. 1569). Oil on canvas, mounted on cardboard, original yellow-edged frame, 40.5 x 38 cm. Kunstmuseum Basel. Photo: Kunstmuseum Basel, Martin Bühler.

fairly unambiguous—the nuances and complexities of her predicament were efficiently stripped of what was deemed officially to have been extraneous detail, allowing for her ready objectification as a victim. In the case of Isaac and Henry, a host of factors militated against a similarly decisive conclusion.

From the outset of the incident, the course of problematization was unyieldingly impeded by the hostile refusal of the involved parties to have anything to do with the responding officers. Years of mutual mistrust and animosity between Isaac's family and the police doubtless contributed to this tense state of affairs. Even in their state of extreme intoxication, physical pain, and emotion duress, Isaac and Henry demonstrated a self-discipline that restrained them from disclosing the actual chain of events that had led to the police response. Bonny, Isaac's girlfriend, had phoned for police assistance; however, once her initial, frantic fear had subsided, she probably concluded that implicating Isaac in the attack on Henry would only result in Isaac's turning on her. It may also be surmised with a reasonable degree of certainty that Bonny felt a certain moral and personal obligation not to cooperate with officers, because Isaac (and, perhaps, Henry) would most likely have perceived this as an act of disloyalty or betrayal. Finally, tactical exigencies and Isaac and Henry's state of heavy intoxication also plainly acted to hamper the efficient resolution of the call.

Despite this confusion and chaos, my colleagues and I quickly determined that the resolution of the incident hinged upon interpreting what Isaac had or had not done. The anguish, hopelessness, and bellicosity that played across Isaac's face, and emerged in his words and actions, were translated by bureaucratic praxis into "resistance to control," "intractability," "unpredictability," and "danger." From the standpoint of a phenomenological aesthetics of encounter, this process of translation is decisive, because it marks the concrete dynamic through which the lived moment of face-to-face interaction assumes its practical significance as a problem. I now turn to Paul Klee's *Senecio* to explore this dynamic, as it occurred in my encounter with Isaac and Henry. *Senecio* offers an extraordinary image of the tensions intrinsic to the process of typifying and reifying human presence, and thereby discloses some of the dangers and enigmas that shape the act of encountering an anguished human being. I am especially interested in showing how *Senecio* and my encounter with Isaac and Henry may both be read as illustrations of Klee's notion of "unstable equilibrium" (*schwankendes Gleichgewicht*).[11]

The principle of unstable equilibrium expresses Klee's attempt "to reconcile the frictions and dissonances within an enveloping tension" (Kudielka, 2002:83). For Klee, unstable equilibrium defines an entire range of relationships between competing or opposing forces, from the physical tension between momentum and gravity at work in a swinging pendulum, to the innermost tensions of the human condition (see Kudielka, 2002:83–85, and Klee, 1961:389). Within the context of explicating my encounter with Isaac and Henry, *Senecio* provides an illustration of unstable equilibrium that reveals parallels to the form of human presence that is often encountered when the police respond to volatile crises, and find themselves struggling to impose control through the containment of situations as discrete problems, definable in terms of a "totality of facts and circumstances."

MAKING PROBLEMATIZATION VISIBLE

Klee's approach to art has an explicitly phenomenological quality, which is expressed in his *Creative Credo:* Art does not reproduce the visible but makes visible (1961:76).[12] This statement shows some of what Klee had in mind as he strived to break with traditional artistic conventions of representation and depiction— what he termed the "optical-physical" (*optisch-physicher*) relation of artist and object—and reveals his radical sense of the *poetic* spirit of art (1961:63).[13]

Senecio conveys Klee's notion of wholeness as a state characterized by intrinsic tensions, which holds the potential for disunity or disintegration. The painting also exemplifies his project of depicting the world from a perspective that transcends the strict representation of an optically "correct" image, and reveals what Grohmann (1967:31) calls the "point of view of totality." *Senecio* consists of a complex juxtaposition of disparate colors, together with a contrasting geometry that combines straight lines with circles and curves. The resulting image presents in its total effect what might otherwise seem in the abstract as contradictory and irreconcilable: childhood and old age; humor and anger; movement and stasis; resoluteness and urgency. Joining these interrelated compositional and thematic tensions with the absence of an immediately self-evident "subject," viewers of *Senecio* find themselves facing the gaze of an enigmatic presence. Projecting what Hall (1992:48) characterizes as an "almost hypnotic power," which virtually compels the viewer of *Senecio* to wonder about the significance of its mysterious and vaguely discomfiting image. On first impression, a number of viewers find that the bright colors and outward simplicity of *Senecio* elicit a feeling of whimsy or fantasy. However, a more sustained consideration quickly finds these reactions tempered and eclipsed by an unsettling awareness that the painting projects a sense of enormous tension.

The sharply demarcated circle of the head is softened by the contrasting grid pattern of *Senecio*'s face, neck, and upper torso (Jordan, 1984:184). The entire background of the canvas is a field of orange and orange-red tones. Is this fire, sunlight, autumn color, or a symbolic representation of emotion? Where they meet the top of the head, these background colors blend into a range of yellow, orange, and light brown, forming a crown of hair, which seems all the more childlike when regarded together with the two pink cheeks. The mouth comprises two dark violet, diagonally offset squares (the upper of the two is actually slightly rectangular) sitting on opposite sides of a horizontal line, which separates the pink field at the center of the face from the much more subdued white and gray coloring of the lower face and "jawline." Looking at the mouth, one is unsure if it conveys impishness or anger.

The most conspicuous feature of the painting is undoubtedly *Senecio*'s off-set eyes, which are darkly outlined by a sharp "figure eight" or "infinity sign" (Jordan, 1984:185), and contrasted further by the white triangular "brow" above the right eye, and the curving brownish-green one above the left.[14] Each eye is painted with a deep red iris, imparting to *Senecio* the central attribute of its remarkable psychological impact (Jordan, 1984:185). Within the iris of the left eye, it is possible to discern two dark, fine lines. These are absent in the right eye. The overall effect of the painting is one of "somberness" (Jordan, 1984:184) and "solemnity" (Verdi, 1984:142). Yet, the image is without a sense of repose or quietude.

Burnett (1977:16) affirms an idea similar to Klee's notion of unstable equilibrium, describing *Senecio* as a "dynamic resolution of contrasts" and suggesting how the painting may be viewed as a split image. The most obvious way to approach *Senecio* is to imagine the face as staring directly outward, looking with both eyes at the observer. However, by focusing on the left side of the canvas, it is also possible to see the painting as a left-facing profile view. Covering the right side of the canvas heightens this effect; covering the left side, by contrast, shows clearly that the phenomenon is not bilaterally symmetrical. Burnett sees further evidence of the "dynamic resolution of contrasts" in the way Klee has set *Senecio*'s head on a "base" of the three primary colors (red, yellow, and blue), together with white and a rich, earthlike brown (Burnett, 1977:17). The tensions depicted in *Senecio*'s contrasts between left/right, dynamism/stasis, interior/exterior, self/other, and earth/cosmos assume a temporal dimension in the image's apparent evocation of both youth and old age.

Klee begins from the abstract idea of unstable equilibrium and discloses its manifestation in the flesh of a face. For my purposes, this quality of *Senecio* offers an aesthetically grounded avenue to the existential foundations of human crisis. The painting accomplishes this transcending of mere affect or empathy to create something akin to what Bachelard calls a "poetic image," through which "we learn to know, in one of its tiny fibres, a becoming of being that is an awareness of the *being's inner disturbance*" (Bachelard, 1994:220, emphasis original). It is this ability to depict the "tiniest impulse of the psyche" (Jardí, 1990:27) that constitutes the disclosive capacity of *Senecio* and its relevance for a phenomenological exposition of my encounter with Isaac and Henry.

THE FACE OF UNSTABLE EQUILIBRIUM

In order to develop a phenomenologically grounded answer to the question, "what happens when the police respond to a domestic violence call?" we might well begin by studying an image such as *Senecio* and pondering what it reveals about the experience of an officer's coming face to face with a fellow human being in crisis. Were someone to ask me, "from a police officer's perspective, what is it actually like when someone first opens the door at a domestic violence call?" one of my responses would be, "it is akin to the experience of looking at this painting." In astonishing fashion, beyond what a mainstream social scientific description or practical police training course might convey, *Senecio*'s depiction of unstable equilibrium makes palpable something of the experience of standing before the visage of enigmatic anger and disharmony.

To behold *Senecio* is to discern something of the inner nature of that moment of initial encounter on a domestic violence call, or other such instance of human crisis. As a means of interpreting my encounter with Isaac and Henry, deliberatively studying *Senecio* helps to disclose some of the subtle conditions of interaction, which are often overlooked both in the exigencies and routinization of police praxis, as well as in the analysis of that praxis by mainstream social science. Most of all, the painting contributes to an understanding of some of the ontological conditions that make it so intractably difficult to step into the midst of human crises and impose bureaucratically dictated resolutions upon them.

Senecio challenges and unsettles the viewer in the way that it resists any attempts neatly to discern and categorize an objective "matter at hand." Is the face in the painting looking at the observer, or not? Is the person genuinely attentive to the observer? What happened to this person? What is "really going on" with this person? What is the person "really" thinking? Are those thoughts rational? Are the person's answers to the observer's questions truthful? Are the person's emotional reactions to the interlocutor genuine, deceptive, or even delusional? Is this person mentally disordered, or under the influence of alcohol or other drugs? How should the viewer reconcile the appearance of the eyes with the face's other features? The act of focusing on the childlike features of the pink "cheeks" and blond hair cannot avoid being struck by the haunting, discomfiting sadness, pain, and anger of the red eyes. Is the mouth projecting a smirk, a frown, or a genuine smile? Perhaps the person is trying to suppress the urge to cry, or to conceal the effect of red eyes that are the aftermath of crying? Is the person potentially violent? What emotions predominate in his or her mind? Which aspects of the gaze in this face are based on events that occurred prior to the observer's arrival, and which of them are influenced or even caused by the presence of the observer?

Each of these questions echoes the experience of translating human presence during the opening moments of a police-citizen encounter, in which officers can never know with absolute certainty what they are truly *facing*. These junctures mark the occasion for some of the most immediately tangible realizations of bureaucratic predictability and controllability. This is especially the case in potentially hazardous and rapidly fluctuating situations, such as my encounter with Isaac and Henry. Gazes in encounters of this kind meet suddenly, with a reciprocal tautness, energy, suspicion, and confusion that cannot be wholly concealed or inwardly suppressed. *Senecio* asserts the same kind of foreboding and unsettled presence that was instantly apparent to my fellow officers and me in our encounter with Isaac and Henry. The unstable equilibrium that the painting discloses thus parallels the sense of conflicting emotions, tensions, and ambiguities the police officer literally faces upon entering the scene of a call. *Senecio*'s powerful evocation of ambiguity and tense confusion re-creates the fear and mystery that accompany the experience of coming face to face with an unknown situation occasioned by human turmoil. The face in *Senecio* projects a sense of reacting to the intrusion of another presence, as if posing the challenge, "what do *you* want?"

This was the reaction that my colleagues and I got from Isaac and Henry, and it was an altogether expected one. When my fellow officers first discovered Isaac and Henry grappling on the floor, they were unable to clearly determine the nature of the situation. At this early point in the encounter, such ambiguity was predominantly regarded as a tactical concern, rather than a legal or investigative one: Isaac was handcuffed not because he was legally under arrest but because he was judged to have posed a threat to Henry and to my colleagues. Establishing this kind of physical control, on the basis of which officers could then advise the dispatcher that "the scene is secure," marked the transition to the next stages of the encounter, in which, among other things, fire department personnel could safely attend to Isaac's and Henry's injuries, and formal, investigative processes and other elements of problematization could commence.

"Securing the scene" is exactly what the phrase suggests: an operational establishment of physical control over an officially demarcated space. However, securing a scene does not equate to assessing, let alone comprehending, the more elemental nature of the actual situation. Although securing a scene is tactically necessary to protect the immediate safety of the involved parties—both officers and citizens—the very means by which this is accomplished can exercise a powerful and often negative impact upon the entire dynamic of the encounter. This is one of the reasons why the shift from tactical control to formal problematization is among the most difficult stages in any police-citizen encounter. The transition demands that officers adjust their interpretive frame of reference by taking the now-secure scene and objectively regarding each of the people within it from a bureaucratic standpoint in order to identify, approach, and solve an underlying problem.

The intensity of the presence radiating from *Senecio* mirrors the overwhelmingness of what a police officer faces, even after an encounter is nominally "under control." What was previously seen largely as a potential or actual threat of violence must now be heeded with respect to attaining the ends of bureaucratic praxis. Although the physical danger posed by a suspect to officers never completely disappears until he has been remanded to the custody of jail personnel, it does, of course, diminish substantially once a person has been handcuffed and searched. It is at this moment of initial security that a new (and far more complex) kind of control must be established that goes beyond tactical domination. With this in mind, the transition from tactical control to complex bureaucratic control requires a practical understanding that the more coercion or physical force was initially required to secure the scene and the disputants, the more difficult it becomes to move to the next stage of the encounter, which necessarily demands establishing some kind of rapport with the involved parties.

Experienced police officers are mindful of this tension, even when they have no consciously intended purpose beyond the imposition of bureaucratic order, and will therefore often accompany tactical actions (such as pointing guns, using physical control techniques, applying handcuffs, and so forth) with gestures and language that recognize the human presence of those at whom these actions are directed. For example, this is why I acknowledged Isaac by name, and attempted to win his cooperation by appealing to our personal relationship, which he and I had established over the course of years of contacts. The viewer of *Senecio* can likewise easily imagine how a dialogue with the person behind the cryptic presence of this otherwise decontextualized face might be safer and simpler if one knew the person's name, or had some other basis for familiarity. It is not only officers who employ this technique. Suspects, too, will often take steps during encounters with officers aimed at winning preferential treatment, or getting officers to "drop their guard." As a result, both parties in a police-citizen encounter find themselves involved in a dialectic of mutual suspicion.

This interpretive ambiguity emerges in *Senecio*'s gaze, and once again helps to illustrate the dynamic at work in the contact with Isaac and Henry. Isaac apparently read my attempt at familiarity as an opportunity to present me with the false claim that it was "Frank" who had actually assaulted his father. Isaac related this story with the clear subtextual message that if I were really his friend, or genuinely cared about him, I would accept it as true. On the other hand, my unwillingness to accept his account of the incident would have cast doubt on the underlying ethical basis of our relationship. Thus, when I voiced skepticism to Isaac about the veracity of his story, he did not address himself to its factual merits, but rather appealed to our personal relationship.

The fact that Isaac's story was not true is beside the point. Beyond trying to avoid getting into trouble with the police, he also seemed to be acting on a desire to convince himself of his own innocence, or at least to rationalize in his own mind what he had done. Isaac projected a sense of being torn between the role of an angry, vengeful son, who since his teenage years has repeatedly assaulted his father, and the role of a contrite son, who perhaps really wanted to believe that "Frank" was his father's true assailant, rather than he himself. During the span of my encounter with Isaac and Henry, Isaac repeatedly vac- illated between looking at his father with remorseful affection and glaring at him hatefully. In any event, the vociferousness of Isaac's claims about Frank did not overcome my sense that he was being untruthful.

This moment in the encounter, when Isaac protested his innocence, and surged from one emotional extreme to another, is a powerful manifestation of unstable equilibrium. Stated otherwise, the most indubitable aspect of Isaac's presence was the depth of his instability. A crucial distinction emerges at this point that centers on whether we approach Isaac's instability in phenomeno- logical terms or through its objectification as a "problem." The former approach attends to the fullness of human presence by recognizing some of the same qualities Klee depicts in *Senecio*. The latter approach, on the other hand, seeks to contain that presence, and to encounter it as an entity that is literally *subject* to practical manipulation. Here, the interpretation of instability and its transla- tion into an object for praxis is decisive, because it establishes a radical divide between the significance that Isaac and Henry attached to the moment and its significance for the police officers acting as bureaucratic agents. The inner laceration and self-estrangement that appeared in Isaac's gaze were translated otherwise for the attainment of bureaucratic ends. The same state of unstable equilibrium marked Henry's presence. Despite his evident anger at Isaac, Henry could not bring himself to tell my colleagues and me what had actually occurred. These emotional convolutions were most poignantly displayed when Henry threw himself at Isaac before walking outside the house to the ambulance. This moment seemed to bring together the unstable equilibrium of father and son, and revealed the stark limitations of bureaucratic praxis. Henry and Isaac acted consciously to preclude my colleagues and me from developing probable cause for assault, which would have made Isaac subject to arrest.

The meaning of being "subject to arrest" is clear enough in a legal and bureaucratic sense; however, its ontological foundations remain less readily apparent. Earlier, in chapter 1, I considered Heidegger's argument (2001:214–15) that human being regarded as "subjectivity" is effectively reduced to the status of an abstract substratum that merely becomes the repository for various predicates. In the case of Isaac, it was his being understood as a "subject" in the ontological sense that made him "subject to arrest" in a bureaucratic and juridical sense. Of course, human beings have been placed under arrest for millennia in one legal sense or another; however, this historical fact should not lead us to overlook the radical novelty of modern bureaucratic praxis, which effectuates arrests on the basis of an instrumental rational approach to human beings.

My colleagues and I attempted to interpret our encounter with Isaac and Henry in such a way that all of the relevant facts and circumstances would "make the case" that Isaac had committed a criminal assault against Henry, for which Isaac would be subject to arrest and removed from the scene. The underlying reality of unstable equilibrium had to be objectified as an abstract entity neutralized to meet the ends of police bureaucracy. As a result, the inherent nature of the struggle between Isaac and Henry never came under direct consideration. From an immediately practical standpoint, their respective states of intoxication and injury would have made this difficult to accomplish, even had the will to do so been present. When my colleagues and I eventually left the scene of the call, we had no clearer understanding of the underlying nature of the situation than we did upon our arrival. Neither Isaac's nor Henry's state of unstable equilibrium had been officially acknowledged, other than as an impediment to resolving the situation. The bureaucratic approach that was taken toward the disputants in "handling" the incident remained trapped at the level of instrumental praxis. Any aspect of human presence that defied or resisted ready problematization was confined to a peripheral significance. *Senecio* and *A Bar at the Folies-Bergère* illustrate the challenge of attempting to reawaken consciousness to existential fullness of the human condition. They show the superabundance of presence, which a naïve reductionist approach will always overlook when it excludes perception of "the anger or pain which I nevertheless read in a face" (Merleau-Ponty, 1962:23–24).

FIVE

The Policing of Childhood: Encounters with Juveniles

Who can say nowadays that his anger is really his own
anger when so many people talk about it and claim to know
more about it than he does? A world of qualities without a
man has arisen, of experiences without the person who
experiences them, and it almost looks as though ideally
private experience is a thing of the past, and that the
friendly burden of personal responsibility is to dissolve
into a system of formulas of possible meanings.

—Robert Musil,
The Man Without Qualities, vol. I, 1995

INTRODUCTION

The close interaction between police officers and juveniles is hardly a new
phenomenon; however, the end of the twentieth century and the beginning
of the twenty-first have been marked by a transformation and expansion of
police contacts with children, apace with sea changes in the social structure
of late modernity. A decisive consequence of the intensified police involvement in the daily lives of children is that, at the most practical and intimate
level, officers bear witness more than ever before to children's struggles for
meaning, security, and self-identity, especially when those struggles unfold
violently. Whether it is during encounters with children or adults, the more
closely police officers become involved in the everyday existence of the public,
the more delicately attuned they must become to predicaments and circumstances that fall far outside their nominal mandate of crime fighting and
order maintenance. In taking stock of the growing involvement of police in
the lives of children, and considering the inherent limitations of the bureau-

cratic response to their predicaments, this chapter applies a phenomenological aesthetics of encounter to police contacts with juveniles. My focus will be on the genre of the novel, juxtaposing narratives of several police-juvenile encounters with passages from Fyodor Dostoyevsky's *Crime and Punishment* and Robert Musil's *The Man Without Qualities*.

In chapter 4, I considered the role of the gaze in police-citizen encounters in order to begin illustrating how the conflicting ontological notions of co-presence and intersubjectivity actually unfold in concrete situations. In the case of Melissa, I showed how her gaze became a "matter of fact" and was translated into an ensemble of data. In the case of Isaac and Henry, I explained how the clash between co-presence and intersubjectivity could be illustrated using Klee's notion of unstable equilibrium. Now, we are in a position to consider the specific interactive dynamics by which bureaucratic problematization occurs. Although I will be focusing on these dynamics using police encounters with children, the general premises at issue are applicable with little or no modification to a much wider range of police-citizen encounters with adults.

In the first half of this chapter, I explore an encounter that I had with "Laura," a runaway girl, in order to illustrate and analyze the phenomenon of *the violence of abstraction*. The violence of abstraction refers to the entire spectrum of dehumanizing effects potentially associated with instrumental rational social praxis.[1] Within the context of the policing of juveniles, the violence of abstraction describes the reification and problematization of childhood into an ensemble of pathologies and risks. I use a short passage from Dostoyevsky's *Crime and Punishment* to illustrate how the violence of abstraction occurs in the concrete dynamics of human encounter and traces its roots to the logic of problematization. The passage explores the nature of social interactions that are founded upon the reduction of human beings to objects or ciphers.

The second half of the chapter explicates a series of several encounters with children, each of which involves a different form of resistance to the presence of the police. Using Robert Musil's idea of "an impassioned struggle for self-assertion," I interpret these encounters in a way that attempts to show how the dynamics of resistance manifest complex predicaments that usually remain out of the view of the bureaucratic gaze. I use the analysis to suggest how the problematization of children's predicaments can lead to outward acts of rebellion, which, if misconstrued, leave the broader precipitating causes of juvenile violence ignored.

Encounter #5-1: Laura

At 1:00 A.M. on a warm July night, I was driving up and down side streets in a residential neighborhood looking for suspicious activity. After a short while, I happened upon three young teenagers standing around a car, which they had somehow managed to drive up onto a large rock. None of the teenagers, a boy and two girls, looked old enough to drive. I stopped to investigate the situation.

It turned out that the car belonged to the boy's father. The boy explained to me that he was trying to take the car so he and the two girls could run away. He went on to explain that one of the girls, "Laura," was supposed to enter a state foster home the next day. She and her two friends were determined to keep this from happening by driving to California. The boy's woeful driving skills kept the teens from making it out of his backyard, where the car had been parked. At my request, the boy went inside his house and returned with his father. I explained to the boy's father what had happened to his car. He gave his son a look of annoyed exasperation and told me he would have the car towed off the rock later in the morning.

With the boy back home, and the matter of the car resolved, I turned my attention to determining where the two girls belonged. Laura's friend gave me her name, date of birth, a local address, and other information for which I asked. The experience of being questioned by the police seemed new to her. By now, another officer had stopped by to check on me. I asked him to give the girl a ride home.

When I asked Laura for her name and date of birth, she gave me her name without hesitation, but paused nervously before reciting a date of birth. I immediately suspected that she had lied to me, probably because she had an arrest warrant, or had run away. I asked Laura if she would prefer to give me her real date of birth. She lowered her eyes to the ground, smiled sheepishly, and gave me the correct information.

I checked Laura's name using the computer in my car, and found that she had indeed been reported as a runaway. It is not a crime for a child to run away; however, when police officers find runaway children, they are legally obligated to take them into protective custody and return them to their families, take them to a shelter, or else turn them over to a state social worker for placement in a foster home. I explained all of this to Laura, and told her that although she was not under arrest, she would have to come with me. She was very polite and cooperative, and agreed without hesitation.

I put Laura in the back of my patrol car, tuned to the radio station that she requested, and began completing an incident report. Sitting in the car, looking at my computer screen, my back was literally turned to Laura as I began the official process of documenting the event of my having found her. Her presence barely registered at a practical level, other than as a source of a fact here and there for my report, and as a potential threat and liability to be monitored with an occasional glance in the rear-view mirror. Almost all the information that I needed for my report was available from the patrol car computer, listed in a format that had neatly fragmented and objectified a teenage girl's existence into so many pieces of data categorized and arranged on the screen according to "fields," each one marked by a standardized, three-letter abbreviation. The "SMT" field, for example, lists scars, marks and tattoos. Any information beyond that fitting in the pre-given fields is placed in the "MIS," or "miscellaneous" field. Here, one might find a statement such as "suicidal hx," meaning a history of suicide attempts.

According to standard protocol, the police department to which Laura had been originally reported as a runaway would have to meet with me to pick her up. This is called a "field transfer," or "meet." An officer from that department would then take her home. My dispatcher called the other agency to make the necessary arrangements. The other agency, however, declined to meet, and told my dispatcher that Laura was a ward of the state who had run away from a foster home. The foster home should send someone out to get her, advised the other agency. My dispatcher phoned the foster home. "We're not responsible for Laura anymore," they said; "she runs away all the time, and we don't want her back here." Laura confirmed this with me. "They put me on thirty days' notice to stop running away, or else leave the foster home. I kept running away, and that's why I'm supposed to go into a new home tomorrow."

Since running away from her foster home, Laura had been living with her adult half-sister and father. Even so, she was still listed as a runaway, because in the eyes of the state, her family no longer had legal custody of her. So, the agency that reported Laura as a runaway would not take custody of her, and neither would the foster home where she had been living. I really could not take her back home, either. I wanted to talk with Laura's caseworker, but she could not be reached at that late hour.

I took Laura back to the police station until I could figure out where she could safely spend the night. It was not lost on her that the bureaucracy was failing miserably in its attempts to deal with her. I apologized to Laura for the delays and confusion. She acted nonchalant and accustomed to being in this situation. She seemed amused that someone, especially a cop, was trying to be nice to her. I offered Laura something to eat or drink. She refused politely and looked at me quizzically, as if I was naïve to the ways of the world.

I had previously dealt with Laura's family. Her mother and several other *relatives were addicted to heroin. State social workers had removed Laura from her family home for her own welfare, owing to what they deemed an unsafe environment caused by her mother's behavior. I wondered if her mother was still living at home: if she was not, I might have been able to take Laura there, because this was where she wanted to go anyway. "How's your mother?" I asked Laura. "Oh, she died in April." I had not heard this, and told Laura that I was sorry. "That's ok," she said. It turned out Laura's mother had died from hepatitis, which she had apparently contracted from using contaminated hypodermic needles. She was forty-one.*

Laura reiterated that she really wanted to go home, and, although I was not hopeful that this would be possible, I promised to call her family to see if the environment might be stable enough for her to stay there. No such luck: Laura's father was dying of complications related to chronic alcoholism and could not care for himself, let alone a teenage girl. Laura's adult half-sister, who had severe medical problems of her own, candidly told me that she simply could not cope with Laura, as all her attention was devoted to tending to her father.

Having learned these facts, I told Laura that I could not let her go back home, and advised her that, regrettably, she would be taken by child protective services and placed in another foster home. "I'll just run away again," she told me. I told her that I knew she would, and tried to change the topic of conversation.

I asked her the same general questions I typically asked other kids: what made her happy, what she hoped for, what she dreamed about, where she saw herself being in a few more years. Like so many hopeless children, she had no answers, and had little sense of the future. She flatly told me that she neither liked anything, nor did anything make her happy. Her reply seemed matter-of-fact, rather than gratuitously rebellious. Sensing that my questions seemed mostly meaningless to her, I turned to more mundane topics, such as a favorite food or favorite color. Here, too, Laura shrugged and replied with languid and dispassionate indifference. She seemed confused and a bit wary, as if she could not quite tell whether my questions were genuine or whether they were a deceptively innocuous prelude to a more formal interrogation. I offered reassurance. "You think I'm crazy, don't you?" I asked her. "Yeah," she laughed.

"It gets better than this, I promise it does," I told her. Laura's eyes began to well up. She averted her gaze from mine, smiled feebly, and then assumed a look of stoic resignation. I wished Laura good luck before closing the door to the holding cell where she sat alone, and then walked down the hallway to the locker room. I took off my uniform, told my dispatcher that I was "out of service," and went home. I learned the next day that Laura had finally

been picked up at 4:00 A.M. by a social worker and placed in a foster home. She ran away again the following day.

After my encounter with Laura, she continued to run away over and over again. Her troubles with the legal system escalated as well, leading to three arrests within a span of several months. The first arrest was for burglary, after Laura and another girl broke into a house. Her second and third arrests were for joyriding with friends in stolen cars.

One of the more remarkable moments in this encounter came when Laura had difficulty naming her favorite color for me. Her silent hesitation was finally broken by a quietly spoken response: "Blue." I was left to wonder if this answer was genuine or just a polite attempt to offer a reply to a question that was apparently regarded as largely irrelevant. I persisted: "What kind of blue?" Laura seemed unsure. "How about blue like the sky?" She shook her head and said she did not know.

At thirteen, Laura is world-weary, distant, and detached. Sitting quietly in a police station holding cell, she seemed to be the living embodiment of Nietzsche's characterization of the modern condition as a world in which "everything is so wild, so disordered, so colorless, so hopeless" (1964:136–37).[2] Laura has little sense of wonder or enchantment; such things must strike her as utterly useless. Laura, too, it seems, is apparently useless. She is "nothing but trouble:" so she has heard from the society that regularly confers these sorts of descriptions upon her.

Laura epitomizes the kind of child frequently characterized, experienced, and understood by late modern society as being "useless," or a "problem." Agents of the criminal justice system and other bureaucracies, and members of society at large, encounter a girl like Laura and wonder, "what are we going to do with her?" She constantly runs away, rarely attends school, and commits crimes. She loiters in public, spending aimless hours "hanging out" with friends and strangers. She smokes, drinks, and uses illegal drugs. In all likelihood, she is sexually active, and hence at risk of becoming pregnant or contracting sexually transmitted diseases. Taking all of this in the aggregate, Laura's visible presence is effectively reduced in significance to the status of being a disruption of society's self-imagined order and stability; and, in being so regarded, she comes to be experienced by police officers and other bureaucratic agents as a "problem," if not even less charitably as "useless."

My encounter with Laura encapsulates at a microcosmic level one particular instance of this broader dynamic of problematization. Whatever elements of empathy, compassion, or general curiosity might have led me to regard Laura otherwise—perhaps with an eye toward determining her "real story"—were accidental aspects of the encounter, insofar as it was regarded as an instance of bureaucratic policing. Such that this is the case, an attitude of compassion and empathy, or whatever else might be seen in policing as contributing toward a positive "bedside manner," does not by itself suffice to disprove or undo the logic of problematization.

In Laura's situation, it is clear that the operational expectations and objectives of the police bureaucracy would have been successfully met, as long as the appropriate processes of problematization formed the basis for rational action. Hence, to the extent that I or any other police officer succeeded in recognizing that, with respect to the instrumental rational interpretive stance of policing, the objective significance of Laura's presence was her legal status as a runaway, the "correct" response would predictably ensue, and the incident would therefore be properly handled. This notion is captured in the moment when I first placed Laura in the patrol car and was writing my report by gathering information from the computer screen. At this point in the encounter, Laura's human presence in the back seat had quite literally become "incidental," in the sense of being subordinate or parenthetical, because her being there was of significance only insofar as she was the "subject" of an official police incident. The existential state of her *co-presence* with me was effectively subsumed by bureaucratically determined *intersubjectivity*.

Her objective presence in the patrol car merely constituted the physical locus of the data describing her on the computer screen. In a distinctly ontological sense, she had truly become the *subject* of an investigation, of which various categories and facts were then predicated. This effect was amplified by the circumstance that, given the interior configuration of the patrol car and the location of the computer, Laura could read the computer screen from the back seat, yet could not see my face, other than by looking at its reflection in the rear-view mirror. As a practical result, this aspect of the encounter between Laura and me was "triangulated" by the intermediary presence of the computer, at which both of us stared rather than looking at each other.[3] Her physical containment in the back seat of a police car was echoed and reiterated by her factual containment in a police database. For the duration of the encounter, as her own actions demonstrated, she became increasingly aware of her objectification and encipherment. This was apparent in Laura's nonchalance (and even her utter resignation) in the face of bureaucratic manipulation, and in her remarkable conversancy with the law enforcement and child welfare systems.

DOSTOYEVSKY: THE REASSURANCE
OF "NICE LITTLE WORDS"

In his classic study of Dostoyevsky's poetics, Mikhail Bakhtin points to Dostoyevsky's striking ability to visualize the human condition in terms of elaborately detailed moments of coexistence and interaction (1984:5–46). Dostoyevsky takes the "cross-section of a given moment" and reveals its multiple layers of complexity, ambiguity, and contradiction (Bakhtin, 1984:30). These layers emerge through the dialogical interaction of characters, who speak for themselves in a "plurality of consciousnesses" that exists beyond the diktats of authorial power (Bakhtin, 1984:6–7). Most important for Bakhtin, Dostoyevsky's polyphonic dialogue responds to the ineluctability of coexistence with implications that are at once both moral and aesthetic: his creation of characters who are the autonomous sources of their own meaning affirms "the dialogic nature of life itself" and challenges the inadequacy of objectification (Bakhtin, 1984:293).[4]

Such a challenge is front and center in the passage from *Crime and Punishment* (1866/1991:80–85) that I will use to analyze my encounter with Laura. Consistent with Dostoyevsky's approach, the passage illustrates how abstract ideas occur as "live events," played out in moments of human encounter (Bakhtin, 1984:88). The passage describes an encounter between Raskolnikov, an anonymous teenage girl, her would-be attacker, and a police officer. As Raskolnikov walks along a deserted St. Petersburg street, he encounters a drunken teenage girl being followed at a distance by a "man-about-town" with evident designs upon her. It is obvious that the girl has already been sexually assaulted. When she sits down on a bench, the "man-about-town" impatiently lingers in the background, waiting for Raskolnikov to leave. Outraged at what, but for his presence, would happen again, Raskolnikov angrily confronts the man, nearly coming to blows with him before a police officer intervenes.

Raskolnikov explains the situation to the officer, who quickly surmises that Raskolnikov has accurately read the man's criminal intentions. The officer attempts to learn the girl's address so he can summon a cab to take her home; however, she is belligerent and uncooperative. As the officer tries to find a way to get the girl to safety, he feels a keen sense of embarrassment, compassion, and indignation (1991:83). He continues his efforts to assist her, but she becomes impatient and walks away. As Raskolnikov watches the girl stumble off, followed by the police officer and the would-be rapist, his sentiments suddenly reverse, turning from mercy and outrage to cold cynicism. He shouts out to the bewildered officer: "What's it to you? Forget about it! Let him have his bit of fun!" (1991:84). While the officer tries to catch up to the girl and the man-about-town, Raskolnikov settles down on a bench and mutters angrily to himself over the loss of twenty kopecks, which he had given to the officer to pay the girl's cab fare.

As Raskolnikov's thoughts wander, his anger dissipates. He reflects further on the plight of the girl and what her lamentable future likely holds. His mind grapples with the brutal misery, which he surmises will consume her remaining few years, as she is cast adrift, floating between brothels and venereal wards. Raskolnikov pauses to find some underlying cause of such manifest tragedy, and sees in the girl's story a near-inevitable fate, foreordained by her luckless circumstances. He becomes repulsed by the convenience with which her suffering could be neatly dismissed: "Pah! So be it! It has to be like that, they say. They say that each year a certain percentage has to go off down that road . . . to the devil, I suppose, in order to give the others fresh hope and not get in their way. A percentage! Nice little words they use, to be sure: they're so reassuring, so scientific. Just say: 'percentage,' and all your troubles are over. Now if one were to choose another word, well, then . . . then things might look a little less reassuring."(Dostoyevsky, 1991:85).[5]

Dostoyevsky's narrative suggests at least two notions of immediate relevance for interpreting my encounter with Laura. First, it reveals the potential implications of the violence of abstraction, showing how the reductive translation of a human being to a statistical cipher expedites forms of praxis in which moral effacement is normalized and passed over in silence. Second, Dostoyevsky identifies a causal nexus between ontological principles and ordinary action, which is apparent not just in Raskolnikov's encounter with the drunken girl, but also in his justification for the murder of Alyona, the pawnbroker.

In the immediate context of Raskolnikov's encounter with the girl, Dostoyevsky notes that when Raskolnikov first saw her, he regarded her no differently from "any of the other objects that had flitted before his gaze" (1991:80). Yet, perceiving something amiss, and against a sense of reluctance that bordered on annoyance, Raskolnikov was drawn to the girl (1991:80). As the scene unfolds, his ethical sensibilities change in precise coincidence with his objectification of the girl. Throughout the encounter, the girl's name and address remain a mystery, reinforcing the logic that she is nothing more than a social atom—an anonymous quantum of the "certain percentage." However much this logic effaces the girl's human presence, it cannot wholly obliterate it; and once that presence is *recognized,* the dynamic of the encounter shifts.

Raskolnikov's shifting responses toward the girl reveal the deep conflict between calculative rationality and an absolute moral responsibility that lies at the heart of *Crime and Punishment*. In fact, his encounter with the anonymous girl parallels in reverse Raskolnikov's justification for the murder of Alyona: "One death to a hundred lives—I mean, there's arithmetic for you! And anyway, what does the life of that horrible, stupid, consumptive old woman count for when weighed in the common balance? No more than the life of a louse, a cockroach, and it's not even worth that, because the old woman is harmful" (1991:102). Albeit with different consequences, this line of reasoning follows the same logic that enabled the nameless girl on the boardwalk to be reduced to an abstract quantum of the "certain percentage," whose potential demise, however regrettable, nonetheless "gives fresh hope to the others" (compare Offord, 1983). The reduction of Laura to the status of a "useless problem child" reflects an identical line of thought.

Dostoyevsky contextualizes this kind of moral reasoning within the lived actuality of human encounter, and thus shows speculative ideas become realized in social praxis. In phenomenological terms, it may be said that Dostoyevsky frames the move from idea to praxis as a question of intentionality—how consciousness orients itself toward the presence of another. When Raskolnikov tries to ignore the girl, and rationalizes her misfortune, her suffering nonetheless continues to plague him. In this response, he reacts to something in her presence that defies objectification. Likewise, when the police officer first encounters the girl, "a sincere compassion showed itself in his features" (1991:82). At one level, the officer has an immediate, duty-bound interest in ensuring the girl's safety; however Dostoyevsky makes it unambiguously clear that at a higher level, his actions bespeak the recognition of a human presence that reduction to a nameless atom of that "certain percentage."

There are clear parallels between the situation of Dostoyevsky's nameless girl and my encounter with Laura. In her being encountered and "found" through the matching of her name with a database entry, Laura's legal and bureaucratic classification changed from "missing juvenile" to "located runaway." I had first found her physically, in the most literal sense of meeting her; but this experience assumed administrative and legal relevance in the subsequent process of his locating her *as a runaway*, named in a database entry. I accomplished this merely by asking Laura her name, which from a strict bureaucratic standpoint was not a gesture of ethical recognition but an attempt to gather a piece of data that would serve an instrumental function. Like so many other people who learn to conceal their true identities from questioning authorities, Laura initially lied about her name, because she knew it would be listed in police databases. This moment in the encounter alone suffices to demonstrate how self-conception can be altered through bureaucratic interactions. Laura's knowledge of police procedures, and of their prior effects on her, led her to conceal the truth. Unlike the girl in Dostoyevsky's story, Laura quickly acquiesced—perhaps out of resignation, fear, or both—and provided her name.

Once I had appropriated Laura's "real" identity as a bureaucratically meaningful fact, her inner nature as conceived by a vast nexus of official organizations emerged: she was a runaway, a clearly defined problem admitting of various solutions. Functioning as an agent of the state, I had located a problem and, however temporarily and imperfectly, solved it, or at least identified and contained it. As a result of this effort, I was also able to count Laura's "pickup" from the street as a statistic, or "stat." She had become a symbolic quantum of my efforts for the night, quantifiable evidence that I had "done something." In the eyes of the police department and the community, I had "made myself useful" by taking a runaway child off the street, and thwarted another child's attempt to steal his father's car. At least to some extent, this was a positive outcome. Yet, as the narrative of my encounter with Laura makes clear, her "problem" was not really "solved" in any meaningful way: the fact that she ran away again the next day amply illustrates this point.

One decisive part of understanding the failure of bureaucracy in Laura's case is to consider that insofar as the policing and child welfare systems could not wholly engage her as a matter of institutional praxis, the resulting effacement of her identity ended predictably. Put in terms of Schutz's phenomenology, the typification of Laura went too far: "Typification is progressive in the same proportion as the personality of the fellow-man disappears beyond the undisclosed anonymity of his function" (1971:71). The logic of bureaucratic problematization dictated that Laura needed to be "placed." Ironically, the very crises in Laura's life that brought her to the attention of the state impeded ameliorative action: the social worker who came to the police station to pick up Laura told me that, because of Laura's history, she would be "difficult to place." The child is "placed" as one places an object, a notion that is reinforced with the completion of an official "Transfer of Custody" form. Completing the "Transfer of Custody" form legally shifts responsibility for the child from a law enforcement officer to a state social worker. Officers dealing with runaway children eagerly await this moment, which allows them to say, "the kid's not my problem anymore." Whatever degree of compassion accompanies the transaction, it still amounts to what Heidegger calls a "concerned handling of objects" (2001:215).

MUSIL: "AN IMPASSIONED STRUGGLE
FOR SELF-ASSERTION"

As Laura's actions demonstrate, one of the more far-reaching implications of such praxis is its transformative effect on the self-conception of those who become its "objects." From lying about her name to her expressed resignation at being entangled in a bureaucratic web, the cycle of running away and getting picked up had become an intrinsic part of her modus vivendi. Beyond their concatenation into a chain of officially recorded bureaucratic incidents, each of Laura's instances of running away constituted a moment in the struggle of a child to seek a sense of purpose and place. With this idea in mind, I turn now to several other encounters with teenagers, which I will interpret using Robert Musil's notion of "an impassioned struggle for self-assertion" (1995:166). By recasting the friction between the police and juveniles as moments in such a struggle, it becomes possible to illuminate the ontological dynamics overlooked in bureaucratic praxis.

ENCOUNTER #5-2: COLETTE

Toward the end of a busy, late summer night shift, several officers and I were dispatched to investigate a rape. We arrived at the run-down house and were met by Cynthia, a woman in her mid-thirties. Cynthia called 911 after her nine-year-old son reported finding his thirteen-year-old sister, Colette, in bed with the babysitter. The babysitter, it turned out, was a nineteen-year-old man, whom Cynthia had hired to watch Colette and her two younger siblings. Cynthia admitted that she barely knew the man: she had recently met him at a neighborhood convenience store, and thought he seemed "nice enough." Cynthia arranged to have the man move into her house.

Like the majority of people questioned by the police, the man quickly waived his right to remain silent and admitted to one of the responding officers at the scene that he and Colette had engaged in sexual intercourse. He was placed under arrest for investigation of rape of a child (statutory rape) and taken to the police station for further interviews and processing. Several other officers and I remained at the scene to gather evidence and speak with Colette.

Colette was extremely defiant and uncooperative. Even though my colleagues and I were well accustomed to such reactions, Colette's combination of vulgarity, anger, and nonchalance led us to exchange discreet glances of disbelief. She lashed out furiously at her mother, and at my fellow officers and me, displaying a demeanor more common for someone twice her age.

She refused to answer any questions, offering no replies other than a stream of obscenities. I told Colette that I was only trying to determine the truth of what had happened to her. "You can't handle the fucking truth," she said in a flat, dismissive tone. Despite sustained attempts by each of the officers present to establish a rapport with her, and to win her trust, Colette remained resolutely sullen and hostile. Every approach and form of entreaty was rebuffed with sarcasm and vitriol. Standing amid the piles of clothing, personal belongings, and trash that covered her bedroom floor, Colette glared with cold defiance at anyone who tried to speak with her.

Here, my fellow officers and I faced a deeply uncomfortable quandary. Colette needed to go to the hospital for a sexual assault examination; and owing to her status as a minor, she did not have the final word in the matter. A colleague and I looked at each other, silently sharing our mutual dread at the prospect of having to physically restrain Colette and take her into protective custody. Fortunately, she eventually relented, and agreed to go to the hospital. Once at the hospital, however, she again changed her mind, and refused to cooperate with medical staff or a sexual assault counselor. She was then taken back to the police station, where investigators interviewed her. Colette said everything that had happened between her and the babysitter was consensual. She gave no indication of having been coerced or tricked, and seemed utterly indifferent to the entire situation. Later in the day, one of the investigators convinced Colette to return to the hospital, and she finally agreed to medical treatment and evaluation. The babysitter admitted that he had known Colette was only thirteen years old. He subsequently pled guilty to rape, and was sentenced to prison. Several months later, Colette was raped again, this time by one of her mother's boyfriends.

Encounter #5-3: Anthony

One Saturday afternoon, a sergeant and I responded to a semi-secure, inpatient mental health facility that houses children who have been diagnosed with serious behavioral disorders. Many of the children also have extensive criminal records. Staff members at the facility frequently call for police assistance to deal with escaped or "out of control" children. Such was the case on this day.

When we arrived at the facility, we were informed by a staff member that fourteen-year-old Anthony had assaulted her and crudely propositioned her, and was now refusing to return to his room. According to Anthony's records, his mother had sent him to the facility because of a severe "anger management problem." She had "run out of options" for dealing with him, a staff member told me. His father was dead, the staff member continued, and no other relatives would take Anthony into their homes, fearing his violent behavior. Unable to keep him under control and afraid for her own safety, Anthony's mother had him committed to the facility.

The staff member said that Anthony has frequent violent outbursts, but that day's had been extreme. She explained to me that she and several co-workers had succeeded in containing Anthony in a lounge area, the doors to which had been locked, pending the arrival of police. The staff member escorted the sergeant and me to the lounge and opened the door. Anthony was standing in a corner, fists clenched at his sides, crying and nearly hyper-ventilating. He was quite large for his age—I estimated that he was nearly six feet tall, and weighed at least two hundred pounds.

Anthony's arms bore numerous scars, where he had intentionally cut himself with sharp objects. Blood streamed from his nose, the apparent result of bashing his head against his bed frame. I tried to initiate a conversation with Anthony. After a few tense moments, he agreed to sit down in a large armchair. I initially approached him cautiously, both to gauge his response and to reassure him of my own peaceful intentions. He gradually grew calmer. "What do you want?" I asked him; "what's going to make you happy and resolve this situation?" "I want to go home," he replied. "Yeah, I can understand that," I told him, "but I'm not sure that's possible." I tried to change the subject in order to keep Anthony from getting angry again. "Why are you here?" I asked Anthony. "I have an anger problem," he said. He described his furious outbursts, and confided in me that although his mother did not know it, he used drugs extensively.

Once Anthony had calmed down, fire department personnel treated his injured nose. It was then decided that Anthony posed too much of a safety risk to remain at the facility, and arrangements were made to transport him via ambulance to a more secure institution. By now, Anthony seemed too tired and resigned to react violently to a decision he obviously did not like. The staff member whom Anthony had hit declined to press any charges against him.

Encounter #5-4: Thomas

Shortly before 4:00 A.M. on a busy night shift, several officers and I were dispatched to a report of a group of gang members brandishing a gun. The call came from a large apartment complex to which officers regularly responded to fights, disturbances, and other such incidents. As one of the officers arrived in the area, he saw a car leaving the apartment complex. The occupants fit the description of the group with the gun. Several colleagues and I assisted the first officer in conducting a "felony stop," or "high-risk stop" of the car, in which the occupants are methodically ordered out at gunpoint.

For gang members and other people accustomed to frequent encounters with the police, the procedures for a felony stop are quite familiar, and to be involved in one is commonly accepted with a degree of equanimity, if not even nonchalance. There are mutual, unspoken expectations on both sides. Gang members and other potential suspects know how to "play the game" by following the rules that shape these expectations: listen to the cops, keep your hands up, no sudden movements, and so on, and you will probably be on your way, unless you have weapons or warrants for your arrest. For their part, police officers learn from experience that rigorous attention to safe tactics and an assertive presence, tempered with a bit of humor and a willingness to overlook minor offenses, such as possession of alcohol and marijuana, can build the kind of positive rapport and trust that help minimize violent confrontations.

In the present case, all of the five young male occupants were cooperative, except for one. Sitting in the back seat, he deliberately ignored commands to remain still and keep his hands in view. He repeatedly slumped down in his seat until he nearly vanished from sight, and appeared to be digging about in the interior of the car. When his hands were visible, they were either flashing gang signs or else his middle fingers were extended in an obscene gesture. All of this was accompanied by raucous, profane taunts directed at my colleagues and me. As might be expected, the passenger's actions raised our stress level. We could not tell if he had any actual hostile intent; and we already knew that the incident to which we were responding supposedly involved a gun.

When the unruly passenger finally decided to emerge from the car, he refused to keep his hands up and would not lie down on the pavement. Instead, he began dancing in the middle of the street, screaming profanity and flashing more gang signs. The passenger's defiance seemed to be a calculated dare: like most people closely familiar with police tactics, he knew that despite being challenged at gunpoint, officers could not, in fact, actually shoot him without a life-threatening provocation. Rather, they would have to fulfill his challenge to "come and get me!" In a move that officers do not like, because it forces them to leave cover and thereby compromise their safety, two of my colleagues ran from behind their patrol cars and forced the passenger to the ground and handcuffed him.

Once the unruly passenger was in custody, and before anyone had even questioned him, he volunteered, "the gun is mine, it's under the front seat; I put it there. It's my baby, my .45 [caliber pistol]." An officer retrieved a stolen .45–caliber handgun from the car. Despite his proud, defiant admission that the gun in the car was his, the uncooperative passenger would say nothing else, and refused to identify himself. He was eventually identified as

"Thomas," a seventeen-year-old member of a local gang. While my colleagues and I were dealing with Thomas and his friends, another officer went to the scene of the original call and contacted a man who said Thomas had shown him the gun and threatened to shoot him. Thomas was booked into juvenile detention for felony assault and possession of a stolen handgun.

ENCOUNTER #5-5: GEORGE

On an unseasonably cold, snowy November afternoon, a colleague and I responded to a disturbance at a house known to be an active site for the dealing of crack cocaine. Mark and his girlfriend, Annette, rented the house. Both of them sold and used crack. Mark's seventeen-year-old nephew, George, had been arrested for assaulting him the previous day, and had immediately returned to the house upon his release from jail. When George showed up, Annette called the police. George worked for Mark selling crack. I had previously dealt with George and Mark, and knew them to be hostile and uncooperative toward police. I had taken a concealed handgun from Mark on a previous contact, and one of my colleagues had recently found a handgun in Mark's car.

My partner and I arrived at the call and saw George and Mark standing face to face on the front porch of the house, engaged in a heated confrontation. As soon as George saw us, he turned away from Mark, who retreated to a position just inside the front doorway. When we came closer, George tensed up and assumed a fighting stance, and cocked back his fist. He screamed obscenities and threatened us. At 6'4" and 190 pounds, George was a fast, wiry kid. We knew he would be a handful in a fight, especially if he was sober, as he appeared to be. We tried to calm him, but he completely ignored us and quickly turned back toward Mark, who taunted him from the doorway. George shoved Mark hard, knocking him back into the house.

Among other things, I had visions of Mark taking out a gun and shooting George. To keep the situation from deteriorating further, I doused George's face with a large burst of pepper spray. My partner and I then quickly grabbed his arms, swept his feet out from under him, and wrestled him to the ground. George continued to struggle and attempted to turn onto his back, a position from which it is easier to fight. We eventually subdued and handcuffed him. Once the adrenaline of the fight had worn off, the pain of the pepper spray hit George. He began to scream and cry. Despite the cold weather, George gasped with relief when I used a garden hose to rinse the pepper spray from his face.

My partner and I took George back to the police station. He was eventually booked into juvenile detention for assault and resisting arrest. When I searched George, I found more than three thousand dollars in cash in the front pocket of his jeans, which he claimed was from "selling a truck."

HOW HUMAN PRESENCE BECOMES A PROBLEM

Although the exercise of bureaucratic authority ultimately "resolved" each of the preceding encounters, it is apparent that as with Laura, these resolutions failed to engage the essential nature of the children's predicaments. In each encounter, the turmoil of adolescence assumed a different face: Colette, the sullen, withdrawn rape victim, who gave the impression of not having been victimized at all; Anthony, the "uncontrollable" boy confined to a mental institution; Thomas, the defiant gang member; and George, the violently belligerent crack dealer. Each of these episodes reflected the common presence of "an impassioned struggle for self-assertion" (*ein leidenschaftlicher Kampf um Geltung*) (Musil, 1952:157, English passage at 1995:166).

"Self-assertion" is the translation of the German *Geltung*, which literally means "value," "validity," or "worth." The key to understanding the significance of the term lies in the phrase that follows it in the text of *The Man Without Qualities*, where Musil characterizes the struggle for self-assertion in terms of the inward contest between a "heightened sense of self" (*Ein höheres Gefühl von seinem Ich*) and the "uncanny feeling" (*unheimlichen Gefühl*) of self-estrangement, which he describes as the sense that one is not "settled inside his own skin" (*nicht fest in seiner Haut*) (Musil, I.40, 1995:166/1952:157). *The Man Without Qualities* offers a monumental exploration of the "impassioned struggle for self-assertion" with a level and detail of character development that Peter Berger praises as having "an almost ethnographic exactitude" (1970:215). The novel describes a year (1913–14) in the life of "Ulrich" (whose surname the reader never learns), and uses the tale of his intellectual, political, emotional, and spiritual peregrinations as the center of an elaborately complicated and often bitingly clever narrative. The tale frames Ulrich's own "impassioned struggle for self-assertion" against the backdrop of the broader struggle of the waning Austro-Hungarian Empire to affirm its own identity in the face of pandemic banality and a growingly acute civilizational shallowness.[6]

Musil's Ulrich is a "man without qualities" precisely because he exists solely as "qualities without a man" (I.39, 1995:156–59). He is the modern "subject" par excellence, an agglomeration of possibilities, with no intrinsic nature or essence of its own. This paradox of modern life, that personal identity is reduced to an identity-free state of abstract potentiality, is the everyday social form of personal existence born of the ontological reduction of human being to pure subjectivity. The implications of this paradox, as they cut across the entire swath of modern society, play out in the pages of *The Man Without Qualities*. It is these same implications that manifest themselves in the existential undercurrents at work in the moments of human crisis that occasion police-citizen encounters.

In terms closely paralleling each of the encounters above, Musil describes how life's circumstances can trap a person in the same way an insect gets stuck on flypaper—gradually, and at first imperceptibly, but once noticed, acknowledged with a panicked struggle to escape that only hastens what is perceived too late as an inevitable demise. For Musil, life's struggles can transform and obscure human self-identity, just as the frenzied thrashing of the insect continues "until it is covered by a thick coating [of glue] that only remotely suggests its original shape" (I.34, 1995:137). In words that could describe any of my encounters above, Musil writes of this diminishing and loss of self-identity as it often occurs in youth: "[t]he mockery of the young, their revolt against institutions, their readiness for anything that is heroic, for martyrdom or crime, their fiery earnestness, their instability—all this means nothing more than their struggle to escape" (I.34, 1995:137). In the process of this struggle, even fatuity and ridiculousness can seem to hold forth the promise of meaning and security, and offer a way to shake off the weight of the "heavy world" (*schwere Welt*), or to break through the "unstable, shifting mist" (*haltlos beweglicher Nebel*) that clouds the human spirit (I.34, 1995:137/1952:131–32). Like sparrows pouncing on crumbs for sustenance (I.34, 1995:137), the human soul hungers for anything that presents itself as a potential source of authenticity, anything that "offers that moment of self-realization, of balance [*Spanungsgleich-gewichtes*] between inner and outer, between being crushed and exploding" (I.34, 1995:138).[7]

The phrase "an impassioned struggle for self-assertion" appears in *The Man Without Qualities* within the context of an episode involving a drunk, disorderly man yelling in the street and taunting the police (I.40, 1995:165–67). Seeing that he has drawn the attention of the police, "an impassioned struggle for self-assertion began" (I.40, 1995:165). When an officer tries to arrest the man, a fight ensues, and the officer gets punched in the face. Other officers arrive to assist their comrade, and the man is eventually subdued and arrested. Ulrich witnesses the fracas, and remarks aloud that because of his state of extreme intoxication, the drunken man ought not be held responsible for his actions. The already upset officers become even angrier when Ulrich's comments re-agitate the man, whereupon Ulrich himself is arrested.

Musil reveals the clash between the loutish drunk and the police officers to be something far more than a simple criminal act of disorderly conduct.

The drunken man, albeit without the same finesse, intelligence, or aplomb, is doing precisely what Ulrich does throughout the book: engaging in "an impassioned struggle for self-assertion." In the face of what, however? Musil precedes his narrative of the drunken man's outburst with an observation about the "spooky" or "ghostly" (*Gespenstisches*) quality of "living constantly in a well-ordered state," with its omnipresent forms of bureaucratic surveillance and order maintenance that reach so deeply and totally into every aspect of existence as to be like the air we breathe (I.40, 1995:165). Musil remarks, "But all these things that one denied, these colorless, odorless, tasteless, weightless, and morally indefinable things such as water, air, space, money, and the passing of time, turn out in truth to be the most important things of all, and this gives life a certain spooky quality" (I.40, 1995:166). In the face of that "spooky quality," people sometimes react in a violent panic, as does the drunken man in Musil's narrative.

Though Ulrich does not become violent, he reacts with similar discomfiture. Following his arrest, Ulrich is transported to the police station, where he tries to explain his situation to the duty sergeant. The sergeant responds with a silent and dismissive stare, leaving Ulrich with "a sense of infinity" (I.40, 1995:167). As the scene unfolds, Musil makes it clear that for Ulrich, the most discomfiting aspect of the police bureaucracy is not its power of physical coercion but its ability to encipher a human being into an abstract assemblage of data. Standing before the sergeant, and presuming that his presence has not yet even been noted, Ulrich is startled to learn that his arrest has already become the subject of meticulous documentation. Now, all that remains is to fill in the happenstance data, which will come to constitute the entirety of Ulrich's being, insofar as it is deemed to be bureaucratically significant. As the sergeant questions him, turning his name into a datum, and his face into "an aggregate of officially describable features" (I.40, 1995:168), Ulrich contemplates the logic that makes all this possible: "So he could, even at such a moment as this, himself appreciate this statistical demystification [*statistische Entzauberung*] of his person and feel inspired by the quantitative and descriptive procedures applied to him by the police apparatus as if it were a love lyric invented by Satan" (I.40, 1995:169).

The word *Entzauberung*, which Wilkins and Pike translate as "demystification," is the same term Weber uses to characterize the "disenchantment" of the modern world under the sway of secularism. Given the echoes of the Weberian critique of bureaucracy in Ulrich's encounter with the police, the common use of the word by both Weber and Musil should not escape notice.

In this decisive respect, Ulrich's experience of demystification is clearly insepa-rable from the broader social process of disenchantment. Further to the point, Ulrich perceives with irony that the police bureaucracy is effectively doing to him from without what he inwardly does to himself. In tracing Ulrich's thoughts during his encounter with the police bureaucracy, Musil illuminates this complex dialectic between social praxis and self-conception (compare Marcel, 2001:183–84).

Like Ulrich and the drunken man on the street, each of the children whom I encountered was asserting a claim for recognition, manifest in acts and words that essentially transmitted the message, "Here I am! You ignore me at your own peril!" Musil's narrative echoes the reality of the street: the response to alienation and estrangement is most aggressive and unpredictable among people whose lives are already in a state of crisis or chaos. This is an abiding aspect of police work, and a source of some its greatest perils.

Similar to the instant and intuitive judgment diagnosis that someone is mortally wounded, my colleagues and I knew right away that Colette was a profoundly troubled girl. Everything about her, from her facial expressions, body language, and speech patterns, to her interactions with her mother and officers, revealed her to be a girl whose life was so manifestly disordered that any action on the part of the police would barely lift the crushing burden from her shoulders. Out of the overwhelming complexity of Colette's predicaments, my colleagues and I abstracted a repository of potential forensic evidence and social risks. Her physical presence became the site (*lieu*) of a crime, the victim of which was Colette, less in her own right than in her formal embodiment of the legal interests of the state (compare Foucault, 1977). Those interests encompassed the criminal investigation of an alleged sexual assault, and the assessment of various social risks that Colette would run away from home, refuse treatment (be an "uncooperative victim"), or otherwise create liabilities for the law enforcement and social services bureaucracy that it could not will-ingly accept.

At one point in my conversation with Colette, after attempts at empathetic engagement had seemed to fail, I tried to raise some of these bureaucratic concerns with her in a personal way: "Look, I need you to help me out and do me a huge favor. I know you don't want to go to the hospital, but if you don't, I'll get into a lot of trouble." This line of argument was aimed at giving Colette a sense of power over her destiny; yet, conversely, it may only have served to reinforce the ultimate nature of the bureaucracy's real interest in her situation, and inflamed her will to resist. Her "impassioned struggle for self-assertion" thus continued: "Why should I give a shit if you get fired?" she snapped. She dismissed my further entreaties with a curt request for a cigarette.

Despite its initial tension and violent prelude, my encounter with Anthony proved far less contentious than the one with Colette. Anthony's initial state of frenzied anger seemed to occur for him as a loss of self-control that he did not like. Once settled down, he spoke with precision about his institutionalization, before lapsing again into despair when he learned that he could not return home. Like so many other teens in his situation, Anthony demonstrated a facile awareness of the pathological light in which he was seen by clinical praxis, along with an expressed understanding that his own family feared him. Interestingly, despite her having sent him to the institution, Anthony did not express any feelings of hostility toward his mother: to the contrary, he seemed more downcast than angry when he kept telling me that he wanted to return home to her.

During the initial stages of the encounter with Thomas, my colleagues and I viewed him almost exclusively in tactical terms as a potential threat, because the incident reportedly involved a gun. Secondarily, we read Thomas's taunting actions and uncooperative demeanor as signs of disrespect for police, elaborately performed at least as much for his friends as for the officers. Once in custody, Thomas steadfastly refused to engage in any kind of dialogue. As my colleagues and I contended with Thomas's stream of obscenities and threats, his friends, who stood nearby watching, began to snicker and joke among themselves at his apparent expense, which suggested that as much as they probably admired Thomas for his tenacity, they knew that his actions were unfolding pointlessly to his own detriment.

Prior to releasing Thomas's friends, I photographed all of them in accordance with policies for gathering gang intelligence. As in the case of the high-risk car stop, they were accustomed to this ritual, and stood cooperatively in the kind of confrontational but dignified poses that gang members overwhelmingly choose to adopt, knowing that their photographs are going to circulate among police departments and in police "gang albums" or be displayed on squad room bulletin boards. Thomas, on the other hand, treated the process of being photographed as an opportunity for conspicuous rebellion, making a scowling, angry face from the back seat of the patrol car into which he had been placed. The effect was preposterous, and doubtless hardly what Thomas had intended to convey.

Yet, the key moment in the encounter with Thomas came with his boastful pronouncement that the stolen handgun in the car belonged to him. If his pre-arrest theatrics constituted a "devil-may-care" display of pride, admitting ownership of the gun elevated the gravity of these sentiments to a higher level, by attaching to them the price of a felony conviction. A street-savvy gang member like Thomas would certainly have known that although the gun was found in the immediate area where he had been sitting, prosecution of the case would be difficult, absent further evidence (such as fingerprints or witness statements) proving the legal standard of his "constructive possession" of the gun. Though a utilitarian calculus might view Thomas's unsolicited admission as irrational or unconsidered self-defeating behavior, this ignores the alternative possibility that it was a gesture of self-affirmation, one rendered all the more authentic by its attendant sacrifice of personal liberty. In this respect, Thomas acted much like the drunken man in *The Man Without Qualities*. As a form of a passionate struggle for self-assertion, Thomas's actions would seem to have been intended less to exculpate himself than to demonstrate the bona fide nature of his gang affiliation, and its place as the symbolic center of his rejection of social and legal conventions.

The most conspicuous difference between the episode involving George and the rest of the encounters is that George was the only one of the juveniles who was physically violent toward my colleagues and me. By assaulting Mark in our presence, George decisively rejected our authority. With the act of returning to Mark's house after his release from jail, George had made a willful decision to confront him. George needed to retrieve some personal property from Mark; however, he certainly knew from the judge who released him that the proper way to go about this would have been to have police accompany him. In point of fact, George's overarching concern appeared to have been to confront Mark to rectify what he interpreted as an act of disrespect or dishonor.

When my partner and I arrived at Mark's house and approached George, he instantly perceived a threat, and probably sensed that he would soon be headed right back to jail. George stood his ground and reacted to our encroachment upon his space. He could not afford to retreat in seeming obedience to the police, and thereby lose face to us in the presence of his uncle. Indeed, to have acquiesced to police authority not only would have destroyed his credibility with Mark, but also would have foreclosed the immediately present opportunity to avenge the previous day's act of disrespect. To turn and flee both from the police and from Mark would have been the worst option, because that would have left him appearing weak in the eyes of both opponents.

The mere possibility that such an interpretive process could even have occurred illustrates how interlocutors seek reciprocally to manipulate the ways that they imagine their presence will be construed by each other. The encounter with George further suggests something about the unpredictable nature of violence that emanates from alienation and a diminishment of self. In a passage that foreshadows the drunken man's "impassioned struggle for self-assertion," Musil points out early in *The Man Without Qualities* (I.3, 1995:7–8) how Ulrich, in a moment of fatalistic resignation in the face of the perceived futility of his actions, suddenly and violently lashes out at a punching bag that hangs in his room. The connection between the ontological and the concrete cannot be expressed with sharper clarity.

EXCURSUS ON LANGUAGE AND THE
INTERPRETATION OF PRESENCE

In composing the narratives above (and for that matter, all of the narratives in this book), I often found myself reverting to customary habits of writing police reports. Although at some points I have deliberately used bureaucratic phrasing to convey the underlying logic of problematization, there are other points at which I have been struck by the fact that, despite all my efforts to adopt the stance of retrospective philosophical commentator, the logic of bureaucracy continues to assert itself. It seems to me that the compositional challenge of interweaving bureaucratic and ethnographic descriptions ultimately brings into play ontological questions of approach that exceed stylistic considerations.

Musil consciously attends to similar dynamics in *The Man Without Qualities*, and uses them to wonderful effect. The book opens quite oddly, with language that shifts between traditional literary prose and a narrative form more common to scientific writing. The resulting tensions establish a polarity between "objective knowledge" and "experiential knowing" (Jonsson, 2000:100–108), which is rooted not least of all in Musil's grounding in phenomenology. From the opening sentence, Musil plays with the reader's expectations of how a novel should be written: "A barometric low hung over the Atlantic. It moved eastward toward a high-pressure area over Russia without as yet showing any inclination to bypass this high in a northerly direction" (I.1, 1995:3). After outlining more meteorological and astronomical details, Musil abruptly shifts his language, and reports that "[i]t was a fine day in August 1913" (I.1, 1995:3). However, at the precise moment when Musil finally seems to have struck a familiar, literary tone, he continues to tease the reader, at first providing additional facts as if to set the scene, only to qualify or withdraw the proffered information a moment later: Yes, we are on a busy street in Vienna, but does it really matter? We could just as soon be in any modern city. And, as for those two well-heeled people walking down the street, might they be Ermelinda Tuzzi and Arnheim? Well, perhaps, "but then, they couldn't be, because in August Frau Tuzzi was still in Bad Aussee with her husband and Dr. Arnheim was still in Constantinople; so we are left to wonder who they were" (I.1, 1995:4).

Musil next takes his disequilibrated reader to the scene of a traffic collision involving a truck and a pedestrian, where the nameless couple is standing among a crowd of onlookers. As the woman looks at the injured victim lying in the street, she is momentarily overcome by a wave of nausea, "which she credited to compassion" (I.1, 1995:5). Her male companion ventures a factual explanation of the frantic scene: "The brakes on these heavy trucks take too long to come to a full stop," he opines (I.1, 1995:5). The German text uses the technical term *Bremsweg* ("braking distance"), a word the woman finds at once both confusing and reassuring: She did not really understand, or care to understand, the technology involved [literally "what a braking distance is"] as long as his explanation helped put this ghastly incident into perspective by *reducing it to a technicality [einem technischen Problem]* of no direct personal concern to her (I.1, 1995:5, emphasis added). As the woman watches the accident victim being loaded into an ambulance, the man recites statistics on the injuries and fatalities caused by traffic collisions. However, her momentary detachment from the reality of the accident passes quickly, and she can no longer suppress her lingering sense that something is horribly wrong.

Musil's narrative suggests how this kind of shift in meaning, attitude, and emotion does not occur by happenstance, but instead coincides with transformations in the elemental interpretive premises with which a situation is approached. Intentional shifts are never a simple progression, in which one interpretive stance exists to the mutual exclusion of all others. Rather, for Musil as for Schutz, every encounter incorporates a range of shifting interpretive stances and forms of typification. At a technical level, it is valuable to know that the underlying cause of a traffic collision may be related to braking distance; however, as the woman's reaction to the injured pedestrian demonstrates, this kind of interpretation only goes so far.

SIX

The Poetry of Policing:
Encounters from the Drug War

All other creatures look into the Open/with their whole eyes.
But our eyes, turned inward, are set all around it like snares,
trapping its way out to freedom.

—Rainer Maria Rilke,
Duino Elegies and The Sonnets to Orpheus, 1975

A PHENOMENOLOGICAL REFRAMING
OF THE "WAR ON DRUGS"

Critics of the "war on drugs" have long called attention to its reduction of an insuperably complicated sociocultural crisis to a literal target of juridical and administrative power. To be a target in the context of warfare is to exist as an object whose practical significance is reducible to its role as a source of threats and harm, and to its concomitant availability for destruction. In the street-level prosecution of the war on drugs, this logic of targeting compounds the logic of bureaucratic problematization by collapsing many of the ethical and operational considerations that would otherwise preserve the distinction between a "problem" and an "enemy."

For the police officers who fight the drug war, the term "problem" is used to describe and name people, houses, or even entire apartment complexes and neighborhoods. At shift briefings, for instance, sergeants might tell their officers, "We need to target Joe Smith; he's becoming a real problem"; or, "I want you guys to work on that problem house at 385 Main Street." The logic of effacement implicit in this approach breeds a methodical numbness and clinical disconnect among the police, and a reciprocal futility and resentment among drug users. It is with good reason, then, that officers frequently compare their response to drug-related calls to shoveling sand off the beach: the patterns of late-modern drug addiction and its correlational forms of crime recur in an unrelenting, tidelike fashion, which defies all punitive efforts aimed at stemming its effects. Within this dynamic, there is a profound spirit of fatalism animating people who use illegal drugs, which seems to lead them to expose themselves so incautiously to police intervention. Police officers, for their part, find it difficult to tell if this kind of behavior is a reflection of hopelessness or a devil-may-care attitude that seeks to flout their authority. Either way, the interactions between police officers and people who use and sell illegal drugs are far too often marked by an uneasiness born of mutual mistrust and contempt. Perhaps the most dangerous unintended effect of this dynamic of the war on drugs is its creation of "justifications of necessity" for punitive actions, which in the context of more traditional warfare might be understood as manifestations of *Kriegsraison*. Michael Walzer (2006:138–51) compellingly argues that the logic of *Kriegsraison* becomes much harder to justify in the face of the sorts of battlefield encounters that shock us into realizing the humanity of the enemy, such as happening upon a naked soldier (compare Katz, 1988:6–7, and Brown, 2005). For police officers fighting the "war on drugs," comparable moments can force them to engage the innermost moral and ontological tensions of the bureaucratic paradox, and to consider how the unfettered logic of punitive action and unbridled "necessity" might well lead to defeat.

In the first half of this chapter, I use Rainer Maria Rilke's poem, "The Panther," to interpret my encounter with Michael, a homeless resident of the area I patrolled. Because he is homeless, Michael's lifelong struggle with alcohol and drug dependency has unfolded largely in full public view, making him a constant object of police attention. Each official police contact translates Michael's crises into manageable chaos, in a process that is at its heart poetic—a dynamic creation of meaning. I explore the poetics of translation in greater detail in the second half of the chapter by applying several of Wallace Stevens's poems to the interpretation of two additional encounters from the "drug war." In particular, I draw on Stevens's explorations of the limits of metaphor, and consider the wider relevance of his arguments for understanding the poetry of policing.

ENCOUNTER #6-1: MICHAEL

One summer afternoon, I was on patrol and saw Michael standing in the parking lot of a convenience store. Several months had passed since our last encounter. Michael stood out conspicuously in his brightly colored winter coat, which was far too warm for the weather. He was chatting animatedly with David, a young man of about nineteen, who both used and sold crack cocaine. I drove into the parking lot and stopped to speak with Michael. Neither he nor David seemed especially disturbed by my presence, so I concluded that they probably were not doing anything illegal. I parked a short distance from Michael, rather than pulling up closer to him and angling my patrol car in a way that would block his path or "box him in," which likely would have conveyed to him that I was initiating an enforcement-related contact.

I got out of my patrol car and began to approach Michael. He closed the distance, meeting me halfway from the point where he had first been standing. I extended my hand and casually greeted him: "Michael, how the hell are you? It's been a while; when's the last time I saw you?" Michael offered a friendly reply, though one that was sufficiently gruff and boisterous to convey clearly to David, or to anyone else who might be watching, that he was not merely currying the favor of the police: "Hey, Wender, what's going on?" His bloodshot, deep-set eyes lit up a bit, as their aimlessness momentarily abated and returned my gaze. The lines on Michael's leathered face lifted into a semblance of a smile as he took my hand and gripped it strongly. He pumped my hand for a second or two longer than a customary handshake, and gave me a look that seemed unable to connect wholly with one emotion or another. It was hard to know how much this had to do with his degree of intoxication. Michael was never completely sober, and the odor of cheap beer or malt liquor always hung in the air around him.

I asked him if he was still working as a short-order cook at a nearby bar and grill. His eyes dropped and he shook his head. Michael looked exhausted and beleaguered. He told me he was back to drinking heavily again, and had lost his job. I had heard from several colleagues that Michael was also regularly smoking crack cocaine, but I did not have the heart to ask him about it, especially in front of David. I also did not want to give the appearance of being on a "fishing expedition" for information. Instead, I took a more casual approach, which I felt would respect Michael's sensibilities while also conveying to him and David that I was well aware of their ongoing illegal behavior. "Are you keeping this young guy out of trouble?" I asked only half jokingly, nodding toward David. Michael seemed to take my point and added to it a further gravity of his own, as he looked intently at David *and left unspoken what Michael and I both seemed to have in mind: that neither of us wanted David to end up in Michael's situation.*

As I made my comment, I recalled to myself how several years earlier, during a brief period of sobriety, Michael and I had talked about the rising prevalence in the area of drug use, drug-related violence, and especially of the conspicuous involvement of teens and young adults in all of this. Michael offered some boisterous, joking comments about how he would try to "keep David in line." At the same time, a vague awkwardness and discomfiture seemed to cross Michael's face. Perhaps what I had intended as a genuine appeal to Michael to exercise influence over a younger man inadvertently gave him a heightened sense of his own accreting weakness, both inwardly and with respect to his credibility on the street. Either way, I sensed that my continuing the conversation would be to no good end. I wished Michael well, admonished David to heed his advice to stay out of trouble, got back into my car, and drove off.

In bureaucratic terms, my encounter with Michael was classified as a "social contact." Under United States law, social contacts are encounters in which citizens have no legal obligation to participate, and from which they therefore have the right to disengage at will, without official sanction.[1] Officers in most police agencies are encouraged to initiate social contacts with the general public, and especially with known or potential offenders. The latter type of social contact serves as a powerful means of informal social control, and offers an excellent source of intelligence and investigative leads. For these reasons, social contacts play a key role in prosecuting the "drug war" by offering a relatively unobtrusive means of developing relationships with drug users and dealers, which facilitate (or, in some cases, help obviate) subsequent enforcement action.[2]

Though many of the social contacts that inevitably occur during an officer's shift pass unrecorded, and hence never become "official incidents," others are deemed worthy of documentation, either for intelligence or investigative purposes, or simply to produce a "stat" to be counted among the other tangible pieces of work an officer performs. Following my contact with Michael, and with both of these goals in mind, I filled out an index card–sized "field interview report," more commonly known as a "FIR card" (pronounced "fur"), or simply, "FIR." FIR cards record the identity and a detailed description of the person interviewed, or "FIRed," along with a short narrative that provides a summary of the contact. On the back of the FIR card that I completed to document my encounter with Michael, I wrote in block letters, "SOCIAL CONTACT. VERY DRUNK. NOT LOOKING GOOD AT ALL." The information on FIR cards is entered into records databases, and serves as a tool for criminal intelligence and investigations by contributing additional "facts" to the official, bureaucratic biographies of people contacted by the police.

My initial encounters with Michael occurred in the early 1990s, when he was still working full time and living with his girlfriend and her son in a small house owned by Michael's father. Over a relatively short period of time, Michael lapsed into a pattern of heavy drinking, drug use, and domestic violence. He eventually ended up living on the street. My colleagues and I regularly contacted him, usually for relatively innocuous matters such as trespassing, public intoxication, or disorderly conduct. All of this was to little avail: in varying ways, Michael was either unable or unwilling to ameliorate his situation. In much the same way that Laura (chapter 5) represents a paradigmatic "problem child," Michael exemplifies modern society's suspicious and unsympathetic vision of the homeless "street person," whom it reifies as a discomfiting object of human detritus (compare Wilson and Kelling, 1982). Objectified as a bureaucratic problem, Michael's presence is reduced to an impediment to order and efficiency.

RILKE AND THE PHENOMENOLOGY OF PRESENCE: PERSON OR SUBJECT, THING OR OBJECT?

For my immediate purposes, the value of Rilke's poetry centers on its illumination of the ontological unity of the world and human consciousness (see Rilke, 1984:xi and 2001:5)[3]. Rilke believed that ordinary perception and consciousness yield an attenuated view of reality, and used his poems to shatter conventional notions of what it means to encounter things in the world. Rilke's poetry reveals the distinction between "things" and "objects," which bears an essential affinity to my own distinction between co-presence and intersubjectivity.

"The Panther" exemplifies Rilke's use of poetry to reverse the structure of the ordinary experience of things in the world. This reversal leads to the creation of a poetic vision that enables the experiencing of a thing "from the inside out" (Strauss, 1980:67; Schwarz, 1984:xi). "The Panther" was the first among Rilke's famous "thing poems" (*Dinggedichte*), with which he sought to go beyond the expression of subjective, emotional responses to the world (Brodsky, 1988:84) and write prose that would be the poetic analogue of the forms created in painting or sculpture. Rilke's predominant inspirations in this endeavor were Cézanne and Rodin, whom he deeply admired for engaging the world as more than passive, reified objects of perception (see Ryan, 2001:129).[4]

In transcending the supposed divide between subject and object, "The Panther" and the other *Dinggedichte* challenge the reader to become open to a different way of seeing. Rilke's disciplined rejection of emotionalism casts aside any notion that the new way of seeing he creates is merely a species of empathy (see Ryan, 1999:50). Rather, truly to engage alterity is to come away heeding the imperative, "You must change your life," with which Rilke ends "Archaic Torso of Apollo," another of the *Dinggedichte* (Rilke, 1908:2–3). Within the context of bureaucratic praxis, Rilke's words serve as a reminder that sentimentality and empathy do not suffice to recast an approach that is ontologically flawed.

THE PANTHER

In the Jardin des Plantes, Paris

His gaze has from the passing of the bars
grown so tired, that it holds nothing anymore.
It seems to him there are a thousand bars
and behind a thousand bars no world.

The supple pace of powerful soft strides,
turning in the very smallest circle,
is like a dance of strength around a center
in which a great will stands numbed.

Only sometimes the curtain of the pupils
soundlessly slides up—. Then an image enters,
glides through the limbs' taut stillness,
dives into the heart—and dies.

DER PANTHER

Im Jardin des Plantes, Paris

Sein Blick ist vom Vorübergehn der Stäbe
so müd geworden, daß er nichts mehr hält.
Ihm ist, als ob es tausend Stäbe gäbe
und hinter tausend Stäben keine Welt.

Der weiche Gang geschmeidig starker Schritte,
der sich im allerkleinsten Kreise dreht,
ist wie ein Tanz von Kraft um eine Mitte,
in der betäubt ein großer Wille steht.

Nur manchmal schiebt der Vorhang der Pupille
sich lautlos auf—. Dann geht ein Bild hinein,
geht durch der Glieder angespannte Stille—
und hört im Herzen auf zu sein.

(Rilke, 1907/2001:62–63)

"The Panther" creates an openness in which the normal "object" of perception is experienced anew from the inside out. Rilke takes the "observable facts" of the panther's presence and elevates them to the level of metaphysical insight (Mandel, 1965:65). From its opening line, the poem builds on the reversal of inside/out: the panther has long ceased actively gazing at the bars of his cage; instead, they move across his field of vision (Leppmann, 1984:214). The physical reality of the bars has effectively caged the panther's inner existence. The ensuing monotony is reinforced by the rhythm of the prose—*Stäbe gäbe* (Wood, 1970:71). The panther lives in a state of near-total enervation and emptiness. Its physical power comes to naught, because its heart has been inwardly stilled. We surmise in reading the poem that the panther has not always been like this: it seems instead that years of confinement have exacted a devastating toll. It is not difficult to see that the panther's experience has a universal quality that readily lends itself to wider application in a human context.

Standing before someone like Michael, one knows immediately what Rilke meant when he wrote of the panther's tired gaze that "holds nothing anymore." Despite its lingering vestiges of proud rage, Michael's gaze had also become empty. Beyond what the single encounter could adequately convey, I had witnessed this transformation over a period of years. In an earlier episode, some ten years prior to the one recounted above, I arrested Michael for domestic violence assault after he returned home from work, got drunk, and struck his girlfriend. Michael was belligerent and defiant; and although he did not resist arrest, he certainly knew how to project an intimidating and uncooperative presence to my colleagues and me. I still remember moving quickly to handcuff Michael as he stood in his living room, tense and clearly ready to fight if given the slightest provocation. His hard, animated stare has since become an empty gaze, not least of all, it may be surmised, because of the ravages of alcohol and drugs, and the self-fulfilling state of disharmony they perpetuate. Michael exists with a disconnect between his body and will that parallels the tragic life of the panther. Just as the panther's might and strength are turned inward, to no purpose other than an endless pacing, Michael's existence is reduced to the perpetuation of a stupor from which he no longer knows how to extricate himself.

Unlike the panther, whose physical boundaries are wholly determined by a cage imposed from without, Michael seemed to have confined himself to a small geographical area in which he spent nearly all of his time. Rarely did my colleagues and I encounter Michael beyond a radius of several blocks, the hub of which was an intersection with a busy convenience store on one corner and an automotive repair shop on another. Michael spent most of his time traveling back and forth between the two locations, where he was a well-known presence. The convenience store was the source of most of Michael's alcohol, and its parking lot and several nearby houses offered ready access to illegal drugs. At times, he served as an unofficial watchman and caretaker for the automotive repair shop, living behind it on and off in a small trailer or wrecked car. When the weather was mild, he slept in a nearby park frequented by other homeless people, or in the backyards of friends, whose tumbledown rental houses were all within a short walk of Michael's corner.

For a period of time, Michael used to walk about half a mile to a strip mall for his cook's job, but this had likely become for him the memory of a distant world. Before he lapsed into heavy drinking and drug use, Michael had also been an avid outdoorsman. He spoke with me several times of the delight he took in escaping from his drab surroundings to go hunting and fishing. Gradually, however, the range of his travels grew smaller. This self-restriction seems to have paralleled an inner sense of resignation, and revealed itself in his gaze. In this essential respect, a phenomenological reading informed by "The Panther" suggests how Michael's actions and presence may be read as a projection of the state of being in which he found himself.

Rilke shows explicitly in the opening line of the poem that the panther's will has weakened to the point that its everyday experience of the world is now all but completely determined and controlled from without, by "the passing of the bars." The panther appears to have lost any sense that its own movement and gaze affect the phenomenon of the passing of the bars. It has so internalized the presence of the bars that their "external reality seems to converge upon the existence or inner self of the panther" (Jayne, 1972:68). The panther's existence has devolved into a state of passivity and monotony, which are inwardly experienced as a dulled reflex. Michael's mundane existence centered on passing the time of day and finding the substances that made this condition somewhat more tolerable. As Michael himself knew and forthrightly admitted, the former and the latter were effectively one and the same, giving his modus vivendi a circularity that endlessly turned upon itself while constantly threatening to spiral further downward.

Michael might have remarked in a moment of self-reflection that, like the bars before the panther, "life was passing him by," or that in fact, it had already effectively done so. In this sentiment, one finds a human version of the relationship between the panther's gaze and spirit. From a rational, everyday standpoint that structures the normal comportment toward the givenness of reality, and informs the parameters for the precepts of mainstream social conduct, Michael's actions cannot but strike most people as utterly aimless. To some, his actions might be regarded even more critically as lazy, stupid, or self-defeating. Others may take a different view and attribute them to biological, psychological, or social factors, over which Michael might be seen to have no ultimate control. All of these assessments, whatever their practical value or analytic relevance, have nonetheless prematurely reified human presence in an effort to make sense of its obtrusion upon what is generally regarded as normalcy and order. Against such a hasty reification, a phenomenological reading of my encounter with Michael based upon "The Panther" suggests that the dull and directionless quality of his gaze must first be understood on its own terms, from within, as it reveals itself, rather than from without, as a "problem" or "datum."

To say, as Michael might have, that "life is passing me by" may be paraphrased in this way: "As I am here, experiencing the fact of my own existence, I feel empty and powerless in the face of all that occurs before me." "I merely bear witness to a world in which my participation is utterly pointless and without real consequence." With these words, and with the gaze that matches them, Michael and others of like spirit emerge as a presence that evades the grasp and ken of instrumental rational praxis. In encountering Michael, whatever the outside police observer qua bureaucrat may think, and however these thoughts become transformed into practical action, for Michael, as for the panther, "It seems to him there are a thousand bars/and behind a thousand bars no world. (*Ihm ist, als ob es tausend Stäbe gebe/und hinter tausend Stäbe keine Welt.*)"

Ihm ist literally means, "*to him* it is": to him, as he sees it and lives it, from the inside looking out, it is "as if" (*als ob*) there are a thousand bars, and beyond the bars, an empty void—"no world." Rilke's language thus establishes in the first stanza of the poem a clear link between the panther's tired gaze and the innermost elements of its being. By doing so, Rilke takes what might otherwise be abstracted as a "fact" and amplifies its significance with respect to an unseen center. When, in my official capacity, I approached Michael in the parking lot of the convenience store, was I able to attend to the analogous aspect of his presence, which was ultimately more real and irreducible than whatever judgments bureaucratic praxis might venture? Problematization does not engage these broader possibilities and farther horizons. Yet, this interpretive economy comes at the price of an incomplete vision, with a resulting attenuation of practical action. Rilke, on the other hand, reverses the subject/object relationship, and starkly brings forth the heart of the panther's existence with a forceful proclamation: *to him* it is this way; and because this is so, his gaze can hold no more. For Michael, moving from point to point in his constellation of disharmony, these peregrinations must create for him what the passing of the bars creates for the panther. Viewed in this light, his pacings to and fro, his loitering, all emerge with a *newly seen* profundity. Spatiality in the encounter assumes an existential significance (see Bachelard, 1994).

As I approached Michael in the convenience store parking lot, he closed the distance, not shrinking or shying from the contact, but acting so as to cement its inevitability. An announcement of presence, a gesture of free will—all of these may be found convincingly in Michael's apparently simple act of approach. The "dance" that ensued between Michael and me—the exchange of handshakes and greetings, the initial flurry of rough jocularity, gave expression to a presence that used to assert itself with far greater force. These actions are the analogue of the panther's "dance of strength" (*Tanz von Kraft*). There is also for Michael, as for the panther, a center around which the dance occurs, a center "in which a great will stands numbed" (*in der betäubt ein großer Wille steht*).

The verb *betäuben* carries a special relevance for understanding Michael's situation, given its varying connotations of intoxication, deadening, or anesthesia. In German, one of the terms for a narcotic is *Betäubungsmittel*—literally, a "means of deadening." For Michael, everyday life consists largely of wandering within the confines of his foreshortened horizons, and seeking the means to deaden himself against the effects of his own actions. The endless circling continually unfolds around a center, which perpetually seeks to escape the knowledge and awareness of its predicament. The will is thus not so completely numbed as to have forgotten its own existence. To the contrary, it is the void and pain between states of numbness that gives impetus to the search for escape, which for Michael can be held in his hand, in the form of a crack pipe or an oversized bottle of cheap malt liquor.

Nur manchmal—"only sometimes": once in a while, there comes a moment when the "great will" gains a degree of energy or self-confidence, by means of which it imagines fleetingly that it might regain what it has lost. The narrative above describes how the encounter seemed to arrive at a crucial point when I suggested to Michael that he take some steps to "keep David in line." Momentarily, perhaps, at the sound of this suggestion, Michael might have realized a notion of his erstwhile power and reputation. I knew that as a long-standing presence on the neighborhood streets, Michael had a degree of credibility, albeit one that had diminished in recent years. In any event, Michael found himself presented with an acknowledgment of his credibility, or a certain recognition of his authority. At the same time, however, this recognition conveyed the acknowledgment that this was largely attributable to Michael's own transgressions.

Perhaps, as with the panther, an image entered Michael's mind as he looked at David and me. The image expanded as the mind reflected upon its possibilities—here was the moment when Michael turned to David and offered an impromptu bit of avuncular counsel. For an instant, Michael might have recalled within himself another time, when he had been genuinely jocular and sociable. He used to seek me out, waving to me as I drove by in my patrol car, and would engage me in conversation from time to time. Now, it appeared almost as if Michael sought to erase these memories; or, perhaps he had just grown more wary of me, or was even embarrassed to talk with me. The encounter above was one of the more amiable contacts between Michael and me for some time; yet, it still had a marked quality of strained artificiality. Did Michael, for a fleeting moment, envision a way out of his captivity and sense the possibility of a restoration of self and dignity? Perhaps; although it seems, as with the panther, when it entered his heart, the vision ceased to exist.

Michael's gaze is the panther's: the alienation and fatalism with which the panther looks out, *as if (als ob)* there were no world "out there," corresponds to the modern, urban landscape, where the foreshortened horizon of a disenchanted world blends imperceptibly with the bars of a Weberian "iron cage." Michael's inner laceration, instantly palpable in the dissonance between his aggressive, proud handshake and the feebleness of his watery gaze, is matched to no small degree by the paradox embodied in the armed, uniformed bureaucrat, whose outward trappings of power hold forth a promise of solace, which is never delivered.

What, then, does one "truly see" in standing before Michael, and how does the police officer translate that vision into "facing the facts" of a social crisis? One answer might be found in the circular structure of "The Panther" (see Brodsky, 1988:88). The German text begins and ends with a pair of homonyms: respectively, *sein* (his) and *sein* (to be). The reader is thus brought back to the same point of departure, following the pacings of the panther. In the encounter between Michael and me, the final moment is one of mutual dissatisfaction and vague melancholy. Here, Michael's experiences and mine elide into something that cannot be explained by empathy alone. As "The Panther" shows, what is seen determines the possible range of responses to the presence to which one bears witness. The amazing power of Rilke's way of seeing lies in its disclosure of the ontological qualities of ordinary action. He thus offers a perspective from which complacency, indifference, and routinization might be overcome, or at least contextualized. "You see how difficult it becomes," wrote Rilke, "when one tries to get very close to the facts" (1985:82).

Having gotten "close to the facts" of Michael's situation, many of my colleagues viewed him with a pathos that made them decline to take all but the most necessary enforcement action against him, and to chide their peers who did more than this. With the same view in mind that would regard the "hunting" of a caged panther as intrinsically unjust, many of my fellow officers intentionally passed up opportunities to arrest Michael. I also shared this perspective, which led me on more than one occasion to drive right past Michael with the knowledge that he had an outstanding arrest warrant for some minor offense or another. On other occasions, I merely reminded Michael casually that he needed to remember to show up for his court dates.

One afternoon approximately a year after my encounter with Michael and David, two of my colleagues arrested Michael for a misdemeanor warrant, apparently because they needed an "easy stat" on what had been an uneventful shift. They were later chided by one of their peers, who demanded to know why they were "messing with Michael" and wasting their time arresting him for a "chippy, bullshit warrant." They also inveighed against the officer who had issued the original citation for property damage that resulted in the warrant. From a supervisory and personal standpoint, I voiced my agreement with the position that Michael ought to be left alone, unless he did something violent.

Encounter #6-2, Sunday Morning at a Crack Motel

On an uncharacteristically busy Sunday morning, I responded to assist several colleagues at an extended-stay motel with a reputation for chronic drug dealing, prostitution, and other criminal activity. My fellow officers had responded to the motel after a woman called 911 to report that her adult granddaughter, Jennifer, was staying at the motel, and was suicidal. The woman told the 911 operator that Jennifer was addicted to crack cocaine, and was depressed because she had run out of drugs and money. She expressed concern for Jennifer's welfare and asked that officers find her. Unfortunately, the woman did not know Jennifer's room number, which left the responding officers to figure out in which one of the dozens of motel rooms she might actually be staying.

One officer who responded to the call had received information that a wanted fugitive was dealing crack cocaine out of one of the rooms. While keeping the room under surveillance in hope of catching him, the officer had noticed several people milling about inside it. He thought it would be worthwhile to see if Jennifer was in the room. With assistance from another officer, my colleague checked the room and found Jennifer, along with two other young women, Paulette and Sonya. The fugitive was not there, although his wallet and driver's license were sitting on the counter in the kitchenette.

By the time I arrived at the motel, two officers were leading Sonya away in handcuffs. They had arrested her for an outstanding warrant, which had been issued after she failed to appear in court on a prostitution charge. I walked upstairs to the room where two of my colleagues were waiting, along with Jennifer and Paulette. The room was strewn with clothing and assorted personal belongings. There were crack pipes, syringes, and condom wrappers everywhere. A cabinet in the kitchenette contained baking soda, a scale, butane torches, and other paraphernalia used to make and smoke crack cocaine. A walkie-talkie sat on the dresser by the front door—it was probably used by a lookout to report the comings and goings of customers and, more important, police cars.

Jennifer lay silently on one of the beds, curled up in a fetal position. She was semiconscious, and could barely speak. It was obvious that she desperately needed to get high. Paulette scratched feverishly at the scabs that covered her entire body. According to her driver's license, she was twenty-four years old, although she looked closer to forty. I asked her how long she had been using drugs. "Forever," she deadpanned. I told Paulette what she already knew: that hanging out with a violent felon who was selling crack and prostituting her was a sure path to disaster. "Look," she snapped angrily, "I know I have a problem, ok?" I told her that I was not trying to lecture her, but was only attempting to understand her situation. "How can you understand me?" she asked, "I don't even understand myself."

Paulette was utterly annoyed by the police presence in the room. She tried to climb into one of the beds, but I would not let her, for fear that a weapon might be hidden beneath the blankets and clutter. "One of the other cops already looked, ok?" she said in an annoyed, impatient tone. After confirming this with one of my colleagues, I told Paulette that she could get into the bed. She dismissed me with a vexed glare, and protested that she had to check out of the room within an hour. As my colleagues finished searching the room for evidence, drugs, and weapons, I stood by, watching Paulette, who in turn watched me, all the while sitting in a chair and scratching anxiously at her scabs. My colleagues eventually amassed a large quantity of paraphernalia. We later disposed of it without filing criminal charges, which we knew would consume time and paperwork and accomplish absolutely nothing.

Because Jennifer had threatened to kill herself, an officer drove her to the hospital for a psychiatric evaluation. All three of us knew that she would be right back on the street within a few hours. Paulette remained alone in the room. She sat forlornly on the bed, staring at the piles of clothing strewn all around her, and realized the impending arrival of the motel's checkout time. "I've got an hour to pack up all this shit and check out," she said in exasperation. It was obvious that the fugitive crack dealer had left it to Paulette to gather up his belongings for a later rendezvous.

I tried to end the encounter on a note of optimism, however farfetched. "You're not fooling me, I know you're really a nice girl," I said to Paulette with a smile as I walked out the door. Paulette chuckled gently. Once out of her earshot, I turned to one of my colleagues and remarked, "Gee, I bet now she's going to quit smoking crack." "Well," I added, uncomfortably trying to refute my own sardonic comment, and before the other officer could answer, "all we can do is try."

Later that afternoon, two of my colleagues found Paulette and Sonya sleeping in the fugitive crack dealer's car on a side street behind the motel. Paulette had checked out of the room, and the arresting officers had released Sonya after the agency that had issued her arrest warrant declined to pick her up, probably owing to a lack of jail space. A short while later, the fugitive and another man showed up. A high-speed pursuit ensued, during which the fugitive drove the wrong way up an interstate freeway. He was eventually captured and returned to prison. Paulette and Sonya were interviewed, and once again released.

Encounter #6-3, Cecilia and Albert— "Crossing the Threshold"

Early one weekend morning, a colleague and I responded to an assault at an apartment complex. A maintenance worker told us he had heard sounds of fighting from one of the units. He went inside and saw a man striking "Cecilia," the tenant who lived there. The worker pulled the man from the apartment and chased him off. I found the man sitting on the curb at the complex's entrance. I recognized him from a couple of recent contacts as "Albert."

I recalled that Albert suffered from a heroin addiction and a host of mental disorders. Among other things, he experienced hallucinations. Albert also had an odd penchant for collecting women's cosmetics. Beside him on the curb where he was sitting was a large, plastic garbage bag, which overflowed with clothing and other belongings. When I tried to speak with Albert and check him for weapons, he became agitated and tried to pull away from me. My partner and I handcuffed him after a brief scuffle.

Once we had safely secured Albert in a patrol car, I went to contact Cecilia *at her apartment. She opened the door cautiously. The apartment was filthy, with the floor barely visible beneath the clutter. Cecilia looked pale and horribly sick. Like Albert, she was addicted to heroin. She also told me that she had severe, chronic medical problems, for which she was taking numerous prescription drugs. Cecilia said that she was not romantically involved with Albert, and characterized him as "just a friend." She told me Albert had been visiting her and had tried to steal her cash and pain medications. Cecilia said he assaulted her when she tried to stop him. She did not complain of any injuries. Cecilia said she felt sorry for Albert, and did not want to press charges; she just wanted me to retrieve her money and medications.*

Cecilia cried as we spoke. I explained to her that Albert was in custody, and told her she had nothing to fear. I asked her what was upsetting her so much. Cecilia shook her head for a moment and then replied, "Nothing, I'm just so sick." I went outside to retrieve her cash and medications, which my partner had found in Albert's coat pockets. I returned to Cecilia's apartment and gave her the money and pills. She set them aside and thanked me. Cecilia was still crying. I asked her if she would be all right after I left. She looked at me silently and then reached out, took one of my hands with both of hers, held it to her cheek, and closed her eyes. I did not say anything. After a few moments, she released my hand. I asked Cecilia if she wanted me to stay for a while. She shook her head, and I left. Given his apparent lack of mental competence, and Cecilia's refusal to press any criminal charges, Albert was taken to the hospital for a psychiatric evaluation instead of being booked into jail.

Bureaucratic police praxis in drug-related encounters reflexively acts to typify and encipher human presence into the abstract entity of "the doper." "Dopers" are merely the incidental human vessels within which various forms of drug-related behavior are contained. Unlike other terms, such as "junkie" or "pusher," which distinguish between users and dealers, the term "doper" is a generic category that encompasses the entire population of people involved with illegal drugs, whether as producers, distributors, consumers, or any combination of the three. Categorizing people as "dopers" rests upon the unexamined conflation of rhetorical tropes with the reality that they purport to represent. This creation of meaning is an inherently poetic process: it is the essence of "policing as poetry."

Physically isolated in bleak spaces epitomizing the social atomism of modern urban life, the trio of women in the motel room and Cecilia and Albert were already, by virtue of their unitized modus vivendi, that much more amenable to being approached as objects conveniently arrayed before the apparatus of bureaucratic praxis. In the episode at the motel room, my colleagues and I encountered Jennifer, Paulette, and Sonya as the objectified embodiment of the phenomena of drug use and prostitution. For all intents and purposes, the three women were just another set of unpleasant objects that needed to be picked up and removed, like the crack pipes and used syringes that littered their motel room. My encounter with Albert unfolded in similar fashion. The way in which I had found him, sitting silently on the curb next to the trash bag full of his belongings, unsettlingly suggests how for practical bureaucratic purposes, the man and the bag were similarly regarded as potentially danger-ous social detritus—unhygienic and unpredictably harmful. In searching Al-bert's property and in searching him, I took the same clinical approach: I wore rubber gloves to avoid possible contagion, and proceeded cautiously to avoid being stuck by hidden syringes, of which I found many. I had also followed similar procedures in dealing with the women in the motel room. The issue here is not one of challenging the demonstrable need for these sorts of safety measures; rather, it is a matter of understanding the comportment toward human presence that enables the instant translation of one's interlocutor into an abstract ensemble of harms and risks.

The unrelenting logic of this comportment can be disrupted in the most un-expected ways, as when Cecilia took my hand. Her action caught me completely off guard, and was followed by a stark and awkward silence. With her simple gesture, Cecilia challenged me to recognize what bureaucratic praxis could not see: that "[t]he hand is not a bundle of flesh and bone, it is the palpable pres-ence of the other person" (Merleau-Ponty, 1973:116). The act of reaching across the doorway instantly nullified her bureaucratic translation into a "subject" and retranslated it back into the form of co-presence. Cecilia's gesture shows how the simplest act can call into question the entire ontological foundation of bureaucratic praxis and unravel the metaphors it uses to problematize those whom it encounters.

WALLACE STEVENS AND THE LIMITS OF METAPHOR

As Frank Kermode puts it (1980:273), Stevens's poems are created out of a "watching the shining of the commonplace." Through his meditative study of the inseparable relation between world/consciousness, self/other, and fiction/"reality," Stevens illuminates the kinds of ruptures in the ordinary that characterized my encounters with Albert and Cecilia, and the three women in the motel room. Even more than this, Stevens uses his poems to engage the constitutive power of thought and language, not least of all as they unfold in his own acts of poetic creation. In this decisive respect, Stevens's poetry carefully incorporates a self-reflective, metapoetic stance that is phenomenological in nature (compare Naylor, 1988). Questioning modernity's faith in the categorical certitude of notions such as objectivity and subjectivity, Stevens takes a deconstructive stance from which he observes the continuous creation of meaning that defines the poetic dimension of human being (Stevens, 1997:750).[5] In his continual reflection on the power and limits of poetic language, Stevens gives particular attention to the roles of metaphor and translation. It is in this respect that his work is especially relevant for my project of a phenomenological aesthetics of encounter.

"Notes Toward a Supreme Fiction" stands as the apogee of Stevens's metapoetic works, and also ranks among his most philosophically rich poems.[6] As Stevens understands it, the "supreme fiction" is nothing other than poetry itself.[7] In characterizing poetry as the "supreme fiction," Stevens does not mean that it is false, or a mere figment of the imagination (Naylor, 1988:47–53). Rather, he seeks to evoke an awareness of the intrinsic imperfection of poetry and of every other human attempt to grasp the ultimate nature of the world. By applying Stevens's ideas on the boundaries and limits of poetic language within the context of police-citizen encounters, the interpretive actions of bureaucratic policing that reductively frame predicaments as abstract "problems" become readable as a distinct and powerful kind of poetry. Out of their encounters with fellow human beings, police officers poetically create fictions—abstractions and typifications composed by isolating instrumentally univocal meanings out of the unbounded existential totality of presence. If we grant that bureaucratic praxis functions as a form of poetry through the metaphoric transformation of human presence into a "problem," then some of Stevens's reflections on the limits of poetic language should likewise apply to elucidating the sorts of tragically flawed dynamics that drive the poetics of policing.

To secure the basis for this comparison, we need to call attention to the role of metaphor in all discourse, and especially to discourse in the context of social praxis. In light of various philosophical investigations of metaphor (see especially Lakoff and Johnson, 1980, and Ricoeur, 1977), this is relatively easy to do, at least up to the point that most people will acknowledge the existence of a "rhetorical" dimension in various kinds of social discourse, such as jurisprudence and politics. Broadly following Stevens, I want to claim that the realm of metaphor is actually much wider: metaphor is intrinsic to any form of discourse, regardless of its particular semantic rules, and is most powerful where its presence remains unrecognized. To the extent that consciously metaphoric language such as poetry largely "divests" itself of claims of direct representational description, it ceases to be beholden to an epistemological schema of truth as accurate correspondence (Ricoeur, 1977:247). Simultaneously, however, a careful genealogical analysis of metaphor forces us to collapse the putative distinction between "proper" and "figurative" metaphoric tropes (see Ricoeur, 1977:294, and compare Derrida, 1975). As a result, we are able not only to discern the cryptic metaphoric quality of representational discourse (e.g., scientific descriptions) but can also open ourselves to the elemental possibility of the truth content of aesthetic form and "fictional" discourse (see chapter 3).

The police officer creates abstract, formal meaning ("problems") out of the vicissitudes of human predicaments through the use of a complex metaphoric schema. This schema functions on the street essentially as it functions in the composition of formal poetry: by transferring the name of one thing to another, which is ontologically separate from it (see Aristotle, *Poetics*, 1457b:7–25). To appreciate its wider implications, this process must be understood as an ontological event, which cannot be reduced to an abstract linguistic operation. How so? Recall that classical rhetoric distinguishes metaphor from simile on the general basis that a metaphoric comparison does not use the terms "like" or "as." Metaphors thus create comparisons that necessarily incorporate an ontological dimension: it is not merely that "A is *like* B"; A *is* B (see Ricoeur, 1977:24–27). The nature of metaphor is such that its figurative power can transform unnoticed into a means of substantive displacement with enormous practical implications.

The functioning of metaphor becomes clearer if we note how the Greek term *metaphorā* becomes rendered into Latin as *translatio*—a moving or carrying across. In "White Mythology," Derrida engages the unspoken role of metaphor in philosophical language, against its claim to be discursively self-transparent.[8] If Derrida is correct that "[a]bstract notions always hide a sensory figure" (1975:210), the reverse is equally true: figuration is impossible without abstraction. Hence, the question central to reflecting on the role of metaphor in bureaucratic language is how the power of displacement extends beyond semantics and assumes concrete form in the operations of praxis. How, in other words, are the dis-placing (trans-lational) operations of bureaucratic policing—the arrests and other actions that physically move "subjects"—a reinscription and intensification in social space of linguistic tropes?

APARTMENTS OF MISERY

To address this question within the specific context of police praxis, I turn now to a consideration of the metaphoric translation of human presence that occurred during my encounters with Albert and Cecilia, and the women in the motel room. The logic by which each of these people came to be identified as the "subject" of an investigation situated them within an interpretive schema that served as the basis for deciding how they would be "handled." This was achieved by substituting the identity of each person with a form of objectified presence, fitted to a range of potential bureaucratic actions. Unfolding as it does according to a self-conception of objectivity and neutrality, bureaucratic praxis gives little heed to the flaws and contingencies of this sort of translational process, let alone to its readily identifiable effects. The sorts of plaintive or belligerent resistance attempted by those upon whom this process is enacted, such as Paulette's acerbic statements to me, are thus rarely taken as signs of any limitations inherent to the objectifying operations of problematization. Quite the contrary, resistance is deterministically seen as a reconfirmation of their validity: "they're just a bunch of dopers, what do you expect?" The efficient, metaphoric transportation of human presence over to the classificatory schema of the "drug war" thus proceeds unfazed when literally faced with such opposition. As this process unfolds at the scene of an incident, officers decide who among the "subjects contacted" will be kept and which of them will be "kicked loose."

In Albert's case, although I initially determined that he had probably committed a crime, my unfolding interpretations of his mental state and Cecilia's express unwillingness to pursue charges meant that he could not be approached as a criminal and taken to jail. Nevertheless, his violent, delusional behavior defined Albert as an immediate threat to Cecilia, my partner, and me; and simply releasing him also would have posed an unacceptable risk to the general public. In the end, we decided to take him to the emergency room for evaluation of his psychiatric condition, as well as to screen him for a drug overdose. We knew from experience that Albert would be right back on the street within a few hours; however, the decision to "hand him over" to the health-care bureaucracy had at least left us "covered." Similar logic prevailed in the encounter in the motel room, where my colleagues and I had no probable cause to charge Jennifer with a crime. Because she was under the influence of cocaine and had threatened to kill herself, she went to the hospital. The unnamed woman from the motel room was taken to jail for her warrant. Like Paulette, Cecilia was left to her own devices. The manifest futility of the police action taken in these two "drug war" skirmishes is apparent in the fact that two of the three women from the motel room were recontacted by officers within a few hours. Beyond engaging such obvious issues of bureaucratic efficiency at the operational or political level, the ontological and ethical question that remains to be answered is this: what truly was known about the individual situation and predicament of each of the persons in these two encounters?

To see what lies behind the seemingly commonsense approach of bureaucratic praxis, as it unfolded in the events in the motel room and Cecilia's apartment, we might adopt the stance urged by Stevens in the opening canto of "Notes Toward a Supreme Fiction":

> You must become an ignorant man again
> And see the sun again with an ignorant eye
> And see it clearly in the idea of it.
>
> (Stevens, 1997:329)

Stevens's use of the term "ignorant eye" is deliberately ironic: the "ignorance" of which he speaks is the result of attaining a vision of reality that sees through and beyond the ideas that the mind has used imperfectly to describe it, by attempting to name what is ultimately ineffable. What Stevens is prescribing here corresponds closely to the phenomenological *epoché* and its process of bracketing or suspension (see Hines, 1975:145–46; compare Baird, 1968:279–80; also see chapter 1).

Once the eye sees the sun "with an ignorant eye," the wholeness of the sun's presence overwhelms the names with which its existence had hitherto been conflated. Reality eclipses metaphor:

> How clean the sun when seen in its idea,
> Washed in the remotest cleanliness of a heaven
> That has expelled us and our images . . .
>
> (Stevens, 1997:329)

The myths and metaphors that previously attempted to capture the sun thus wither in the face of its light:

> Phoebus is dead, ephebe. But Phoebus was
> A name for something that never could be named.
> There was a project for the sun and is.
> There is a project for the sun. The sun

Must bear no name, gold flourisher, but be
In the difficulty of what it is to be.

(Stevens, 1997:329–30)

To name the sun is to delimit what ultimately defies being bounded, for its "project" exceeds what can ever be said of it. To call the sun "Phoebus" (or, for that matter, to call it "a body of superheated gases") is to try to make reality conform to the limits of the mind's ability to name it. In the end, however, truth overflows the bounds of its containment in names or myths. The duty of the mind, then, is not to bend the world to its will but to know it through an openness that allows it to be "In the difficulty of what it is to be" (see Hines, 1975:148–49).

Stevens recognizes that all language uses names and metaphors—note the ironic insertion of the metaphor "gold flourisher" into his admonition against naming the unnameable (see Hines, 1975:148). His words do not repudiate the poetic gesture, but in their metapoetic stance of metaphor reflecting on its own limits, they describe a posture of solicitude. Elsewhere, in "The Poems of Our Climate," Stevens characterizes the nature of the milieu that is the "climate" in which human beings find themselves existing:

The imperfect is our paradise.
Note that, in this bitterness, delight,
Since the imperfect is so hot in us,
Lies in flawed words and stubborn sounds.

(1997:179)

The modern logic of controlling and dominating the whole of reality, and the application of that logic in the social world, clashes headlong with the kind of thinking expressed in Stevens's words.

His reflections on the imperfections of metaphor bear directly on the bureaucratic approach to human predicaments and its practical application through the "poetry of policing." Imagine that the police officers who encountered Albert and Cecilia, or the three women in the motel room, were to assume the stance of Stevens's "ignorant man" in order to reveal the metaphoric processes informing their approach. From this new vantage point, which is essentially phenomenological in its orientation, it becomes possible to suspend the interpretations ordinarily attached to the most mundane aspects of these encounters. Suddenly, something as naturally taken for granted as the physical setting of the encounters discloses its ontological foundations, and leaves us astonished:

It is the celestial ennui of apartments
That sends us back to the first idea

(Stevens, 1997:330)

To perceive the blandness and isolating vacuity of drab human dwellings as "the celestial ennui of apartments" is to discern something far more elemental about the state of existence in which Cecilia, Albert, and the three women in the motel room live out their days, than can ever be said in the matter-of-fact language of bureaucracy. It is, in the most radical way, "to approach the scenes" of the two encounters, other than with respect to their precise location in the abstract, rationalized, Cartesian space of computerized police dispatch grids.

"The celestial ennui of apartments" evokes the isolation of modern, urban life, marked as it is by a stark *apartness*, whose architectural incarnation is the apartment. The regulation of social order in this eerie configuration of human beings, each one existing in a "world apart" from the others, falls disproportionately to the police, who are called upon to handle the "ennui of apartments" and all that it engenders. Applying this kind of attentiveness to the phenomenological interpretation of the outwardly unproblematic "scene" of police-citizen encounters demonstrates what may be accomplished in following Stevens's use of poetry to solicit meanings out of space that might otherwise remain occluded.[9]

In the context of my encounters with Cecilia and Albert and the women in the motel room, the physical setting of each episode manifested an innate ontological relation to the forms of praxis carried out within it. The anonymity and isolation of modern social space inevitably help shape the practical nature of the police response, right down to the need to determine in an orderly manner in which lonely motel room a lonely woman could be found. Yet, the success of the official response, as evaluated by Jennifer's being located, and then relocated, did not attend to her presence other than in an objectifying manner. The panicked anguish and desperation of a young woman were efficiently translated and broadcast over a police radio as a problem: "go find the suicidal drug addict in the motel room." In my encounter with Cecilia, her gesture of reaching beyond her doorway turned it into a threshold she could only dream of crossing. Although it was true that Albert was gone, and that she had gotten back her stolen medications, the moment of calm that marked my initial attempt at ending the encounter turned quickly to despair: as if animated by the crushing realization of still "being here," Cecilia reached out to seek from human presence what bureaucratic presence had failed to give.

One way to summarize the shortcomings of bureaucratic praxis in its encounters with Cecilia, Albert, and the trio in the motel room is to say that, in our capacity as bureaucrats, my colleagues and I did not *realize* the nature of the predicaments before us. Within this context, "realizing" is not the act of making real, in terms of actually creating an entity itself, but rather is the act of creating meanings commensurate with the nature of the approach being taken toward the presence one encounters. To reiterate what I have previously explained, the creation of meaning is, in a strict sense, a form of poetry; and what it produces exists largely as metaphors. Policing as poetry creates meaning, albeit of a kind oriented toward fulfilling the bureaucratic mandate of making decisions *sine ira ac studio* (Weber, 1978:975). Thus, in the poetic processes that shape its approach, bureaucracy in effect *realizes* very little of the existential complexity of the quandaries it encounters, because its ontological stance precludes it from doing so.

The ensuing situation, which characterizes the self-fulfilling inefficacy of a bureaucratic approach to an intricately complex, multifaceted social predicament such as drug addiction, finds apt expression in "Notes Toward a Supreme Fiction":

> Not to be realized because not to
> Be seen, not to be loved nor hated because
> Not to be realized.
>
> *(Stevens, 1997:333)*

Stevens points here to a hollow inattentiveness to the presence of the other person. The presence we fail to realize is the presence that our approach has precluded us from seeing; and what we fail to realize is neither loved nor hated, but is simply ignored and passed over in silence. In the end, for Stevens—and here his argument bears a clear relation to the idea of the hermeneutic circle—inattentiveness to the world traces itself back to the metaphors used to describe it: we do not name what we do not see, and vice versa.

Ultimately, then, the creation of meaning is inseparable from the self-interpretation it confers upon its own approach. This is the metapoetic narrative either overtly or cryptically contained in any body of discourse. In Stevens's metapoetics, language heeds its own limitations:

> But to impose is not
> To discover.
>
> *(Stevens, 1997:349)*

Such a sentiment is the antithesis of the bureaucratic approach and its inseparable dialectics of knowledge and control. Stevens's dictum is exemplified in
the remarkable quality of police bureaucracy to control so much while knowing so little.

As a political or sociological argument, the preceding point may suffice
to explain the limitations of police praxis in situations such as drug-related
encounters. However, for the purposes of a phenomenological aesthetics of
encounter, it still remains to consider how these limitations are themselves an
indication of the existential nature of human presence, on the basis of which
it resists reification. Stevens's "Study of Two Pears" (1942/1997:180–81) offers
a phenomenologically oriented meditation on the intrinsic resistance of presence to containment through metaphor, analogy, or classification (see Baird,
1968:189; Hines, 1975:99; and Eeckhout, 1999):

STUDY OF TWO PEARS

I

Opusculum paedagogum.
The pears are not viols,
Nudes or bottles.
They resemble nothing else.

II

They are yellow forms
Composed of curves
Bulging toward the base.
They are touched red.

III

They are not flat surfaces
Having curved outlines.
They are round
Tapering toward the top.

IV

In the way they are modelled
There are bits of blue.
A hard dry leaf hangs
From the stem.

V

The yellow glistens.
It glistens with various yellows,
Citrons, oranges and greens
Flowering over the skin.

VI
The shadows of the pears
Are blobs on the green cloth.
The pears are not seen
As the observer wills.

The pears may be described in a multitude of ways; however, they ultimately exceed all of the terms and meanings that might be used to capture their appearance: "They resemble nothing else." The poem thus offers us a methodological meditation on artistic representation. The reader of Stevens's poem can discern that the pears appear in a painting. Even in their painted form, they still exceed the boundaries of aesthetic representation: "The pears are not seen/As the observer wills." The pears emerge in the wholeness of their being, against all efforts to render them less than what they are.[10] As Eeckhout remarks in his analysis of the poem, "a pear is a pear is a pear—and not a metaphor" (1999:7).

The further relevance of the poem lies in its metapoetic quality. It is written as a self-conscious poetic attempt to engage the presence of two pears—a presence that is already itself the "object" of aesthetic representation. As an interpretation of an interpretation, "Study of Two Pears" thus engages a range of hermeneutic questions that may be readily extended to the analogous dynamic that occurs in social scientific or bureaucratic praxis, or, for that matter, in any form of human interpretation.

Of course, as soon as one begins to speak of human beings, and not pears, an immeasurably more complex set of existential conditions obtains, which are grounded in the reflexive, reciprocal, and dialectical qualities of the poetic process. It is impossible to overstate the psychological, moral, and social intricacy of a moment such as the one that occurred when I tried to speak with Paulette about her drug use and was met with the response, "How can you understand me? I don't even understand myself." Like Cecilia's reaching across the doorway, this kind of astonishing utterance disrupts the logic of instrumental rational praxis by calling into question its approach, and thus, by extension, its entire foundational ontology. Paulette's poetic self-interpretation became the object of the poetry of policing. In turn, the resulting hermeneutic process becomes subsumed within another poetic creation of meaning when it is approached as an object of intellectual attention, as it is in the pages of this book. To ignore this self-defining creation of meaning, which is intrinsic to every form of action and expression, is to foreclose the possibility of engaging precisely what must be engaged if praxis is to have any meaningful ameliorative effects.

SEVEN

Encountering the Drama of Mental and Emotional Crisis

That instant traumatized my whole existence. Since . . . since
then, I am no longer myself . . . I don't even know who I am.

—Gabriel Marcel,
Gabriel Marcel's Perspectives on "The Broken World," 1998

INTRODUCTION

The resolution of police encounters with people in states of mental and emotional crisis involves working through intricate and often conflicting interpretations in order to decide what is "really" going on, and to determine for bureaucratic purposes what another person is "really" thinking. These encounters require a dynamic comportment toward uniquely enigmatic kinds of human presence, whose inner nature is particularly resistant to straightforward interpretation. Across the entire spectrum of such encounters, officers face the challenge of establishing a meaningful rapport with a fellow human being, whose relation toward reality is, in one way or another, held to be at variance with the "natural attitude" (see Bittner, 1990:63–88). At the same time, the underlying instrumental logic of the encounter can undermine such attempts at communicative authenticity. The resulting conflict pits the existential actuality of psychological disharmony against its bureaucratic objectification.

Obviously, when an encounter is characterized by the participants' radically dissonant comportments toward ordinary reality, the potential for confusion, misunderstanding, and violence can be very high. This circumstance defines the operational parameters of many police encounters with people who are in a state of mental or emotional crisis and suggests why the outcome of these encounters can at times even be fatal.

Drawing on representations of emotional and mental disharmony in the dramas of Luigi Pirandello and Gabriel Marcel, my aim in this chapter is to develop insights into the nature of police encounters with people in psychological crisis. In the first half of the chapter, I use Pirandello's play, *Così è (si vi pare)* [*Right You Are (If You Think You Are)*] to explore the conflicting comportments toward human presence that marked my encounter with a man having a flashback to an episode of wartime combat. The second half of the chapter develops the issue of comportment in further detail by using dialogue from two of Marcel's plays, *The Broken World* and *The Votive Candle*, to interpret concrete aspects of the objectification of human presence that occurred in my encounter with a man who had escaped from a psychiatric hospital.

Intentionally diverging from analyses that uncritically presume much of the descriptive and normative content of social scientific and clinical articulations of mental and emotional crisis, the phenomenological analysis I present here takes these articulations to be secondary to a more elemental (and often unacknowledged) engagement with human presence. I have therefore purposely refrained from using, on their own ordinary terms, classifications such as mental "illness," "disease," or "pathology," "insanity," and taxonomic systems (most notably the various editions of the American Psychiatric Association's *Diagnostic and Statistical Manual* [DSM]) that are inconsistent with the theoretical notions central to a phenomenological aesthetics of encounter.

ENCOUNTER #7-1, PHILIP

On a summer morning, I responded to a high school with two of the officers on my squad for a report of a Vietnam War veteran having a combat flashback. I suspected that the person in question was Philip, who worked at the school as a janitor. Philip was widely regarded by teachers and students as a kind man with a troubled soul. Officers who had been assigned to duty at the high school all got along well with him, and knew he was someone whom they could rely upon for support and assistance. I had spoken with Philip on several prior occasions, though not in recent years. I remembered that he always kept a loaded pistol in his car. This fact was an obvious cause of immediate concern, which I shared via radio with the other responding officers.

When my colleagues and I arrived at the school, staff members told us that Philip had telephoned the school district's head office to report to his senior supervisor that he was experiencing a flashback, and asked to have a friend, who was also a coworker, drive him home. The supervisor declined his request, apparently because it violated school liability procedures. Instead, she told Philip to stay on the phone, and said she would call an ambulance. Philip panicked, and drove away on his own. School staff members reported that he had not made any threats to harm himself or anyone else; however, standard police protocols for "community caretaking" dictated that my colleagues and I make a reasonable effort to locate Philip and ensure that he was all right. One of my colleagues requested that an officer from a neighboring agency attempt to contact Philip at his house. He also began to gather the necessary information to have the communications center broadcast an "attempt to locate" for Philip, directing any officer who found him to stop him and check his welfare.

I left the school and was driving back to the police station with the hope of taking a lunch break when I saw a car parked on the side of the road with its hazard lights flashing. Thinking that it was probably just a disabled motorist, I pulled directly alongside it to see if I could be of assistance. Doing this was an unsafe tactical error, and I knew it, inwardly chiding myself: officers are taught never to pull abreast of another car but rather to park behind it, so it can be approached safely. I instantly realized that the driver of the car was Philip, and quickly backed up. I told my dispatcher that I had located Philip.

Using my public address system, I called out to Philip. At the same time, I drew my gun and kept it at my side. I asked Philip if he was all right. "Hell no, I'm not all right!" he shouted. "I'm fucked up, man!" I told him to put his hands out the window of his car. He complied. I told Philip that I just wanted to check on him, and assured him that he was not in any kind of trouble. I tried to overcome the impersonal nature of our incipient contact by appealing to our past encounters at the school. "It's Wender," I said, "you remember me, right?" Philip seemed unsure and became increasingly agitated. I asked him if he had his gun. "Yeah, it's right here, cocked and locked," he yelled.[1] This obviously did not bode well for the situation. I now trained my gun on Philip as he sat in his car. I requested backup, and asked the dispatcher to restrict radio traffic.

I told Philip to keep his hands extended out the driver's door window, and asked him where his gun was located. "It's on the seat, next to me," he shouted back. Despite my commands, he withdrew his hands into the car and said, "Here it is." A moment later, he extended his left hand back out the window. A semiautomatic pistol was dangling from his index finger by the trigger guard. I could see that the hammer was cocked back. Aside from the obvious concern that Philip might intentionally fire the gun, I was equally *worried that he might simply drop it, and possibly cause an accidental discharge. I ordered Philip to place the gun on the roof of his car. Much to my relief, he complied. As all of this was occurring, another officer arrived to assist me.*

As we held Philip at gunpoint and ordered him to remain inside the car, my colleague and I began discussing how we could safely retrieve the pistol from the roof without allowing Philip to get to it first. We decided that with help from other officers, we would approach the car from behind a ballistic shield and take the gun, after which we planned to secure Philip. While we waited for more help to arrive, Philip opened the driver's door of the car, and got out. "Shit!" I muttered to my colleague, as we glanced quickly at each other, silently sharing the realization that we might end up having to shoot Philip. Philip stood between the open door and the car, within instant reach of the pistol on the roof. The other officer and I trained our own guns on him and told him not to move for his pistol. "Don't do it!" I loudly implored, "don't do it!" Philip stood there for a moment, looking very tense and bewildered. He then backed away from the open door, around the front of the car, and up onto the sidewalk. I immediately moved forward and took the gun from the roof of Philip's car. I unloaded it and locked it in an equipment vault in the trunk of my patrol car. Meanwhile, other officers had begun to arrive, and were trying to keep Philip contained on the sidewalk, in order to prevent him from "going mobile"—walking down the street uncontained.

Philip seemed utterly terrified. He looked rapidly and warily all around him, and moved tactically, like a soldier in battle. "Don't come near me! Stay back!" he yelled. He acted as if he feared being ambushed or attacked. He tracked every car that drove past him, and nervously watched officers' every move. My colleagues and I kept our distance as we tried to find a way to contain Philip in a small area without provoking a fight. Not least of all, we were concerned that he might have another gun or other weapon. Armed or not, Philip posed a serious threat in his own right: he was a large, burly man, and especially in his state of mind, would be extremely difficult to subdue physically. I finally succeeded in convincing Philip to sit down on the sidewalk, with his back up against a chain-link fence. Once Philip was seated, one of the officers who knew him well established a rapport with him. The officer convinced Philip to surrender a knife that was in his pocket.

Philip then began to recount in intricate, vivid detail the incident in Vietnam that was the recurrent focus of his flashbacks. The helicopter on which he served as a door gunner was shot down over North Vietnam. When the helicopter was struck, one of his fellow crewmembers had been killed, and another had been gravely injured. Philip sobbed as he told the story. He recounted how he tried to hold in his friend's disemboweled intestines. "Guys," he said, looking at me and my colleagues, "there's twenty-five feet of intestines inside a man, and once they come out, you can't get them back in." After the helicopter crashed, Vietcong soldiers began to close in on Philip and his injured friend. Philip hyperventilated and looked around as he continued his narrative. Philip's friend knew he was going to die, and asked Philip to shoot him. Philip refused. His friend finally put his pistol to his temple, and asked Philip to help him pull the trigger. Philip ultimately relented. As Philip recounted this moment, he dissolved into sobs and told my colleagues and me, "Guys, I helped my friend kill himself. I shot my friend."

As he concluded his horrific story, his attention seemed to move back and forth from what was obviously to him the palpable reality of "being in hostile territory," to recognizing the nature of his immediate physical surroundings. For several minutes, it seemed unclear whether Philip would focus on the immediacy of his presence with my colleagues and me or remain within his state of terrified recollection. Just when he seemed to begin to calm down, an officer in an unmarked car came driving up the street, and turned his vehicle sideways to block traffic. This instantly provoked a reaction from Philip, who yelled at us, "Get him out of here!" I told the officer to move farther up the street, out of Philip's line of sight. He was obviously terrified of being cornered or ambushed, which is what had happened to him following the crash of his helicopter.

Philip was eventually able to tell my colleagues and me that he had medication in the car to control his flashbacks. An officer retrieved the pills, and gave them to Philip along with a bottle of water. Philip took several pills, and continued talking with us. Gradually, he began to calm down, as the flashback seemed to recede from his mind. He grew more and more directly attentive to his situation vis-à-vis the officers who were present, and began to apologize profusely as he realized what had transpired. "Guys, I'm so sorry, I'm so embarrassed," he said. We reassured him that no apologies were necessary. Philip requested that a coworker from the school drive him home. One of my colleagues called her, and she arrived at the scene shortly thereafter. She said she had helped Philip before during other flashbacks, and expressed no concerns about doing so again in the present situation.

At the conclusion of our encounter, after Philip was more or less "himself" again, I included him in an impromptu sidewalk debriefing of the incident. I asked Philip how, in the event of future contacts with him of this nature, my partners and I could ensure another peaceful resolution. Philip said, "Well, you guys did the right thing; you gave me my space, and you stayed back behind cover." I then asked Philip a pointed question, which I prefaced with the comment that I was not trying to offend him: "Philip, do you

think that when you're having a flashback like the one you had today, that
you might be capable of shooting at us?" "Oh yeah, definitely," he replied,
without hesitation. "If you'd have come up to my car before, I'd say there's
a 95 percent chance I would have shot at you." I told Philip that I appreci-
ated his candor. As my partners and I had arranged, Philip's coworker took
him home.

Later in the day, I completed the necessary paperwork to have Philip's
name entered in an officer safety database, with a warning that he carries
a gun and has the potential to use it when he is experiencing a severe flash-
back. His comment would continue to haunt me for days. Several hours
after the encounter, I telephoned Philip to see how he was doing. During
our short conversation, he repeatedly apologized for having inconvenienced
my colleagues and me, and expressed his great embarrassment. I protested
that apologies and embarrassment were not in order. A week later, Philip
delivered a bouquet of flowers and a card to the police station for my squad.
The card thanked us for saving his life.

Viewed in the practical, operational terms of a police response, the key issues
in my encounter with Philip demanding resolution were as follows: first, he
had to be physically located after having driven away from the school; second,
for reasons of community safety, it was necessary for my colleagues and me
to interpret his mental state and accompanying intentions with a view toward
evaluating his potential harm to himself and others; and third, the ensuing
evaluation had to be translated into police action that would impose a bureaucratic solution. Together, these steps constituted the bureaucratic approach to
the situation. The first step, of course, was serendipitously resolved when I
happened upon Philip while driving back to the police station. The second and
third steps were unpredictable and dynamic, to a large degree because they were
inseparable from the tactical exigencies of keeping Philip physically contained
and communicating effectively with him. This "real-time" interweaving of operational tactics, dialogue, investigative analysis, and bureaucratic resolution
may be viewed from a phenomenological standpoint as a dramatic process of
street-level hermeneutics, in which an interpretive sequence of remarkable complexity had to be undertaken rapidly in order to determine and implement a
particular course of action.

The central, bureaucratically mandated interpretive task in my encounter
with Philip was primarily one of accurately reading his "true state of mind."
This task was profoundly complicated by the polarities and shifts in Philip's
actions, which made him vacillate unpredictably between states of apparent

rationality and irrationality. However, my colleagues and I were also able to maintain an openness toward him, which helped our efforts at engaging his dynamically transmuting forms of self-presence. At some points during the encounter (and increasingly toward its conclusion), Philip seemed logical and composed, and acted in concert with communicative precepts that were meaningful with respect to our formal objectives. During these moments, he was able to discuss his situation from a clinical standpoint, and to a substantial degree, was able to stand over against himself and his actions. However, at other moments in the encounter (especially when I first contacted him), Philip acted in a way that suggested a near-total loss of self-awareness and self-control.

In some instances, the hermeneutic task of reading intentions and states of mind is rendered far less complicated, or even moot, if other facts provide a basis for action independent of a person's statements and observable actions. On the other hand, a situation such as my encounter with Philip presents police officers with a state of ambiguity they do not like, because it complicates the objective of isolating a fixed, underlying problem, which is readily available for bureaucratic remedy. The process of problematization would have been most efficient if Philip had "given" my colleagues and me "something" that we could have used as the basis for an unambiguous decision, such as a clear statement of suicidal intentions, or threats against us or others. That he did not do so presented us with a quandary.

Instead of merely having to formulate a tactical response to a straightforwardly defined problem, we had to divide our attention between the dual processes of keeping watch over Philip and maintaining a dialogue with him, while simultaneously trying to decide "what to do with him." Although Philip was physically contained on the street, so that his movement was restricted to a small radius beyond which we would not let him move, the far greater challenge was how to contain him bureaucratically. He had neither made any suicidal threats nor had he threatened anyone else. He had not committed a crime of any kind. He also refused to go to the hospital for a voluntary psychiatric evaluation when this option was presented to him. As we considered our various options for resolving the situation, my colleagues and I discussed the stark fact, abundantly clear to everyone present, that to compel Philip to go to the hospital for a psychiatric evaluation would inevitably entail a violent confrontation, and would only result in a clinical reconfirmation of what everyone already knew, namely that he suffered from flashbacks related to his experiences in Vietnam. All of the officers at the scene, and not least of all me as their supervisor, saw little point in provoking a knockdown, drag-out fight that would only delay Philip's release by another couple of hours.[2] In the end, we opted to retain Philip's pistol for safekeeping and sent him home with his coworker.

Should this resolution not be seen as a triumph of bureaucratic policing, especially because it was achieved without the use of force, and without resorting to incarceration or institutionalization? Peaceably containing Philip on the sidewalk and initiating a dialogue that helped get him to the point where he was able to take his medication did, in a certain sense, momentarily "solve his problem." Moreover, after his medication had taken effect, our giving him an active role in deciding how the situation would be resolved recognized the legitimacy of his concerns in an ethically and practically meaningful way.

Upon further reflection, however, it could well be argued that the truly decisive contingency in resolving this crisis was the fortuitous fact that Philip personally knew me and several of the other officers at the scene, thus adding a dimension to the encounter that would otherwise have been missing had the incident occurred with different officers. The added dimension of personal acquaintance might literally have saved Philip's life; and at the very least, it almost certainly contributed to a safer, more peaceful resolution of a dangerous situation. If my argument is correct, it demonstrates the crucial role of the ability to approach people in ways that responded to the whole of their presence, even as they move between the two poles of anguished fury and tentative calm (compare Bittner, 1990:81–82).

PIRANDELLO AND THE INTRINSIC AMBIGUITIES OF READING HUMAN PRESENCE

Luigi Pirandello's dramas explore the ambiguities of human identity and social roles, the nature of truth and illusion, and the crises of isolation that he viewed as endemic to the modern condition (see Krysinski, 1989).[3] He engages these topics with considerable intellectual sophistication, yet does so in relation to the concrete circumstances of ordinary people, as they struggle to cope in a world that is rapidly transforming the most basic aspects of everyday existence (compare Bassanese, 1997:1). Pirandello's depiction of the insular quality of traditional Sicilian life has wider parallels to the isolated existence of people cast adrift in modern society (see Bernstein, 1991:95–107, and Bassanese, 1997). On a more intimate level, his concern with crises of isolation and insanity was deeply affected by the tragic experience of dealing with his wife's violent mental breakdown.[4]

The aptness of Pirandello's work for a phenomenological aesthetics of encounter rests on several points. To begin with, his characters convey a palpable reality that lends their words and actions to seamless integration within an extraliterary context. Rather than treating them as the mere embodiment of his intellectual positions, Pirandello instilled them with a convincing vitality, and presents them in "case study" form (Bassanese, 1997:10). In fact, Pirandello's drama has attracted the attention of phenomenologically oriented social science, most notably in Baumann's comparative analysis (1967) of George Herbert Mead and Pirandello. Erving Goffman (1974) also draws widely on Pirandello's plays (see Bassnett-McGuire, 1983:33).

The particular play that I will use to explicate my encounter with Philip is *Cosí è (se vi pare)* [*Right You Are (If You Think You Are)*] (1917/2000). The Italian title translates literally into English as "thus it is (if it seems so to you)."[5] A phenomenologically informed elaboration of the title might read, "reality is presumed to be of a certain nature, according to the stance that you take toward it," or, more freely, "your approach to the world has a reciprocal influence on how you experience it." In the Italian title, the word *vi* means "to you," and conveys a sense of intentionality that cannot be expressed with a nondeclinable English pronoun. Especially in the arena of social action, the intentional relationship between world and consciousness is at once both analytic and ethical—the attempt to know another human being is a fundamentally moral act, and thus irreducible to "neutral" praxis.

The action of *Cosí è (se vi pare)* focuses on the inseparability of the epistemological and ethical dimensions of social praxis, and shows the danger of ascribing objective certitude to knowledge of one's fellow human beings. According to Bassanese, the play "[p]arodies the possibility of documenting anything human. The heated search for proof, evidence, and logic in this grotesque opus challenges the positivist view that objective knowledge can provide answers, as the title immediately implies" (1997:46). This "heated search," as it unfolds in the action of the play, points directly to the moral and social implications of the reduction of human presence to an abstract ensemble of "facts." The prominent role that Pirandello gives to bureaucracy in this process amplifies the immediate relevance of the play for engaging the ontological foundations of police praxis.

Cosí è (se vi pare) follows the unrelenting attempts by the residents of an Italian provincial capital to learn the "real truth" behind what they regard as the scandalous living arrangements of their new neighbors, Signor and Signora Ponza and Signor Ponza's mother-in-law, Signora Frola.[6] Signor Ponza and his wife move into a seedy apartment building on the outskirts of town, while he rents a separate apartment in the city center for Signora Frola. It appears that Signor Ponza forbids his wife and mother-in-law from directly seeing one another. Signora Ponza never leaves home, even to run errands, and never visits her mother face to face. Instead, the two women communicate through handwritten notes that are passed back and forth in a small basket, which is lowered from the Ponza's apartment to the courtyard below, where Signora Frola awkwardly stands and gazes up at her daughter. Lurid fascination turns to anger when out of supposed inhospitality, Signora Frola refuses to receive her neighbor, Signora Agazzi, whose husband is Signor Ponza's superior officer at the prefecture.

In the opening act of the play, the neighbors, annoyed and curious in equal measure, proclaim their desire to know the real truth behind the newcomers' living arrangements. The underlying philosophical issues at stake emerge in the following exchange between one of the neighbors, Signora Cini, and Lamberto Laudisi, the play's *raisonneur*:

> *Signora Cini:* But all we want is to know!
> *Laudisi:* Know what, Signora? What can we know about anyone? Who they
> are? What they are? What they do? Why they do it?
> *Signora Sirelli:* By picking up bits and pieces. By gathering information. (Pi-
> randello, 2000:6/1953:74)

In the Italian text, Laudisi's question conveys a much stronger sense of the disparity between true knowledge of another person and what is supposedly knowable through "bits and pieces" of news (*notizie*) or factual data (*informazioni*): "*Che possiamo noi realmente sapere degli altri?*" (1953:74). *Altri* connotes difference and otherness, much like the English "alterity." This is amplified by the word *realmente* ("actually," "really"), which is dropped in Mueller's translation. In the original text, *realmente* serves to amplify the disparity between attempts at "knowing" other human beings and the fullness of their actual existence. In this crucial respect, Pirandello's characters are grappling with the same competing ontological notions of co-presence and intersubjectivity that police officers face in their encounters on patrol.

Pirandello shows throughout the play that the obsessive desire of the townspeople to neatly "define" the living arrangements of their new neighbors has little to do with knowing who they truly are. In the final scene, this point is symbolically emphasized by Signora Ponza's wearing a "thick, black, impenetrable veil" (*"un fitto velo nero"*) (Pirandello, 2000:52/1953:136), behind which she remains an enigma. Despite all of the probing and interrogation, no one has made an authentic effort to know her and her family. The townspeople's stance exemplifies the kind of reductionist absolutism that Pirandello condemns as fundamentally dehumanizing (Bassanese, 1997:48; Bassnett-McGuire, 1983:77). For Pirandello, the mystery of the other person creates a moral imperative that demands an approach grounded in openness and solicitude (see Moestrup, 1972:149–51).

In the context of interpreting my encounter with Philip, it is worth considering how Pirandello specifically addresses the enigma of human identity in relation to crises of mental and emotional disorder. As the play unfolds, Signora Frola implies that Signor Ponza might be mentally ill (2000:14); and one way or another, the neighbors have already made up their minds that he is a "monster" (2000:6, 16). When he speaks, Signor Ponza's eyes appear "hard, fixed, and sinister" (*"duri, fissi, tetri"*) (2000:16). Later, in Act II, Pirandello describes him as "quivering with near-animal fury" (*"tremito quasi animalesco"*) (2000:35).[7]

Against Signora Frola's suggestion that he might be mentally disturbed, Signor Ponza protests to the neighbors that it is actually *she* who is insane, gripped by the delusional belief that his wife is her daughter, Lina, when in fact Lina had been killed four years earlier during an earthquake. Signor Ponza explains that the woman whom Signora Frola believes to be Lina is actually his second wife, Julia. No sooner than Signor Ponza leaves after offering this explanation to the neighbors, Signora Frola returns, only to protest and reiterate that it really *is* Signor Ponza who is deranged. She explains that Lina had to be committed to a sanatorium, which led Signor Ponza to believe that she had died. When Lina was released a year later, he refused to believe that she was truly his wife. Signora Frola says that the story of Lina's death and Signor Ponza's remarriage to Julia was a compassionate fabrication intended to keep Signor Ponza from going insane. This flurry of claims and counterclaims by Signora Frola and Signor Ponza leaves the inquisitive neighbors even more confused, and even more driven to discover the "real truth."

This constant vacillation, heightened by Signor Ponza's aggressively animated behavior during his interactions with his neighbors, parallels the kind of shifting self-presentation that marked my encounter with Philip. In either situation, the process of interpreting disequilibrated emotions can only succeed if it opens itself to the human presence of which the emotions are only a transient manifestation. The characters in Pirandello's play failed to do this, which ensured the futility of their approach, to say nothing of its ethical bankruptcy. This did not occur in my encounter with Philip. I hasten to emphasize that the approach my colleagues and I took toward Philip was strongly influenced by the fortunate coincidence of our personal familiarity with him, which was extrinsic to the underlying logic of bureaucratic action. As the narrative suggests, however, there was no mechanism *intrinsic* to bureaucratic problematization, which could have ensured that a similar positive outcome would have been otherwise replicable. To the contrary, in an anonymous encounter, officers would have been forced to rely on whatever data they might have gathered from Philip, from witnesses, or from police databases.

In *Cosí è (se vi pare)*, a similar fact-gathering process occurs when an official inquiry is made to the police commissioner in the town from which Signora Frola and the Ponzas have moved. However, the inquiry proves fruitless, because the earthquake that supposedly killed Signora Frola's daughter also destroyed all public records. But Laudisi argues that even so, relying on documentary evidence ignores the fact that the abiding reality of human circumstances cannot be isolated from the actual thoughts and sentiments of the people involved: "Reality, for me, is not to be found in pieces of paper, but in the minds of *those two! Those two* into whose minds I have no possible entry, except for the little they choose to tell me!" (Pirandello, 2000:25). Of course, for a police officer facing someone who is incoherent, even this may be impossible, thus forcing the delicate and arduous task of reading human presence for conflicting signs of fact and delusion.

Such confusion abounds in the last act of the play, when Signora Ponza finally appears. Although she is the only person who can affirm whether it is Signor Ponza's or Signora Frola's version of events that is true, her pronouncement dashes all expectations and compounds the mystery that the neighbors had desperately hoped she would solve. Signora Ponza announces that *both* accounts are correct: she is Signora Ponza's daughter, as well as Signor Ponza's second wife. When the neighbors protest that this is impossible, and demand that she proclaim herself to be one or the other, she replies, "No. Not at all. I am the one you believe me to be" (Pirandello, 2000:53). This closing scene, where Signora Ponza affirms the ambiguous nature of her true identity, effectively leaves the reader in the same situation as the police officer, who faces a human presence that will not (or cannot) reveal itself. As Baumann observes: "The real meaning of the drama *Cosí è (se vi pare)* is not an illustration of appearance as a mere sham, but of appearance as a *form of existence (Erscheinungsweise eines Seins)*" (1967:596, emphasis added). The events in *Cosí è (se vi pare)* echo what occurred during my encounter with Philip: it was a process that unfolded poetically, as an unpredictable creation of meaning occasioned by the enigmas of alterity. During his moment of crisis, the immediate reality for Philip of his vivid memories of combat was existentially inseparable from his "actual" or "objective" spatiotemporal situation. This is why my colleagues and I simply could not afford, even for tactical reasons, to diminish the ontological reality of Philip's recollections. I do not know if every detail of his story was true; however, such facts are ultimately irrelevant to the urgency and tangibility of his responses. Indeed, to have focused on searching for external, objective evidence would have ignored the broader situation, both ethically and tactically. Whether it is Philip's case or that of someone else in turmoil, police officers learn from experience that dismissing the perceptions, thoughts, and emotions of the people whom they encounter does little to address the predicament at hand, except in the most superficial or fleeting way.

What ultimately proved to be decisive in my encounter with Philip was neither the power of law nor that of clinical psychiatry. To be fair, there is a risk that this analysis might sound self-congratulatory, by implying that I had some kind of insight into Philip's situation that enabled me to arrive at a resolution that might have otherwise been impossible. However, as I already suggested, whatever the particular combination of knowledge, skill, and experience that my colleagues and I brought to bear, the decisive factor in safely resolving this situation was the fortuitous condition of personal familiarity. Part of what facilitated the peaceful resolution of Philip's crisis was the practical acknowledgment of the truth and reality for him of his perceptions. To Philip, at the moment of his flashback, all other aspects of reality receded into the background. Once Philip realized that my colleagues and I were open to the truth of his perceptions, and that we were in effect "covering his back" until he could reorient himself, the possibility of violence was markedly reduced.

This is precisely what did not happen with Pirandello's characters. Rather than *face* the mystery of the Ponza family and Signora Frola in the fullness of its ontological and moral complexity, the intrusive neighbors responded by reducing their presence to the abstract embodiment of aberration. In a further parallel to Philip's situation, the action in *Così è (se vi pare)* reveals the hermeneutic dialectics of social encounter. Philip's reaction to his flashback was shaped by the presence of my colleagues and me, and vice versa. Indeed, one of the most remarkable moments in the encounter came at its conclusion, when I invited Philip to participate in the unofficial post-incident debriefing. Most significantly, my decision to include Philip in this conversation represented an unusual "metabureaucratic" moment for everyone involved, and perhaps fleetingly revealed to us a horizon beyond the official gaze.

GABRIEL MARCEL: LIVING AS A PROBLEM
IN A BROKEN WORLD

As in Pirandello's plays, the tragic implications of the objectification and effacement of human presence figure prominently in the work of Gabriel Marcel. Though Marcel remains best known as a philosopher, he was also a prolific playwright, with more than two dozen dramas to his credit. Marcel's plays complement and vivify the theoretical positions articulated in his philosophy, and lend an "empirical" quality to his work that defies the traditional conventions of social science and literature alike.[8] Most of all, rather than seeking to illustrate abstract ideas, Marcel *begins* his search for metaphysical principles in moments from everyday life.[9] I am especially interested in drawing on Marcel's key distinction between "mystery" and "problem" to interpret my encounter with Robert, whom I contacted after he had escaped from a psychiatric hospital.

For Marcel, drama and metaphysics are two complementary aspects of a common interpretation of human existence (Chenu, 1948:178).[10] Nowhere is this entwinement of drama and metaphysics more immediately evident than in Marcel's decision to publish as a single volume his play, *The Broken World* (1933), and his philosophical essay, "Concrete Approaches to Investigating the Ontological Mystery." Ranking the play above the essay, Marcel argued that the play is not meant to illustrate a philosophical thesis so much as the essay is intended to serve as the philosophical analysis of a human situation, which the play presents in its "raw complexity" and in a manner that ultimately defies reduction from a *mystery* to a *problem*.[11]

This distinction between mystery and problem is central to Marcel's thought (see Marcel, 1998:178–82/1933:267–74) and is important for my own purposes because it closely corresponds to my distinction between intersubjectivity and co-presence. For Marcel, "[a] mystery is a problem that encroaches upon its own data, that invades the data and thereby transcends itself as a simple problem" (1998:178).[12] The intellectualization of a mystery always runs the risk of "degrading" it to the level of a problem (Marcel, 1998:178). Within the context of reflecting on police-citizen encounters, it is especially instructive to note how Marcel considers the implications of this process in relation to the human experience of evil (see Davignon, 1985). The ontological totality of any such human experience, once it has been rendered abstractly into facts, ceases to be known in terms of its mysteriousness (see Prini, 1984, especially pp. 225), and loses its quality of *astonishment*. Moving against this reductionist current,

Marcel portrays the crises of his characters with a vitality and realism that forecloses their objectification as clinical conditions or technically manageable problems. A number of his characters exhibit psychological states that might be viewed today as clinical pathologies, such as manic depression. Against this kind of quick reductionist instinct, Marcel challenges us to engage illness, emotional distress, and anxiety in the fullness of their relation to the ontological conditions of human existence (see Lazaron, 1978:172). In the analysis that follows here, I draw on two of Marcel's plays, *The Votive Candle*, (*La Chapelle ardente*, 1950) and *The Broken World* (*Le Monde cassé*, 1932), in order to attempt just such a wider engagement with emotional crisis, and to move beyond its inauthentic problematization.

Encounter #7-2, Robert

Early one evening, I was dispatched to contact a woman who wanted to report that her thirty-four year-old son, Robert Brown, had escaped from a secure mental hospital, where he had been placed by court order. She was concerned that Robert, who had a long history of violent, delusional behavior, would show up at her house. The 911 operator who took the call from Mrs. Brown apparently did not realize that Robert had already arrived. As a result of this misunderstanding, I merely thought that I was going to allay Mrs. Brown's concerns and tell her to call back if Robert actually came home.

My partner and I arrived at the Brown residence, and Mrs. Brown showed us to her dining room. She explained that Robert had telephoned and told her that he had left the mental hospital. She did not know what to make of the call. The institution was a secure facility, and was more than fifty miles away; however, Mrs. Brown felt that if Robert had, in fact, left the grounds, he was sufficiently resourceful to make the trip home. As she continued to elaborate upon her concerns, my partner suddenly interrupted me and said, "Hey, is that him?" I looked up and saw Robert peering around the corner from inside the kitchen.

He stood there impassively, blankly gazing at us. My first thought was that Robert's position gave him ready access to kitchen knives. The kitchen lights were off, which made it difficult to see exactly what he was doing. My partner quickly shined his flashlight in Robert's face to constrict his pupils and disorient him. Robert winced, and then stared at me and quietly asked in a monotone voice, "Why did he shine a light in my face?" Sidestepping the question, I explained reassuringly to Robert that my partner was a "nice guy." Robert nodded slowly, as if to show that he was willing to grant me the benefit of the doubt. I convinced Robert to step out of the kitchen and sit down in a dining room chair. At this point, my partner casually but quickly moved off to Robert's side, blocking his path back to the kitchen. I tried to keep Robert's attention focused on me, in order to keep him calm and distracted from my partner. Given his large physical stature and history of violence, I discreetly asked my dispatcher to send two more cars to the call. As I awaited their arrival, I asked Robert how he had gotten out of the hospital. He calmly explained that he decided he did not want to be there anymore, and claimed that he had simply signed himself out at the reception desk. When the other officers arrived, I instructed them to remain with Robert while I made some telephone calls in order to determine his legal status.

I telephoned the mental hospital and confirmed that Robert was a patient there. I then asked the staff member to whom I was speaking if he knew Robert's current whereabouts. He told me that Robert was in the hospital. When I replied that Robert was actually sitting at his mother's dining room table, the staff member quickly transferred me to a senior supervisor, to whom I explained my quandary. I told the supervisor that I needed to verify Robert's legal and mental status in order to be able to decide what to do with him. I explained that I would not risk a violent confrontation by taking Robert into custody unless I had legal evidence that he was a danger to the community or to himself. The supervisor confirmed that Robert was officially considered an escapee from the hospital, inasmuch as he was being held there under a valid court order. I told him that he would have to fax a copy of the order to the police department, so that I would have documented proof of Robert's legal status. He agreed to send the documentation, and further agreed to take custody of Robert at the local hospital emergency room and transport him back to the mental institution.

Now, my colleagues and I faced the delicate task of trying to win Robert's cooperation and take him into custody without a fight. Police officers quickly learn that of all physical confrontations, those with people in a state of mental disorder or emotional crisis can be among the most violent and unpredictable. These confrontations become even more complicated and tense when they involve people who are officially regarded as mentally ill, but understand and refute this very assessment. Such was the case with Robert: here was a man who had been confined by a judge to a psychiatric hospital, yet who demonstrated a set of faculties that allowed him to reflect on his situation and willfully extricate himself from it. Had Robert been completely delusional, catatonic, or otherwise wholly incommunicative, my task would have been different.

I spoke quietly and calmly with Robert, discussing his predicament and his claim to have checked himself out of the hospital. I explained that I did not have the authority to release him, and told him he would have to plead his case to the hospital staff. He replied that he had no intention of returning to the psychiatric hospital. I tried to strike a middle ground by telling Robert that he could address his concerns to the staff members from the institution, who were coming to meet him at the emergency room. As we spoke, I watched him cautiously, but tried not to stare at him or challenge him. A challenging, fixed gaze meant to assert control can trigger immediate and unpredictable violence, particularly when it is directed at someone who is mentally unstable or in a state of emotional crisis. I tried to be accommodating but not acquiescent. My partners and I eventually succeeded in talking Robert into coming outside. As soon as we reached the patrol car parked closest to the house, I signaled another officer to help me handcuff Robert, and we quickly took hold of his arms. Robert turned his head and gave me look of anger and betrayal. "Am I in trouble?" he asked. I assured Robert that he was not, and explained that the handcuffs were strictly a matter of safety and departmental policy. Thankfully, he did not become violent, and my colleagues and I secured him without incident in the back seat of the patrol car.

Robert obviously felt he had been deceived. The officer in whose car we had placed Robert quickly drove away, before Robert had a chance to reflect on his situation and potentially turn combative. The remaining officers and I stood around and chatted for a few minutes, and expressed our satisfaction that we had not had to fight with Robert. However, the ambiguous nature of our "victory" did not go unmentioned. One of my colleagues downplayed these concerns, and remarked, "Hey, what else could we do? No one got hurt—screw it." I later learned that Robert was furious that he had been handcuffed, and had vowed to "take out a cop" the next time he was contacted.

In marked contrast to my encounter with Philip, Robert's situation was more immediately resolvable as a bureaucratic matter, because of the greater ease with which Robert was approachable as an abstract problem. Unlike Philip, whom my colleagues and I had to engage in a prolonged dialogue, Robert had already been legally categorized as an escapee from a psychiatric hospital, which also necessarily meant that he was to be approached as a "potential risk of harm to himself and others." Our stance toward Robert was therefore one of approaching a ready-made problem: little had to be accomplished other than physically taking him into custody. Once I had confirmed as a matter of legal fact that Robert had escaped from a secure psychiatric hospital, the bureaucratically intended outcome of my encounter with him was a fait accompli.

This efficient translation of Robert's presence into a problem subsequently facilitated his movement through the criminal justice and mental health systems. As he was literally handed from one bureaucratic system to another, the constancy of his presence as a problem endured. This coordinated functioning of three bureaucracies—the police, a general hospital, and a state psychiatric hospital—is ultimately traceable to the common ontology shaping their respective forms of technical praxis. Whatever the vast differences and conflicts among their operational stances, each institution assumed a similar unreflected orientation toward Robert's presence.

When my partner and I first saw Robert standing in his mother's kitchen doorway, he projected an outward appearance of eminent calm; yet, he did so in a way that was perceptibly unsettling. Even a person lacking experience dealing with intense emotional disorder would have intuited that Robert "wasn't all there." Most notably, the flatness of his voice and his emotionless gaze seemed to indicate an inner state of disequilibrium.[13] This kind of behavior by itself hardly suffices to demonstrate that someone is in a state of mental breakdown or crisis. However, for my colleagues and me, Robert's actions could not be considered apart from what we presumed were the legal and clinical justifications for his committal to a psychiatric hospital. Accordingly, we judged it necessary to approach Robert with a tactical wariness and suspicion that pragmatically regarded him as "insane." This approach largely determined the communicative process of our negotiating Robert's surrender, and the ensuing tactical procedures used in his physical detention.

Among the more noteworthy elements of this process was my use of deception. My decision to deceive Robert, or at least to conceal from him the inevitability of his return to the psychiatric hospital, rested on two assumptions. The first was that he lacked the rational faculties to accept the inevitability of the resolution my colleagues and I had decided to impose. My second assumption was that, even if one presumed that Robert did have the mental capacity to comprehend what was going to happen to him, the potential for a violent reaction militated against presenting the totality of the facts to him. Although it might be argued that these two assumptions are potentially contradictory, my colleagues and I tried to reconcile them within a broader interpretive schema. From this standpoint, we interpreted Robert's protestations and denials of his clinical diagnosis (schizophrenic, bipolar, manic) as validation of its accuracy. Such situations are quite common in police encounters with people who have been diagnosed with various mental disorders, especially schizophrenia. A person will often take great offense at being regarded as mentally ill, and in so doing will reject the diagnosis with eloquent challenges that can be strikingly compelling.

In many such situations, officers adopt a divided stance of the kind that was evident in my encounters with both Robert and Philip. In each encounter, at the same moment that my colleagues and I were attempting to sustain a dialogue, we were also working to translate our interlocutors' presence into something objectively available for bureaucratic action. However, while our dialogue with Philip actually played a determinative role in deciding the outcome of his situation, in Robert's case, the purpose of keeping him engaged in conversation was purely tactical. Whatever he said would have no manifest impact on the outcome of the bureaucratic process.

In *The Votive Candle*, Marcel considers how actions undertaken for ulterior motives reduce human presence to a passive instrumentality. The play follows the moral and emotional crises of Octave and Aline Fortier, whose son, Raymond, has been killed in battle in World War I. Raymond's mother, Aline, is so consumed with keeping his memory alive that it determines her behavior toward everyone around her. As part of this obsessiveness, Aline manipulates Raymond's fiancée, Mireille, by feeding her grief in the hope of keeping her faithful to him. Aline cannot abide the notion that Mireille might ever fall in love with someone else, and succeeds at getting Mireille to share her sentiment.

Even when her intentions are good, Aline has lost the ability to treat Mireille with genuineness or authenticity. In his comments on *The Votive Candle*, Marcel remarks (1967:109) that Mireille's actual human presence gives Aline no solace: Mireille exists for Aline solely as an objectified memory, through her ostensible continued faithfulness to Raymond. Mireille is thus reduced to a fixture in the house—a devotional object to be displayed, in the same manner as the collection of Raymond's childhood toys, which Aline pointlessly refuses to give to her grandson, choosing instead to enshrine them in a specially made cabinet.

Mireille feels so inextricably trapped by these suffocating circumstances that her entire self-conception becomes warped. When Mireille finds herself attracted to Robert Chanteuil, a handsome, wealthy bachelor, Aline seeks to turn her toward the Fortier's gravely ill nephew, André Verdet, for whom Mireille obviously has no affection. Octave is enraged that his wife would so callously seek to arrange a marriage between Mireille, whose entire life remains ahead of her, and a terminally ill young man. However, Aline is absolutely convinced that she is acting in Mireille's best interest. Aline succeeds in winning over Mireille, and the marriage takes place. Octave is so angered that he leaves Aline. As the play approaches its denouement, it becomes increasingly clear that whatever their good intentions, Aline's actions will end tragically (see Lazaron, 1978:25–26).[14]

As her sense of being trapped deepens, Mireille ends up in a state of psychological and emotional crisis. Even then, Aline responds to Mireille in a manner that is as malapropos as it is imperceptive:

> *Mireille:* . . . But I want to be *free*, don't you understand, or I should despise myself. And I shouldn't *be* anything. And then I would hate you. . . . Oh, when I feel like this I want to move right away and never, never come back.
> [*ALINE moves uneasily. There is silence.*]
> *Aline:* I noticed you seemed rather depressed [*"un peut sombre"*] lately.
> *Mireille:* You're always watching us. (Marcel, 1965:259/1950:83–84)

Mireille's words show the transformative ill effects of Aline's manipulations on her self-conception and self-consciousness. Mireille draws an explicit connection between her desire for freedom and her sense of self-worth: without the former, her very existence would be called into question. She makes it clear to Aline that this inner laceration and its accompanying sense of weakness and powerlessness would manifest itself in the form of a poisonous *ressentiment* (compare Scheler, 1994).

Aline's response to Mireille is startling in its utter flatness, and strikes a "clinical" tone analogous to a bureaucratic encounter. Rather than engaging the substance of what Mireille has said, Aline dismisses her words by reducing them to the passing effects of a bad mood. This cavalier, matter-of-fact reduction of her existential torment to a simple problem is not lost on Mireille, as suggested by her sarcastic rejoinder to Aline. Mireille eventually rebels against Aline's control, and strives to regain her freedom. By the final act of the play, Mireille voices the depth of her feelings against Aline in even sharper terms: "But she swamps everyone. No one can *exist* when she's about" (Marcel, 1965:279/1950:128, italics original).[15] The clash between Mireille and Aline highlights the direct impact of reductive praxis on human self-identity, and illustrates how its impact is nothing short of existential. It is not simply that Aline angers Mireille: her actions prevent Mireille from existing as a human being.

In this decisive respect, Mireille's rage and anguish could just as well have been the result of well-intentioned but hubristic bureaucratic intervention. Much like the bureaucratic approach, Aline's comportment toward Mireille presumes the ability to engage in a kind of "crisis intervention" that reifies emotional predicaments as problems. However, that very comportment, insofar as it can either induce or exacerbate feelings of alienation, shame, disgrace, or humiliation, can have explosive consequences. For the police officer, this dynamic poses an obvious physical hazard, to say nothing of an ethical quandary.

A similar situation arises out of the phenomenon of speaking of other persons as if they were not present, and in the related practice of concealing an uncomfortable truth from someone for fear of inviting an undesirable reaction. Both of these phenomena occurred during my encounter with Robert, and find parallel examples in *The Votive Candle*. In the play and in my encounter with Robert, it quickly becomes apparent that a person who is made the object of either form of treatment experiences a keen sense of effacement, rage, and loss of volition.

When Aline pressures Mireille to marry André, knowing that he will soon succumb to his heart condition, André's ignorance of his own imminent demise injects a cruel irony into his relationship with Mireille, as he blithely imagines their life together. Even André's doctor does not reveal the condition to him, for fear that doing so would induce a dangerous level of stress. This "expert" decision to avoid telling a patient the extent of his own condition, though largely anachronistic in current medical practice, nonetheless offers an instructive analogy to the logic of my decision to keep Robert from learning of his impending detention and return to the psychiatric hospital.

Consider the tensions revealed in the following dialogue:

> *Octave:* It's very lucky that so far we've been able to keep him [André] in the dark. . . . If he felt that knife hanging over his head . . .
>
> *Mireille:* Yes, yes. But it's so humiliating to be made a fool of like that. It's degrading. . . . I know that in his place I . . .
>
> *Octave:* I don't know if Andre's strong enough to face the truth. . . . I doubt it, to be honest.
>
> *Aline:* [*sharply*] Do you think it's very generous to disparage him at a time like this?
>
> *Octave:* I'm not disparaging him, I'm merely seeing him as he is (Marcel, 1965:257/1950:79).[16]

Among the possible reactions to being treated as an incidental element or abstract substratum (subject) of one's own deepest predicaments (predicates), humiliation stands out as the one that is probably the most potentially violent and degrading (compare Katz, 1988). Mireille certainly understands this in voicing her opposition to keeping André in a state of ignorance. Yet, Octave's point is hardly without merit, and is no less well intentioned than Mireille's. Octave protests that he is treating André in a manner consistent with what he *is*. His words bring the immediate relation between ontology and praxis into sharp relief: what André is understood to be as a person determines how best to approach him. The exchange between Mireille and Octave raises some of the same factors informing my decision on how to "handle" Robert. Moreover, just as Octave believed, my colleagues and I felt that our actions were truly being taken in the best interests of another person, whom we had to protect from himself.

Marcel further explores the ontological foundations of everyday human encounters in *The Broken World*. The title of the play comes from the words of its heroine, Christiane Chesnay, which she speaks as she decries the anomic state of her life: "Don't you have the impression that we are living . . . if we can call that living . . . in a broken world? Yes, broken like a watch that has stopped. Its mainspring no longer works. To all appearances nothing has changed. Everything is in place. But if you put the watch to your ear . . . you hear nothing" (Marcel, 1998:48/1973a:121). Faced with this vacuous existence, Christiane struggles to escape by engrossing herself in endless superficiality, which allows her to be, as she calls herself, a "busy woman" (*femme occupée*) (Marcel, 1998:48/1973:121–22).

The play centers on Christiane's psychological deterioration as she struggles to survive in the hedonistic "broken world" of interwar Paris. Her frenetic life as a socialite distracts her from a growing sense of alienation, and masks it from the retinue of admirers with whom she surrounds herself. Most of all, it helps her cope with a loveless marriage to Lawrence, a high-level bureaucrat. Christiane's intimate social circle is populated by friends whose crises and behavior read like reports from a police blotter: suicide, drug addiction, pedophilia, mental breakdown, and psychologically manipulative domestic violence.

As she flits from one social event to another, Christiane's state of perpetual turmoil becomes so disequilibrating and enervating that her friends fear she will suffer a nervous breakdown (*la dépression nerveuse*) (Marcel, 1998:91/1973a:164). Her closest friend, Denise Furstlin, tells Lawrence in Christiane's presence that Christiane probably needs to spend several months in a Swiss sanatorium. Christiane listens silently; and in the midst of the conversation, she "sits down with the dejected, ironic air of a person who is being treated as an object" (*réduite à l'état d'objet*) (Marcel, 1998:91). Christiane's feeling of objectification is only heightened when another of her young admirers, Henry, adds to Denise's comments, which he also directs to Lawrence, as if Christiane were not even present in the room.

What might make for rudeness in this kind of intimate discussion among close friends can unfold with far graver consequence in a situation such as a police encounter with a person in a state of emotional crisis or mental dishar-mony. The bizarre circumstances of my encounter with Robert illustrate this with particular clarity. What began as a conversation with Robert's mother, in which I erroneously presumed that Robert was not present, quickly trans-formed into a potentially critical incident as soon as he appeared. Prior to that moment, Robert was only "present" for Mrs. Brown, my partner, and me as an abstract concern. Once he appeared in the kitchen doorway, it was obvi-ously necessary to shift the entire dynamic of the contact. However, this shift still effectively treated Robert as an objective presence. In my encounter with Robert, his state of confusion and torment put him in a situation much akin to Christiane's, or André's, in the earlier dialogue from *The Votive Candle*. Like both of these characters, who each already had a sense of being alienated, Robert had to sit by passively as his fate was discussed.

In an ironic reversal of the objectification that occurs when Denise confronts Lawrence about Christiane's mental state, Christiane takes a radically differ-ent approach toward Denise when, two weeks later, she finds her in a heroin-induced stupor. Faced with the double crisis of her recently failed marriage to Max, who has a history of pedophilia and drug addiction, and the news that she has now been betrayed as well by her lover, Bertrand, Denise turns to heroin with the general intent of committing a slow suicide. Christiane realizes what is occurring, and confronts Denise:

> *Christiane:* (Going to greet her.) You look awful.
> *Denise:* (In a somber tone.) It doesn't matter.
> *Lawrence:* I believe you want to speak with Christiane. I'll leave you two to-gether. (He goes out.)
> *Christiane:* Have you seen a doctor?
> *Denise:* It's not a medical problem. Your prediction was wrong. Bertrand is going to marry that de Brucourt girl. And that's not all . . .
> *Christiane:* (Looking at her.) Why, Denise, your pupils are dilated . . . you haven't . . . ?
> *Denise:* Yes, I tried to, but failed as in everything else. (She looks around her.)
> (Marcel, 1998:112–13/1973a:183)

The context of the dialogue makes it obvious to the reader that Christiane's approach to Denise is one rooted in a deep mutual understanding. Explained in terms of Marcel's key distinction, Christiane regards Denise as a mystery, rather than as a problem. In my own terms, the encounter between Christiane and Denise is one of consciously acknowledged co-presence, rather than intersubjectivity. This is most clearly apparent in Christiane's authentic openness, on the basis of which she not only realizes the tragedy of Denise's situation, but is also shaken by its uncomfortable similarity to her own life.

Looking strictly at the outward content of the dialogue between Christiane and Denise, it is easy to imagine a similar exchange during a police encounter with someone in emotional crisis. Everything that Christiane says to Denise approximates the kinds of statements police officers commonly make to people who are suicidal or otherwise in a state of profound psychological disharmony. Commenting on outward physical signs of distress, offering medical assistance, and adopting a low-key approach aimed at eliciting critical information, all represent elements of the approach that most police departments would encourage their officers to use in such situations. Yet, considered more closely, the two dialogues unfold according to radically diverging approaches to human presence, and reflect poetic creation of praxis out of ontology.

The poetics of my encounter with Robert reduced our conversation to a process of pragmatic stalling, aimed at keeping him engaged while I formulated a tactical plan to take him into custody. Critically viewed in Heidegger's terms (1996:157–59), one might say that our dialogue was merely "idle talk" (*Gerede*), the purpose of which is to fill time, rather than truly to engage the other person. Further evidence of this approach may be found in my partner's first words upon seeing Robert: "Hey, isn't that him," and not, "Hey, aren't you Robert?" Everything that followed from this moment treated Robert as the subject of bureaucratic action. As the next chapter will illustrate, this tension endures even in encounters with death.

EIGHT

Policing Death:
The Problematization of Mortality

In all this the thing was to exclude everything fresh
and vital, which always disturbs the regular course of official
business, and to admit only official relations with people,
and then only on official grounds.

—Leo Tolstoy,
The Death of Ivan Ilych, 1886

INTRODUCTION: DEATH AS AN OFFICIAL PROBLEM

The awesomeness of death inevitably transcends whatever means are taken to desacralize it and to treat it in a routinized, factual way (compare Eliade, 1959:186). Considered in phenomenological terms, the discomfiture, dread, and awkwardness that police officers experience during encounters with death may be read as a sign of an intuitive awareness of human presence that overwhelms the logic of problematization. Indeed, episodes of death illuminate the difference between co-presence and intersubjectivity in a way that no other kind of encounter can.

Despite popular notions to the contrary, the vast majority of police encounters with death involve unremarkable natural circumstances rather than homicide, suicide, or accidents. In police circles, these "routine" situations are widely known as unattended deaths, or simply "unattendeds." An attended death is one that has been witnessed by a medical professional, who can attest to its scientific cause, and thus demystify and classify it as a distinct clinical, legal, and administrative incident. An unattended death, on the other hand, occurs beyond the gaze of state-sanctioned medical expertise. Such situations present a bureaucratic problem, insofar as modern society demands a rational account of each and every death.[1] In fulfillment of this mandate, death becomes framed as an official event, which must be ascribed to a specific *manner* (natural, accident, homicide, suicide, or undetermined), *cause* (e.g., cardiac arrest, asphyxia, pneumothorax), and *mechanism* (e.g., gunshot, fall, electrocution). For death to be problematized, it needs to be understood beforehand as a phenomenon that can be placed within this kind of juridical and medical taxonomy. The role of the police as first responders to death investigations frequently represents the initial stage in this process of problematization.

Death scenes are rarely the solemn, controlled situations depicted in popular culture, in which police officers hang up cordons of yellow crime scene tape, and then conduct an investigation that proceeds in a systematic, orderly manner. The actual circumstances for police officers and other first responders at the scene of a death are far more unpredictably dynamic, and suffused with an emotional, psychological, and spiritual rawness. To respond to a death as an agent of the state often means having to encounter hysterical, angry, and shock-stricken survivors, and feeling the overwhelming awkwardness of intruding on one of life's two most sacred moments.

How does a police officer explain to a man that he should not go into his elderly father's house, because the stench of decomposition is so unbearable? What does one say to the young woman who returns home to find her boyfriend's body, after he had blown his head apart with a high-powered rifle? How does one physically restrain an anguished father who tries to shove past officers to get to the body of his dead son? These quandaries are typical of the kinds of situations I have encountered at death scenes, and will strike a familiar note to any experienced police officer or anyone else who has dealt "officially" with death. Although the majority of police officers eventually grow somewhat accustomed to facing the physical gruesomeness of death, there is no growing accustomed to the deeply unsettling discomfiture that comes from being in the position of a bureaucrat whose official concern with the worldly end of a human life is but a shadow of its meaning for the family members and others who are present. I suspect that it is more for this latter reason, than out of physical revulsion, that so many police officers dread responding to deaths.

In this chapter, I turn to Leo Tolstoy's novella, *The Death of Ivan Ilych*, and Anton Chekhov's short story, "Sorrow," to illustrate the conflicting poetics of death that emerge out of bureaucratic problematization on the one hand and a holistic engagement with the sacred awesomeness of death on the other. These contrasting approaches to death demonstrate how the ability to problematize death enacts a notion of human presence that is anything but inevitable or innate. Even in death, human being defies objectification and reification.

ENCOUNTER #8-1, VANESSA

On a November night, shortly before 1:00 A.M., a colleague and I were dispatched along with paramedics to a report of an "unresponsive female" in an apartment. "Unresponsive" usually means dead. The dispatcher advised that the caller had returned home to find the woman unconscious, blue, and not breathing. I immediately remembered the address as one to which my fellow officers and I had frequently responded in recent months for drug-related incidents and domestic violence.

As the paramedics, my partner, and I hurried toward the apartment from the parking lot, we could hear the panicked yelling of a male voice: "Mom, wake up, wake up! Start breathing!" We entered and saw a couple in their late teens standing over a woman, who was lying on a thin mattress in the middle of the living room floor. I recognized the couple from several recent contacts as Rick and Theresa, and quickly realized that the woman on the floor was Rick's mother, Vanessa. It was instantly apparent that she had been dead for a number of hours, so the paramedics made no attempt to resuscitate her.

Vanessa was lying on her left side, curled up in a semi-fetal position, with her hands clasped together in front of her face. Her body was cold and blue, with clear signs of rigor mortis and livor mortis (postmortem, gravitational pooling of blood in the lowest points of the body). Near Vanessa's head, there were two pillows stained with bodily fluids, which appeared to have seeped from her nose and mouth. She was clothed in a T-shirt and underwear and was partially covered with a blanket.

The paramedics quickly gathered up their equipment and left, doubtless relieved they would not have to remain at the scene. Surreptitious looks of humor-tinged jealousy were exchanged between the paramedic crew and my partner and me. We escorted Rick and Theresa outside the apartment, which would now officially be considered a crime scene until an investigation was completed. I requested additional assistance from other officers. One officer secured the front door, and I directed another officer to ensure that as witnesses in the investigation, Rick and Theresa remain apart from each other. One of the officers called for a chaplain to help comfort Rick and Theresa and to assist them in contacting family members. Rick sobbed loudly, his crying interspersed with profanity-laced incantations of anger and disbelief: "Goddamn it, Mom, I can't fukin' believe it!" "I can't fukin' believe it!" Theresa, too, was in a state of near-hysteria.

My partner and I tried to elicit general information about the circumstances of Vanessa's death from Rick and Theresa while we waited for detectives to arrive. Their versions of the incident were inconsistent on some points, and outright contradictory on others. There were no signs of a struggle in the apartment, nor did Vanessa's body show any obvious signs of trauma. Theresa claimed she had found Vanessa after returning from a brief trip to a nearby convenience store, and reported that Vanessa started having difficulty breathing. Theresa said she panicked and called Rick, who came over right away to see what was wrong with his mother.

Theresa's calling Rick would have been unremarkable except that a judge had recently issued a domestic violence no-contact order against Rick, which legally barred him from being at Theresa's apartment or even from communicating with her at all. Theresa and Rick had been dating since their early teens, and had a two-and-a-half-year-old child together. Rick's drinking and use of methamphetamine aggravated his violent temper; and following repeated incidents of domestic violence with Theresa, a judge issued the no-contact order, and Child Protective Services took custody of the couple's child. Normally, Rick's being with Theresa, or even his attempting to contact her, would have led to his arrest. However, I told my colleagues that we would overlook the technical violation of the court order, and ventured my opinion that, under the circumstances, to do otherwise would be blatantly cruel.

Rick's anger and violent temper were not only directed at Theresa: on numerous occasions, Vanessa had herself experienced his wrath, both verbally and physically. Theresa and Vanessa had developed a very close relationship over the years that Theresa was dating Rick. Like Theresa's mother, Vanessa had longstanding addictions to heroin and other drugs. Theresa was renting the apartment in which Vanessa died. Vanessa had been staying with Theresa since her release from prison several months earlier, where she had served a sentence for drug-related forgery convictions. With nowhere else to live but the street, Vanessa ended up living with Theresa.

Vanessa's death was devastating for Theresa, whose own mother had died of a heroin overdose only two years earlier. She had been in her early thirties. Theresa told me that Vanessa had essentially become her mother since her own had died. Her stepfather had recently been convicted of selling heroin, and was sent to prison. Theresa's biological father was also in prison, having been convicted of child molestation. Rick had apparently been present when Theresa's mother had died: now the horrific cycle was repeating itself. Theresa stood in the cold hallway outside the apartment, sobbing. "I can't take it any more, I can't fukin' take it!" she cried. "It's all because of drugs, I hate drugs!"

After about an hour and a half, two detectives and an investigator from *the medical examiner's officer arrived at the scene. Vanessa's relatives also begun to show up at the apartment. Several of them quickly became angry with Rick and Theresa, blaming them for what they already knew had been Vanessa's relapse to heavy heroin use following her release from prison. Theresa was too upset to remain at the scene. I escorted her away from the knot of angry relatives, and had her sit in my patrol car. Tempers flared further, and a fistfight nearly broke out between Rick and his uncle. This tense situation lasted for several minutes, until I told everyone that this was not the time to lay blame for Vanessa's death. At the family's request, they were subsequently allowed to view Vanessa and say their farewells before the medical examiner removed her body from the apartment for transportation to the morgue.*

Detectives later took Rick and Theresa to the police station and questioned them about the events surrounding Vanessa's death. They remained vague and uncooperative, as they had at the scene. The medical examiner subsequently ruled that Vanessa had died of bronchopneumonia, caused by an accidental overdose of opiates and cocaine. She was thirty-nine years old.

APPROACHING DEATH

The episode of Vanessa's death vividly illustrates my earlier point that the more unsettling aspect for police officers in their encounters with death often is dealing with the survivors, rather than with the deceased. Had Vanessa been found not by Rick and Theresa but instead, by a stranger, such as a landlord or maintenance worker, the bureaucratic problematization of her death would doubtless have occurred more efficiently and quickly. As it happened, of course, my colleagues and I found ourselves having to contend with the immediate aftermath of Rick and Theresa's discovery of Vanessa's body, and their futile attempts to resuscitate her. In this crucial respect, our approach to Vanessa was operationally inseparable from our approach to Rick and Theresa.

Problematizing Vanessa's death necessarily involved a physical and figurative crossing of thresholds between a neatly contained crime scene and the world beyond it, with the two separated only by the front door of an apartment. Like the crossing of thresholds that occurred during my encounter with Cecilia (chapter 6) when she reached across her doorway and took my hand, the transformation of Vanessa's death into a bureaucratic problem similarly had its ontological presuppositions powerfully challenged by events just on the other side of the door, where Rick and Theresa stood in the cold night air, trying to come to grips with their shock, loss, and anger. This created an interpretive dynamic in which the physical act of passing back and forth through the apartment door moved my colleagues and me between two radically different experiences of and approaches to Vanessa's death.

The police response quickly "contained and stabilized" the situation, but only in a very limited way. For Rick, Vanessa was, as he put it while pointing at the front door of the apartment, "my mother, who's lying dead *in there*." For Theresa, Vanessa was vividly present in her sudden absence as a "lost mother," not only because of what she had been to Theresa in life, as well as for how she had apparently died. For my colleagues and me, acting in our official capacity, Vanessa was "the body." Alone in the apartment with the "subject" of our investigation, we created a sanctuary for bureaucratic efficiency.

Sequestered outside, Rick and Theresa must have experienced the scant distance between themselves and Vanessa as an infinity, and not only because of the physical barrier of the door, but also the fact of its being guarded by a police officer. This moment suggests Bachelard's notion of the profundity of the threshold, where passing from inside to outside has a poetic dimension that transcends the spatial geometry of here and there: "How concrete everything becomes in the world of the spirit when an object, a mere door, can give images of hesitation, temptation, desire, security, welcome and respect. If one were to give an account of all the doors one has closed and opened, of all the doors one would like to re-open, one would have to tell the story of one's entire life" (Bachelard, 1994:224). The interactions among Rick, Theresa, and my colleagues and me are apprehensible as microcosmic moments of exactly what Bachelard describes—a telling of one's life story—in which competing poetics of human presence clash headlong.

Rick and Theresa's immediate state of crisis was part of a deeper, perpetual turmoil, lived out in the near-constant presence of the police. As such, my encounter with them resisted delimitation as an isolated incident. The smallest of issues engaged histories and patterns of mutual mistrust and suspicion. For example, Theresa's simple request for her a coat became translated into a variable in a complex bureaucratic analysis: did she really want the coat to stay warm, or might the coat contain a potential piece of evidence? Might it hold a weapon, to be used against officers? After a careful search of its pockets turned up nothing, the coat was handed out the door, passed by a detective to a patrol officer, who then gave it to Theresa out in the dark stairway, where she and Rick sat.

In addition to being isolated from the crime scene, Rick and Theresa also had to be isolated from each another, following standard procedure for preventing witnesses from influencing each other's statements or memories, and to prevent suspects from concocting alibis. Still, in deference to the utterly tragic nature of the situation, I decided to maintain a more limited degree of separation between Rick and Theresa, which allowed them to interact, albeit in the immediate presence of an officer who remained with them and monitored their conversation. These, then, were the uncanny circumstances within which my colleagues and I tried to engage Rick and Theresa, as we struggled to reconcile the bureaucratic "problem" of Vanessa's death with the actuality of its ultimate existential significance.

One of the questions that might arise in reflecting on my decision to leave Rick and Theresa together is the extent to which such a gesture was truly authentic or only a calculated attempt to encourage their cooperation in the hope of eliciting facts and data about the case. In reality, it was probably neither exclusively one nor the other, but a reflection of the awkward interweaving of multiple intentional stances. When I note how my colleagues and I tried to gather information from Rick and Theresa while "allowing" them to grieve, this suggests an approach different from one that would have accorded priority to their grieving over the need to attain bureaucratic objectives. This dynamic was further complicated by the role of our professionally ingrained skepticism, through the lens of which Rick and Theresa's expressions of grief had to been viewed as potentially inauthentic emotional displays, staged for the benefit of the police, in order to conceal a crime or other suspicious circumstances.

What of the encounter with Vanessa? The initial response to the scene of her death was treated as an emergency involving a potential lifesaving situation. This is because considerations of liability, to say nothing of ethics, dictate the operational assumption that people are alive until definitive proof to the contrary is found. Once it was evident that Vanessa was dead, emergency medical personnel left the scene, and with them departed any official interest in Vanessa's existence as a living human being, except insofar as the final hours or days of her life might be read as a potential source of clues to the chain of events that led to her death.[2] In this way, Vanessa instantly became the "subject" of a formal police investigation, and became approachable as such.

Almost simultaneously, the entire domestic space in which Vanessa had lived out her final months was declared a crime scene, and Vanessa's body was designated the central object of interest within it. Toward the conclusion of the crime scene investigation, the door to the apartment opened again, and my colleagues and I stepped aside, momentarily ceding bureaucratic control to the greater existential reality of death, as we allowed family members to say goodbye to Vanessa. But at the conclusion of this ritual, bureaucracy reasserted itself: Vanessa was wrapped in a body bag and loaded into the back of the medical examiner's truck.

TOLSTOY: BEING IN THE PRESENCE OF DEATH

Harold Bloom characterizes Tolstoy's work in a way that fittingly introduces its value for a phenomenological aesthetics of encounter: "Tolstoy is above all an artist of the normal—the normal, however, so intensified that it acquires a poetical truth and an emotional fullness which we are astounded to discover in the ordinary situations of life" (Bloom, 1986:58). Although *The Death of Ivan Ilych* is most widely acclaimed for its reflections on mortality from the standpoint of its dying protagonist, the story also gives detailed attention to the reactions of Ilych's family and colleagues to his impending and actual demise. There are several key passages in the story centering on encounters with Ilych's dead body and on the reactions of his colleagues to his death, all of which are directly applicable to analyzing the police encounter that followed Vanessa's death. In particular, Tolstoy's emphasis on the matter-of-fact "business" of dealing with death reveals how the actuality of death is circumscribed in ways that make it literally approachable as a certain kind of rational event (see Simmons, 1968:149, and Christian, 1969:238).

Early in the story, Tolstoy marks out the distinction between what may be regarded as existential and social comportments toward death. The former occurs as the immediate, visceral awareness of one's own mortality, captured in the realization that for the moment, one is still alive, and that it is someone else who has died (Tolstoy, 1991:124). The latter is the mundane realization, accompanied by dread and discomfiture, that one must attend to "the very tiresome demands of propriety"—funerals, condolence calls, and the like (Tolstoy, 1991:124). Intermingled with all of this is the awkward awareness that death can create opportunities for the survivors, in the form of promotions, inheritances, and other worldly advantage (see Greenwood, 1975:122). This awareness can engender a powerful sense of guilt, though not as strong as the guilt felt by survivors, who, like Ivan Ilych's widow, cannot help but acknowledge that death can also lift a crushing burden from the shoulders of the living.

The story opens with the reaction among Ivan Ilych's friends to the news of his death. His closest colleague, Peter Ivanovich, goes to view the body and to offer his condolences to Ilych's widow, Praskovya Fedorovna. As soon as Peter Ivanovich arrives at Ivan Ilych's house, he is struck by the discomfiture of the moment: "Peter Ivanovich, like everyone else on such occasions, entered feeling uncertain what he would have to do" (Tolstoy, 1991:125). He opts for the safe and solemn ritual gesture of crossing himself. This initial, overwhelming gravity, which accompanies the arrival at the scene of death, is akin to the police officer's first moments at a death-related incident. Especially when an officer must first encounter surviving family members, there are usually delicate, painful rituals of expressing condolences, and of trying to explain the role of the police at the scene. Having dispensed with these social obligations, the actual encounter with the body may then proceed.

At the scene of Vanessa's death, once the paramedics had left, my colleagues and I quickly escorted Rick and Theresa outside, reassuring them with statements of condolence, but mindful of the need "to get them out of the scene" before they had a chance to assimilate the full significance of what had occurred. Paradoxically, of course, the act of being taken outside by the police has this effect anyway: the utterance, "I'm sorry, there's nothing we could do" begins to communicate the truth of death's finality, of which the mind has already begun to take notice, at least unconsciously. The departure of the paramedics almost immediately after their arrival occasioned statements of condolence from them and from police officers to Rick and Theresa, which acted to reiterate the factual circumstances behind their decision to not make resuscitation efforts.[3]

Once the outside world begins to impinge on the mind and distract its attention, the distraction itself can shock consciousness into the sudden and uncanny knowledge of irreversible loss. It is at this moment when officers must guard against uncontrollable and unpredictable responses, which can at times be physically violent. Simultaneous with all of their efforts to "control the scene" and begin the process of problematizing death, officers, too, find themselves struggling to contain their own existential awareness of what has transpired. However, despite the attempt to formalize and limit their role to that officially prescribed by the occasion for being present, death is such that it overwhelms the mind and the senses.

This is exactly what happened to Peter Ivanovich. As soon as he stepped inside Ivan Ilych's house, he "was immediately aware of a faint odor of a decomposing body" (Tolstoy, 1991:125). Even in a case such as Vanessa's death, when putrefaction had not yet begun, the primordial nature of death seems to exert an almost instinctive effect on the senses, and upon smell more than the others.[4] The mind imagines that the nose smells death, even when "factually" it probably does not. Other smells become amplified, too: bodily excretions, fresh blood, the mustiness of a room, lingering odors of cooking and smoking, and medicinal aromas.

Walking into Vanessa's apartment and seeing her body triggered a hypersensitivity to every aroma in the room. In this onrush of smell, the nose transports the mind "to the things themselves"—to the utmost, inescapable palpability of death. Tolstoy seems to be acutely aware of this experience, which he frames in relation to the struggles of the mind to comprehend the event of death. In the opening scenes of the story, Tolstoy describes (1991:129) the commingled odors of incense, the decaying body, and carbolic acid (a disinfectant used on corpses) that linger oppressively in Peter Ivanovich's brain until he is able to go outside and breathe fresh air. Ivanovich's experience shows how the mind's willful efforts to compartmentalize death through rational reflection clash with a more elemental and involuntary awareness that death resists all such containment. It marks, as such, a clear analogue with the quandary of the police officer, whose stance toward a dead body constantly shifts among a range of ultimately inseparable intentional postures.

Besides his attentiveness to smell as a key aspect of the intersecting existential and sensory experiences of death, Tolstoy treats the "heavy" presence of death with remarkable attunement to what this means in terms of the physical nature of a corpse, as well as to what it signifies for those in its presence. For new police officers, the absolute stillness of death leaves a lasting impression: it is impossible to realize how much a living human being moves until one has stared at a corpse and marveled at its fixed eyes, whose gaze is haunting, precisely because there is no present intention behind it.

The absolute stillness of death becomes a sign for officers, which they learn to read quickly and translate into an awareness of mortality. Unless death has been very recent, the visible perceptibility of stillness and heaviness is intensified even more by the tactile sensation of dead human flesh. Officers are taught that absent decomposition or decapitation, motionlessness alone cannot be used to confirm death. Thus, the living hand must approach dead flesh, and feel for (even if it already knows it likely will not find) a carotid or femoral pulse, or check for reactive pupils. The coldest flesh of a living person resists when pressed, and seems always to radiate faint warmth from within: the coldness of dead flesh, by contrast, shocks the unaccustomed hand with its chill and lack of resilience, and seems to urge the living hand to recoil. The mind that processes what the hand feels in searching for signs of life thus struggles to bracket out its own sadness, horror, revulsion, and fear, as the official judgment is made whether life remains, or not. Expressed in terms of the distinction between co-presence and intersubjectivity, what the police officer attempts to encounter strictly in objective terms, in the formal act of probing for vitality, persists in revealing its existential wholeness, even in death. Here, in the moment of the tactile encounter with death, the notion that a human body can be experienced abstractly, as an objective presence, seems utterly illusory (see Heidegger, 2001:80–89 and 184).

In the case of Ivan Ilych, the absolute stillness and heaviness of death transformed his body into a presence that draws the eye with wonder and trepidation, and undoes any intention to see it as a mere thing. As Peter Ivanovich approaches the body, he notices how "The dead man lay, as dead men always lie, in a specially heavy way, his rigid limbs sunk in the soft cushions of the coffin, with the head forever bowed on the pillow. His yellow waxen brow with bald patches over his sunken temples was thrust up in the way peculiar to the dead, the protruding nose seeming to press on the upper lip" (Tolstoy, 1991:125). Staring at the expression on Ivan Ilych's face, Peter Ivanovich reads in it "a reproach and a warning to the living," though tries to imagine that they do not apply to him (Tolstoy, 1991:125). Nonetheless, his effort to detach himself from the implications of what he sees before him fails, and he quickly becomes unsettled and hurries from the room. A short while later, during the funeral, Peter Ivanovich tries again to remain passive and detached: "The service began: candles, groans, incense, tears, and sobs. Peter Ivanovich stood looking gloomily down at his feet. He did not look at the dead man once, did not yield to any depressing influence, and was one of the first to leave the room. There was no one in the anteroom, but Gerasim darted out of the dead man's room, rummaged with his strong hands among the fur coats to find Peter Ivanovich's, and helped him on with it. 'Well, friend Gerasim,' said Peter Ivanovich, so as to say something. 'It's a sad affair, isn't it?'" (Tolstoy, 1991:129). His perfunctory remark uttered, Peter Ivanovich leaves. The night is still young; he heads to the house of a friend, where he joins a card game that has just gotten under way (see Gustafson, in Tolstoy, 1991:461–62).[5]

Of course, the police officer investigating the death of a stranger stands in altogether different relation to the decedent than a mourning friend or relative. Though Peter Ivanovich's rushing from a funeral to a card game might seem callous, it is perhaps easier to make sense of the state of mind that allows many officers to follow a gruesome death investigation with a large meal shared over the recitation of macabre jokes. In fact, such a meal is often the first opportunity that officers have to drop their emotional guard, which demands especially careful attention in the era of ubiquitous cameras: every police officer under-stands the importance of maintaining solemnity in the immediate presence of surviving family and friends; however, more than a few officers have cringed after seeing their grinning faces on the evening news.

This is one reason why the "easiest" death investigations are often those in which no one is present except for the responding officers and the deceased. In these situations, officers have wider latitude to relax a bit and engage in the irreverent humor they share with other professions that encounter death.[6] Such humor often provides welcome relief from the boring and time-consuming ritu-als associated with death, which are the common province of police investigations and events such as Ivan Ilych's funeral. Protracted encounters with death also become occasions for the incongruous intrusion of life's unavoidable necessities. This is why experienced police officers know that whenever feasible, a bathroom break and snack should precede the response to a death scene.

Even before Peter Ivanovich left Ivan Ilych's funeral, he had surreptitiously chatted with his friend and fellow mourner, Schwartz, in order to decide where they would be playing bridge that night. Similarly, at the scene of Vanessa's death, while Rick and Theresa faced an overwhelming loss, my colleagues and I mixed official matters related to the investigation with small talk about mundane concerns: who was going on vacation for the holidays, annoyance that the death investigation consumed time that could have been used to catch up on accumulated paperwork or take a coffee break, and so forth. When the investigator from the medical examiner's office arrived at the scene, he and I chatted for a few minutes in the parking lot, well out of the view and earshot of Rick and Theresa. Not having seen each other for some time, we remarked how the occasion of death provided an opportunity to "catch up." Seen through a phenomenological lens, such attempts at normalcy cannot help but be "pulled back" to the presence of death. Whether for police officers or for Peter Ivanovich, adopting a posture of forced nonchalance that seeks "to go about one's business as if there weren't a death here" only makes the death that much more palpable.

In a lengthy passage from *The Death of Ivan Ilych* that has been the focus of extensive commentary (e.g., Bloom, 1986), Tolstoy shows how as Peter Ivanovich struggles to console Ivan's widow, he is aware of the smallest things around him, such as the way he sinks into the thickly cushioned hassock on which he is sitting (1991:126–27):

> When they reached the drawing-room, upholstered in pink cretonne and lighted by a dim lamp, they sat down at a table—she on a sofa and Peter

Ivanovich on a low pouffe, the springs of which yielded spasmodically under his weight. Praskovya Fedorovna had been on the point of warning him to take another seat, but felt that such a warning was out of keeping with her present condition and so she changed her mind. As he sat down on the pouffe Peter Ivanovich recalled how Ivan Ilych had arranged this room and had consulted him regarding this pink cretonne with green leaves. The whole room was full of furniture and knick-knacks, and on her way to the sofa the lace of the widow's black shawl caught on the carved edge of the table. Peter Ivanovich rose to detach it, and the springs of the pouffe, relieved of his weight, rose also and gave him a push. The widow began detaching her shawl by herself, and Peter Ivanovich again sat down, suppressing the rebellious springs of the pouffe under him. But the widow had not quite freed herself and Peter Ivanovich got upon again, and the pouffe rebelled and even creaked. When this was all over she took out a clean cambric shawl and began to weep. The episode with the shawl and struggle with the pouffe had cooled Peter Ivanovich's emotions and he sat there with a sullen look on his face.

This passage captures the struggle between sensory hyperawareness and the background events that precipitate the mind's seeming desire to focus anywhere but on death itself. Intentionality shifts to and fro, as the mind poetically attends to the ineluctable fact of its own presence.

Despite his attempts at busying himself with consoling Ivan Ilych's widow, and fixing his attention on sinking cushions and creaking furniture, Peter Ivanovich is carried back to the enormity of the moment: as Praskovya Fedorovna relates the days of horrific pain and suffering that preceded Ivan Ilych's death, Ivanovich grapples with the unavoidable fact that this, too, might be his own fate. His mind moves from one state of consciousness to another, from one form of rationalization to another. In calling attention to these shifts, Tolstoy shows why it is impossible to approach death as a clinical matter-of-fact. Rather, the detachment from death constitutes an unwitting suspension or bracketing. In depicting Ivan Ilych's attitude toward his impending death, and the cultivated detachment of Ilych's friends after he dies, Tolstoy reveals how both stances, whatever their overt intent, nonetheless still amount to acknowledgments of the ultimacy of death.

ENCOUNTER #8-2, LEONARD

Late one Friday afternoon toward the end of my shift, I was dispatched to check the welfare of fifty-four-year-old Leonard, who lived alone in an apartment, and had not been seen or heard from in several days. Leonard's ex-girlfriend had called 911 to report that he was gravely ill, and feared that he had died. She had also contacted the manager of his apartment complex.

I arrived at the apartment complex accompanied by the young, rookie officer whom I was training. Like so many apartment complexes, this one had one of those bucolic names that belied its utter drabness. We met with the property manager, who seemed nervous and distraught, and already knew the reason for our visit. She confirmed that no one had seen Leonard for several days. He was not answering his door, and had failed to return several phone calls from relatives about an urgent family matter. The manager handed me a passkey and led my partner and me to Leonard's building.

We walked toward the building across a small, narrow lawn, which had just received its first mowing of the spring. I looked down at the wet grass clippings adhering to the toe of my boot, and hoped to myself that Leonard would not be dead. I instantly felt guilty as I reflected on the motive for my thoughts: my sentiment, I realized, had more to do with my desire to go home on time (the end of my shift was less than an hour away) than it did with my regret at the idea that another human being might have died. The incongruity of these simultaneous thoughts was striking: in my professional capacity, another person's death occurs for me in no small measure as an inconvenience, a disruption of my plans.

We arrived at Leonard's building. The manager pointed to an apartment on the second of the three stories—"He lives up there," she said. I could see the glow of a television screen through the partially open blinds. "Why don't you wait down here," I told the manager, as my partner and I began to climb the wooden staircase. My intuition told me that I was about to find myself involved in a death investigation.

As I reached the front door to the apartment, I inhaled sharply, checking for the odor of putrefaction, and hoped to myself that the body would not be badly decomposed. I knocked on the door and loudly announced, "Hello! Police Department!" "Leonard, are you in there?" I neither expected a response nor did I get one. After knocking several more times, I radioed the dispatcher that my trainee and I would be entering the apartment. I placed the key in the lock, opened the dead bolt, stepped back, and looked over at my partner—"Okay, you're on," I said to him, directing him to make entry. We drew our guns, standard procedure every time officers enter and search a building under suspicious circumstances.

My young partner opened the door and walked inside. Almost immediately, I heard him shout, "Sir, wake up!" He yelled nervously at me, and started to reach for his portable radio. "I'm going to call for aid [an ambulance]," he said. I entered the apartment right behind the rookie officer, and immediately saw Leonard lying on the floor. "Forget it," I replied, shaking my head, "he's gone." Leonard's body was frozen in full rigor mortis. His eyes and mouth were open, and his face was a dark, purplish-blue color.

His fingernails were nearly black. I estimated he had been dead for close to twenty-four hours.

Leonard had died sitting in a large lounge chair in the corner of his living room, watching television and drinking beer. The television screen cast a flickering glow across his death-stilled face. There was a small, glass-topped table next to the left arm of the lounge chair. The remote controls for the television and VCR sat on the table, neatly placed alongside several empty beer bottles, another partially full bottle, and several bottles of prescription medication. The bottles of beer had been removed from a half-case carton that sat on the floor at the foot of the lounge chair. Leonard had fallen from the chair right next to the box, knocking over several of the bottles, though not breaking any of them.

Leonard was lying on his right side, with his head tilted back slightly. As he fell, one of his bare feet caught the edge of a bowl, which was sitting atop a stack of plates on the floor, not far from the lounge chair. The plates and bowl were decorated with an attractive Japanese motif, and seemed to have been positioned on the floor with some care. Leonard's foot had struck the edge of the bowl in such a way that it was now tilted forward toward him, as if pouring out its contents, and was held absolutely still in this position by his perfectly arched toes, which were frozen by rigor mortis. The scene projected a melancholic beauty. I imagined that if someone had painted it, many a viewer would judge the arrangement to be utterly improbable. I thought, too, how Leonard had died a paradigmatically modern, urban death: alone, in front of a television, in the isolated anonymity of an apartment. These reflections, however, quickly yielded to the official task at hand.

My young trainee had never been to a death scene, so Leonard became a practical lesson for him in the forensic skills he would need to investigate "routine" deaths, which typically are not handled by detectives. These scenes can actually prove more technically and emotionally difficult for patrol officers than situations such as homicides or suicides, in which all they need to do is secure and preserve the scene for detectives. However, in the majority of death investigations, which typically involve elderly or terminally ill people who die at home, officers must handle the situation themselves, which means they must literally handle the body.

First, I talked my trainee through his instinctive reluctance to touch a dead human being: "Let's glove up," I said, directing him to put on surgical gloves. "Go on, touch him . . . there you go . . . see what a cold body feels like?" I tried to channel his reactions to the uncanniness of death in a rational direction, dictated by the needs of the training curriculum: "Try to move him; see, that's rigor mortis." "Do you remember learning in the academy when rigor sets, and when it breaks?" Our lesson continued: I showed my trainee the marks on the body from lividity, and showed him how to check the body for signs of trauma, injection sites, and other noteworthy indications of how the death might have occurred.

As my trainee moved Leonard's body, accumulated stomach gases discharged in a noxious, postmortem belch. I chuckled at my trainee's startled and disgusted reaction, and thereby spontaneously initiated him into the dark humor that allows police officers to "laugh at death." "You've got to be careful to stay away from dead peoples' mouths when you move them," I cautioned him. "Even though they're dead, they can still puke on you."

I paused and we chatted for a minute about the odd juxtaposition of laughter and death. I told the rookie officer that joking about death had its rightful place, as long as he remembered the ultimate solemnity of the moment. His comfort level somewhat raised, I directed him to look at Leonard's eyes. We talked about fixed pupils, and how to check for petechial hemorrhaging—the rupturing of blood vessels on the inside of the eyelids caused by asphyxia, and thus often seen in cases of hanging or strangulation.

I remember having been taught in the police academy to approach a dead body as if they were just another piece of furniture in the room. "Try to forget that it's a person," the instructor had said. I never agreed with this; and when training new officers, I always made a point at death scenes of explaining that a police officer should not and really could not forget that a dead human being was never just an object, and that a body's dignity and sanctity should always be borne in mind. Standing in Leonard's living room, I looked at my trainee and told him that one day, he or I might well be the one dead on the floor.

I was able to reach Leonard's physician, who verified that Leonard had been suffering from generalized scleroderma, a progressive hardening of the skin and connective tissue, which eventually leads to systemic organ failure and death. The doctor agreed to sign Leonard's death certificate, which meant that an autopsy would not be necessary. I relayed this information to an investigator at the medical examiner's office. The investigator conferred with Leonard's physician, and then called me back with what is called an "NJA" number ("no jurisdiction accepted") and authorized release of the body to a funeral home. By relinquishing jurisdiction, the medical examiner's office communicated its confidence that there was no mystery to the death: the "problem" had, in effect, been solved.

A woman soon arrived at the scene and identified herself as Leonard's ex-girlfriend. She said she had been the person who called for us to check on Leonard. She immediately began to explain to me that there were numer-

ous things inside the apartment that belonged to her, and demanded to have them. The woman became upset when I told her that because her name was not on the lease, I would not allow her into the apartment. I told her that the apartment would be turned over to the family, and that any claims of ownership to property would have to be passed along to Leonard's next-of-kin. The woman grew more annoyed. A chaplain soon showed up, as did Leonard's sister-in-law and other family members. The chaplain agreed to assist in resolving the argument over Leonard's property. My partner and I were thankful for this and left the scene, our official duty having been fulfilled.

Later, after returning to the police station to write my incident report, I checked Leonard's name in a records database, and realized that I had previously encountered him several years earlier. According to the record of the incident, which I had long since forgotten, I had found Leonard late one night, passed out drunk, lying in the grass at the front entrance to the same apartment complex where he would eventually die. The record noted that, at the time, Leonard was belligerent, and had almost gotten into a fight with me. The entry jogged my memory, and I started to recollect some of the details of my previous encounter with Leonard. I remembered that he had, indeed, been rude and aggressive. I further remembered how, when I roused him from his drunken stupor, he cursed me for bothering him. I checked his identification, and verified that he lived only yards from where I had found him passed out. Stirred back to consciousness, Leonard ambled unsteadily toward his building. Satisfied that he had made it back home, I left.

GETTING A BODY

Death investigations are a crucial element in the training curriculum for new officers; hence, field training officers often look for the opportunity to "get a body" for their rookies. This can redound to the benefit of senior officers, when their death investigation calls get "jumped" by a rookie officer. For altogether different reasons, officers will sometimes volunteer to handle a call for a colleague who has recently experienced the death of a loved one, or when the circumstances of the death might be particularly upsetting to the responding officer, as was the case when I offered to handle the crib death of an infant for a squad mate whose wife was pregnant. Such offers may or may not be accepted; either way, however, they hint at the artificiality of the bureaucratic stance that officers must adopt at a death scene.

The bureaucratic problematization of Leonard's death began with his ex-girlfriend's call to police. She explained her concerns to a 911 operator, who translated them into an official incident, which the computer dispatch system classified as a "welfare check." When my trainee and I received the call and started toward the scene, we discussed some of the considerations that would inform the nature of our response. Were the caller's concerns legitimate; and if so, would they present us with exigent circumstances, the legal standard necessary to enter the apartment without consent or a search warrant? We thus initially approached the call strictly as a problem of law and liability. Faced with situations of this kind, officers typically weigh liability against privacy, and decide in deference to which one they should act.

As soon as my trainee and I decided to enter Leonard's apartment, the situation became problematized *tactically*, as a building entry and search. Even after we found his body in the living room, the rest of the apartment still had to be "cleared." Once the situation had been tactically resolved by completing the search, I advised the communications center via radio that "The apartment checks clear; this will be an unattended [death]." With my declaration, the situation became translated into an *investigative* problem.

Through all of this, Leonard himself remained at the center of the incident. At first, the question of his welfare had to be answered officially: once it was, through the discovery of his body, his physical presence then became problematized in a new form, as the subject of an investigation. Instantly, the tension between co-presence and intersubjectivity came to the fore. In death, Leonard would have to be objectified for the purpose of forensically determining what had happened to him. At the same time, Leonard's actual human *presence*, which in one respect seemed available for manipulation and analysis, defied that very availability, through the *absence* that his body signified (compare Landsberg, 1966:199–200). This tension is readily apparent in officers' shifting comportments toward a dead human body as a person, and as "remains." For example, police report narratives commonly use differing terms of reference for the person who has died: "Mr. Smith," "Smith's body," or, simply, "the deceased," or "the body." Terminological changes seem to coincide with the shift in the officer's comportment toward the person that occurs once death has been confirmed. For instance, an officer might write, "I responded to a welfare check of Robert Smith," and then, after verifying Smith's death, will abstractly refer to him in the next paragraph as "the body." This progressive abstraction points to variations in second-order interpretations of the experience of approaching death.

CHEKHOV'S POETIC REALISM

Combining insights from his clinical encounters as a physician with his broader interests as a social observer and writer, Chekhov used his stories to examine the relation between the peculiar alienating qualities of modern life and the predicaments of ordinary human beings (Chudakov, 2000:5; see also Eagleton, 2003:236–37). Like Gabriel Marcel (see chapter 7), he rejects the device of authorial omniscience for a more solicitous stance that enables his characters to reveal themselves (see Chudakov, 1983:25 and 2000:7–9, and May, 1985). In particular, Chekhov's characters manifest a self-conscious presence that may be read as a poetic mode of existence.

"Sorrow" (1885) tells the story of Grigory Petrov, a peasant wood turner who is driving his sick, elderly wife, Matryona, to the hospital through a blinding snowstorm. Grigory talks to Matryona and to himself as they hurtle down the rough road, not realizing that somewhere along the way, she has already died. He thus continues speaking to her as if she were still alive. The result for the reader is a feeling of tragic irony, coupled with a heightened awareness of how an encounter with death can reveal the fullness of human presence that had been overlooked during life. The reader initially shares Grigory's ignorance of his wife's death, presuming along with him that Matryona is listening in silence. The realization that she is dead, however, dawns upon the reader before it occurs to Grigory.

Early in the story, Chekhov explains how it was Matryona's gaze that first gives Grigory impetus to seek medical attention for her (see Hahn, 1977:49). A heavy drinker with a penchant for domestic violence, Grigory is shocked out of his ordinarily impetuous attitude when he returns home one night and encounters a gaze from his wife that is nothing like the pained, martyred look to which he is accustomed: "this time she had looked at him sternly and immovably, as saints in the holy pictures or dying people look. From that strange, evil look in her eyes the trouble had begun. The turner, stupefied with amazement, borrowed a horse from a neighbor, and now was taking his old woman to the hospital in the hope that, by means of powders and ointments, [Dr.] Pavel Ivanitch would bring back his old woman's habitual expression" (Chekhov, 1999b:95). Hahn remarks (1977:49) that Matryona's preternatural gaze of impending death begins to bring Grigory to the moral realization that he has mistreated his wife for all of the years of their marriage. Her gaze suddenly reveals to him how he has seen his wife up to this moment, and also presages what is later to occur, as the couple makes their way to the hospital through the snowstorm.

As their journey continues, and Grigory rambles on, he begins to notice that his wife has stopped replying to him: "Does your side ache, Matryona, that you don't speak? I ask you, does your side ache?" (Chekhov, 1999b:96). Then, Grigory realizes that Matryona's countenance has changed: "It struck him as strange that the snow on this old woman's face was not melting; it was queer that the face itself looked somehow drawn and had turned a pale gray, dingy waxen hue and had grown grave and solemn" (Chekhov, 1999b:96). At this point in the narrative, Grigory still comports himself toward Matryona as if she were alive. He finds her appearance unusual, but does not yet seem to grasp what has occurred. Indeed, Grigory's initial reaction is to yell at Matryona, until it begins to dawn on him what he is truly facing: "The turner let the reins go and began thinking. He could not bring himself to look round at his old woman: he was frightened. He was afraid, too, of asking her a question and not getting an answer. At last, to make an end of uncertainty, without looking round he felt his old woman's cold hand. The lifted hand fell like a log. 'She is dead, then! What a business!'" (Chekhov, 1999b:96). The gaze that first led Grigory to realize that his wife was ill has become frozen by death, and he finds himself unable to meet it. After the fact of Matryona's death becomes inescapable, Grigory nonetheless continues on his way, driving into the storm, and barely able to see the road ahead of him. The reader discerns that this journey through the falling darkness and swirling snow becomes a metaphor for Grigory's life, which he laments having wasted.

Grigory's experience recalls elements of the approach of the rookie officer, when he first saw Leonard's body as it lay on the apartment floor. As my narrative of the encounter with Leonard makes apparent, I, as an experienced police officer, had intuited before entering the apartment that Leonard was probably dead. This supposition, combined with my numerous previous encounters with dead human bodies, enabled me to assume a quasi-detached, analytic stance toward the incident, an ability that my rookie colleague had not yet developed. Explained from a phenomenological standpoint, my approach to the incident, beginning especially from my ascent of the exterior staircase, was already shaped by the clear expectation that Leonard's body would be found inside the apartment.[7] The rookie officer, on the other hand, had never seen a corpse, and thus approached the situation in a radically different way. He could not imagine as a simple "matter of fact" that he would enter the apartment and encounter a dead human being. Beyond the obvious elements of surprise and shock, the presence of death initially overwhelmed my trainee's ability to contain it within the bounds of bureaucratic problematization.

In light of the condition of Leonard's body—rigor mortis, lividity, and so forth—the reader might skeptically wonder why the rookie officer's first response was to consider calling an ambulance for someone who was obviously dead. Yet, such a judgment wrongly presupposes about my colleague what readers of Chekhov's story could also say of Grigory, by presuming that he was willfully ignoring the undeniable reality of Matryona's death. The experiences of Grigory and the rookie officer both suggest how, even when death is present as an "objective fact," it is not necessarily approached in this way. In the same way that Grigory could not initially bring himself to turn around and look at Matryona's dead face, I had to gradually help my rookie colleague grow accustomed to Leonard's presence as a corpse before talking with him about the intimate and unsettling gaze of death.[8] Both cases show that death can be factually or rationally acknowledged in a way that falls short of facing the full enormity of the moment. In the encounter with Leonard, my practical decision to proceed gradually in teaching my trainee how to approach the body intuitively accepted that looking at a dead face is more profound than blindly touching dead flesh. As Landsberg describes this situation, "In the open eyes of the corpse we perceive not only the end of life but also the disappearance of the person as spirit" (1966:200).

After Grigory acknowledges that his wife is dead, and continues along through the snowstorm, he eventually falls unconscious from exhaustion. He awakens to find himself in the same hospital to which he had been taking Matryona. To his unimaginable horror, Grigory discovers that all four of his limbs had been lost to extreme frostbite:

> He wanted to leap up and fall on his knees before the doctor, but felt that his arms and legs would not obey him. "Your honor, where are my legs, where are my arms!" Say good-by to your arms and legs. . . . They've been frozen off. Come, come! . . . What are you crying for? You've lived your life, and thank God for it! I suppose you have had sixty years of it—that's enough for you! . . ." "I am grieving. . . . Graciously forgive me! If I could have another five or six years! . . ." "What for?" "The horse isn't mine, I must give it back. . . . I must bury my old woman. . . . How quickly it is all ended in this world! Your honor, Pavel Ivanitch! A cigarette-case of birchwood of the best! I'll turn you croquet balls. . . ." The doctor went out of the ward with a wave of his hand. It was all over with the turner. (Chekhov, 1999b:98)

Grigory's rescue from the storm thus comes to naught: the cold that claimed his limbs now combines with its even more devastating emotional equivalent in the doctor's cold indifference, which dashes what small reserve of hope and vitality Grigory has left. In a reversal of the irony that was occasioned by Grigory's talking to Matryona without realizing she was dead, the doctor's indifference toward Grigory so utterly rejects his humanity that it effectively kills him. The irony goes even further: the doctor approaches Grigory fatalistically, as if he were already dead. By contrast, Grigory, though "objectively" speaking to his wife's corpse, was in actuality addressing her with far greater authenticity and solicitude than he ever had when she was living. After realizing she was actually dead, Matryona's presence became for Grigory something utterly different from what it had been while she was alive. Even after "facing the fact" of her death, and feeling it in the coldness of her dead hand, Matryona's presence in the sleigh became the embodiment of all that transcended her physical being. Only in death did Grigory come to know who his wife truly had been for him.

"Sorrow" thus illustrates how even when death is "factually" acknowledged, the presence of a human body can never be experienced solely in objective terms. In some police encounters with death, although a fellow human being is obviously dead, officers' comportment toward the body retains qualities that suggest an inability to disengage from the existential fullness of human presence. The "anti-gaze" of dead eyes, the tactile sensations and colors of dead flesh, and the kinds of sounds and smells experienced in Leonard's postmortem belch, all illustrate how sensory experience is inseparable from intentional reflections on its sources. In "Sorrow," the most vividly haunting example of this phenomenon occurs when Grigory realizes that the loud, banging sound he hears behind him as his horse rushes along the rough roadway "was the dead woman's head knocking against the sledge" (Chekhov, 1999b:97). The ultimate reality of the sound is clearly of greater significance than anything that might be said of its "objective" occurrence as an empirical phenomenon. This remarkable moment shows that sense perception is never reducible to mere abstract sensation.

THE POETICS OF FACING DEATH

Just as Matryona silently froze while riding along in the sleigh, her death unnoticed until after it had already occurred, Leonard's life ended in a moment not witnessed by anyone else, and left him frozen in rigor mortis on the floor of his apartment. The tragic irony of "Sorrow" centers on the fact that Grigory treats his wife as if she were still alive, when she is actually dead, and even more so on his showing her greater respect and affection in death than in life.

A parallel irony emerges in Leonard's story. The event of his death suggests how Leonard's isolation as an object of investigation was merely one more objectification of a human presence that had already been otherwise isolated in a far more elemental way, in the conditions of his everyday life as a social atom living alone in an apartment (see chapter 6).

The official duty of photographing Leonard's body offers an especially significant example of this isolation of human presence, and its subtle aesthetic and poetic elements. The act of approaching a human body, in order to produce evidentiary images of it that will have symbolic and interpretive value, entails already having created the general meanings that attach to those images. To take photographs of a dead body, as the rookie officer did at the scene of Leonard's death, involves bracketing one's presence in a way that enables the process of investigative photography to occur unhampered by the astonishing realization that occurs with the conscious awareness that, "Here I am, taking pictures of a dead human being." Seeking to assume an ideal bureaucratic stance of "being a disinterested professional, who must gather evidence and determine the truth," the rookie officer followed my instructions for taking photographs. Starting at the doorway, and employing methodical procedures, which he had learned in the police academy for getting a "complete picture" of what happened, the officer collected images that captured the truth of Leonard's death. Or did they?

Returning to "Sorrow," and imagining for the moment that Matryona's death had been officially investigated by the police, and approached as Leonard's death had been, what would have been known, and what would have remained unconsidered? Through a bureaucratic poetics that created the legal and forensic fact of his death, Leonard's demise was given a rational accounting meaningful and responsive to the needs of modern administrative praxis. Left unseen in the transparency of this bureaucratic rendering of death was a spectrum of far more elemental realities about the ultimate sacredness and mystery of human presence. Chekhov's story only begins to suggest how, in Leonard's death, the haunting beauty of the scene created by the unintended final movements of a dying man opens a path toward understanding something that bureaucracy cannot ever know.

NINE

Policing and the Poetics of Everyday Life

The poem is the cry of its occasion,
Part of the res itself and not about it.

—Wallace Stevens,
"An Ordinary Evening in New Haven," 1954

ENDING ENCOUNTERS:
THE PHENOMENOLOGY OF WALKING AWAY

In a strict administrative and operational sense, the police do not respond to people, they respond to calls for service. When police departments measure their workload, they tally statistics of "calls handled," not "people assisted." At the end of their patrol shifts, officers do not speak with their colleagues about how many citizens they contacted but of the relative volume of calls to which they responded. A busy shift is one in which officers get "slammed," "buried," or "hammered" with calls for service. Whether it is expressed at the organizational or individual level, the operational assumption that policing centers on responding to calls reflects a profound attenuation of the idea of response, which largely ignores its underlying ontological and moral significance. The same may be said of the everyday practice of mainstream social science, which often describes its task as being a matter of "responding to what the data tell us." But data are mute abstractions, and calls for police service are the mere ciphers of real human cries.

In either case, whether we are talking about bureaucratic or social scientific praxis, the enthralling effects of the application of power divert our attention from the violence of abstraction, and from the ultimate *un*responsiveness that it creates and propagates. Unthinking abstraction is fatally deficient poetry, a creation of meaning (*poiesis*) that is not only ignorant of its effects but also cut off from the manifold reality of the lifeworld that is its true ontological horizon. Just as the technical and predictive triumphs of natural scientific method lead to the spurious substitution of mathematized "nature" for the lifeworld of which it is a mere abstraction (Husserl, 1970:48–57), so it is that the totalizing forms of control born of modern social praxis foster the illusion that lived human reality is coextensive with its pragmatic objectification. The practical implications of this illusion unfold with tragic effects in the surreptitious transformation of the hermeneutic processes that structure our everyday self-conceptions. Estranged from the lifeworld by the power of its own thinking, modernity builds for itself a "museum of horrors," in which we become artifacts on display (Merleau-Ponty, 1996:43–45). We should not imagine that this is solely a topic of abstruse philosophical reflection: for evidence to the contrary, one need look no further than to the matter-of-fact exclamations of the children who would tell me, "I've got ADHD," "I'm an at-risk youth," or otherwise recite the bestowals of diremption and abstraction. The broader effects of this dynamic of self-estrangement are well known: through a determinism of our own making, we lapse into a fatalistic view of our social conditions, imaging that they are largely fixed and beyond the contingencies of volition (compare Berger and Luckmann, 1966:88–92).

Bound by this false determinism, we attend to human crises by way of practical approaches that *invert* the moral imperative of response. Dirempted from the existential actuality of the lifeworld, modern bureaucracy and mainstream social science effectively respond to themselves, or at best to abstractions and fictions of their own making; and consistent with this logic, they demand that the "subjects" of their attention comport themselves to the predetermined goals of praxis. The subject reduced to the abstract "site" of problems or data is therefore compelled to answer for himself, rather than being approached from a stance of solicitude. This explains to a substantial degree why bureaucratic and mainstream social scientific praxis often tend to respond to complexity, ambiguity, and mystery as just so many forms of intransigence. Is it not telling that in both contexts, practitioners speak of methods for resolving circumstances that "defy" or "resist" control and explanation? Whether it is a police officer in the midst of an encounter on the street that exceeds the bounds of ready categorization, or a social scientist interpreting data that must be "fitted," "smoothed," or purged of "white noise," the process of facing these circumstances unfolds as a series of poetic creations, with all of the ethical and aesthetic ambiguity this entails. Whatever the confident self-descriptions of "method," the police officer and social scientist are poets, tenuously dwelling in the world that they often imagine lies wholly within their grasp.

By contrast, poetic creation at its most attentive understands the fallibility and contingency of its gesture. Consider the example of Jorge Luis Borges's studied engagement with the limits of authorial omniscience, expressed in the following brief passage from his short story, "The End": "A man in the habit of living in the present, as animals do, he [Recabarren] now looked up at the sky and reflected that the red ring around the moon was a sign of rain. A boy with Indian-like features (Recabarren's son, perhaps) opened the door a crack" (Borges, 1998:169). There is a remarkable shift in Borges's narrative from a position of omniscience that knows a character's inner thoughts, to a self-abnegation of the power to declare absolutely the identity of the boy who opened the door. With the juxtaposition of these two sentences, Borges calls attention to the contingencies shaping the author's role as a "privileged observer" vis-à-vis the text that he creates (compare Natanson, 1986:61–67). On the one hand, Borges knows that by authorial fiat, he can impose on the text whatever truths he wishes. On the other hand, however, by limiting himself to stating only a possibility of what *might* be true, and by graphically framing it in parentheses, Borges illuminates the ontological and ethical complexities intrinsic to the act of response, even as it occurs in seemingly straightforward relation to his "own" text and characters. Borges's parenthetical signification of contingency recalls the similar graphical configuration of the title of Pirandello's *Così è (se vi pare)* (see chapter 7). For Borges and Pirandello alike, the use of parentheses to signal contingency creates a phenomenological moment, by suspending the reader's natural attitude and inviting a moment of reflection that challenges our commonsense view of the relation among reader, author, and text.

This reflective moment assumes even greater consequence in its implication of the reader within the creative process. Like the viewer of Velázquez's *Las Meninas* or Manet's *A Bar at the Folies-Bergère,* the reader of Borges or Pirandello is denied the illusion and complacency that come with imagining oneself to be a "neutral observer." To observe is to respond and commit. The expression of this attitude par excellence is Rilke's admonition in the final line of "Archaic Torso of Apollo" (1987:3): "you must change your life." Rilke's imperative comes *in response* to the effulgent presence of the statue, which *demands* something of us as we stand before it. Rilke shatters the illusory control of objectification, and forces us to experience the presence of the statue in its overwhelming boundlessness: "for there is no place that does not see you" (Rilke, 1987:3).[1] In its pretended abdication of a stance, the act of indifference takes one. By suspending the possibility of standing over-against the world in a disinterested manner, Rilke or any other like-minded poet or artist is essentially asking, "How ought I respond to what is present before me, in such a way as to do justice to it?" The power of the aesthetic forms that occasion this question rests in their disclosure of the inseparability of the ethical and the ontological. They illuminate the horizon of the intentional relationship, and show how my being-present with other people and other things is always already an ethical relationship.

The imperative of response in the realm of aesthetic creation is thus at root fundamentally akin to its manifestation in the arena of social praxis, although doubtless with far less immediate ethical urgency. Any act of response, whatever its occasion, emerges out of the acknowledgment of a presence other than my own. When I respond to someone or something, I have already comported myself toward a person or situation in a determinate and meaningful way (see Heidegger, 2001:161–62). As a process that involves the creation of meaning, response is always a poetic act. We therefore cannot "escape" from poetry, nor can we circumvent the ethical imperative it entails: to create and attach meaning to that in the presence of which I find myself is to have taken a course of action that is irreducible to the axioms of pure method. Failing to see something as it truly is in itself is to "do it an injustice," and we cannot collapse this idea into the abstract technicalities of methodological insufficiency.

This is why the bureaucratic act of responding to a call cannot be the same as responding to a human being, whether in ontological, ethical, or practical terms. The answer or response that I *give* to a human being standing before me in the ineffable mystery of his or her existence is impossible to conflate with the delimited response to a call for service, which merely reduces the other person to a "subject" of whom a bureaucratically definable problem is "predicated." By the time they are dispatched as "calls for service," human predicaments have already undergone multiple levels of abstraction, setting into motion a complex poetic process that continues when officers arrive at the scene (see Manning, 1988). Officers find themselves in a situation where praxis has already "set the stage" for what must inexorably follow. In organizing its actions as a formal process of responding to calls, bureaucratic police praxis thus cannot do other than engage human beings as the abstract embodiment of specific problems.

Even so, and as several of the encounters in earlier chapters illustrated, the control of bureaucratic praxis over a given situation is never complete and always tenuous. Beyond the sorts of happenstance events that disrupt the flow of problematization, every police-citizen encounter contains a distinct moment with the potential to overwhelm the logic of an attenuated response, and calls us back to the fullness of human presence. The moment is created when officers conclude their involvement and "depart the scene" or "clear the call." Neither of these peculiar expressions from police jargon reveals what is more fundamentally entailed by this phenomenon, which unfolds in the physical moment that I call "walking away from people's problems." With its echoes of theatricality, "depart the scene" indicates how officers tend to frame and manage encounters as dramaturgical processes (see Manning, 1977), though gives no hint of what becomes of the "scene" after the police disengage and leave. To "clear the call" similarly falls silent with respect to what might remain behind in the wake of officers' departure. This phrase interweaves two meanings of "clear": first, as an act of departing or vacating; and second, as a rendering transparent. The official act of "clearing a call" inseparably links these meanings, insofar as the formal termination of a bureaucratic encounter signals to all involved that the mystery or confusion of the matter at hand has been made sufficiently "clear" to justify officers' leaving. To the extent that bureaucratic praxis reflects on what has been left behind or left unanswered, it only does so with respect to the probability or risk that a person might generate "more problems."

Understood phenomenologically, as an intentional act occasioned by a shift in comportment, ending an encounter and walking away creates more than a physical space. The act of walking away must therefore be seen as a poetic moment in its own right, one that overflows the nominal meaning ascribed to it by bureaucratic discourse. In operational terms, the act of departure signifies the formal decision that an officer's presence is no longer necessary, appropriate, or feasible. Yet, the decision can *reverberate* far more deeply, for the space opened by officers as they physically depart the scene harkens our attention to the reality that this void was already there from the moment the encounter began (see Bachelard, 1994:xvi). Beyond its delimitation by phrases such as "depart the scene" or "clear the call," the moment of walking away thus holds the potential to reveal the fullness and mystery of human presence that bureaucratic praxis effaces. The frustration, anger, sadness, or fatalistic resignation that officers constantly experience upon walking away from encounters constitutes at the very moment of departure a response to what bureaucracy could not answer. Walking away thus disrupts the logic of problematization by challenging the processes of abstraction and typification that are central to bureaucratic praxis. Suddenly, the aspects of human presence that were suppressed for practical purposes no longer remain obscured, and the wider ontological horizon of the encounter comes into view (see Natanson, 1986:55, and Schutz, 1962:42). Brought face to face with the transcendent reality of what one has otherwise subjected to abstraction forces a reaction that amounts to seeing the difference between human being as co-presence, rather than subjectivity (see Levinas, 1979:77–81.)

The tensions created by walking away exemplify the quandary of the bureaucratic paradox, which I first presented in the introduction to illustrate how the ontological foundations of modern bureaucracy militate against holistic approaches to human predicaments. As the reader may recall, the bureaucratic paradox occurs in the following way: although it is their official role that initially occasions their encounters with human beings in crisis, police officers' ability truly to ameliorate the predicament at hand often demands transcending the bureaucratic role, or, at the very least, making it subordinate to more holistic forms of engagement. Explained in phenomenological terms, the bureaucratic paradox reflects an ontological and ethical conflict between diverging intentional approaches to human presence. The presence of the human being before me can either be engaged holistically, as co-presence, or reductively, as reified subjectivity. The bureaucratic paradox centers on the conflicting possibilities for response that emerge and unfold in the poetry of social encounter. In the context of a police-citizen encounter, officers constantly arrive at the realization that their formal actions, oriented toward "responding to a problem," will come up short in comparison to potential efforts to respond holistically to the person, of whom the given problem is a remote abstraction.

The bureaucratic paradox functions as it does because of the existence of an interpretive horizon beyond the immediate one identified by the dictates and intentional stance of formal method. Despite the customary, unreflected efficiency with which bureaucratic policing and other forms of instrumental rational praxis "ideally" proceed, it is neither natural nor instinctive to stand face to face with a fellow human being and literally *look* upon him or her as being a "problem," for which one must then find a "solution." Responding in this way to the presence of another human being is no more inevitable than experiencing the natural world according to its scientific reification as an isotropic ensemble of "objects" or "events." Both responses, on the contrary, are grounded in processes of abstraction and typification, which enable what is manifestly present to be circumscribed with a view toward attaining specific predetermined goals. When the attainment of these goals provides the uncompromising basis for determining the predominant significance of the encounter, and not the other way around, the poetic act fails.

THE ONTOLOGICAL LIMITS OF REFORM

Understood as an intrinsic aspect of human existence, poetry emerges as the grounding ontological possibility for any creation of meaning, whatever its context. Heidegger explains poetry as the precondition for dwelling; Bachelard (1994:xvi) sees it as that which places us "on the threshold of being." Taken together, these ideas clarify an ontological notion of the poetic as that creative process by which the lifeworld always-already *comes to be meaningful* for us. To speak of the poetics of everyday life is to discern the universality of the poetic as a basic ontological feature of human existence. We are therefore mistaken if we presume to delimit poetry in a strictly formal sense, as a particular kind of literary discourse. We are equally wrong to exclude from a phenomenology of the poetic the innumerable intentional creations that occur in mundane moments such as police-citizen encounters. Any practical engagement with the lifeworld is *eo ipso* a poetic gesture. Structuring as it does the relationship between ontology and praxis, poetry is at once both boundlessly sublime and boundlessly powerful. For Heidegger (1971:222), poetry is that which allows us to experience death by taking the measure of our own finitude, and thus creating the possibility of existence as mortality. But as Wallace Stevens warns us in the final line of the unsettlingly titled "Poetry is a Destructive Force," "[i]t can kill a man" (1997:178). These reflections surely give pause: what kind of poetry is created by bureaucratic or mainstream social scientific praxis, and how might it ever be otherwise?

More specifically, is this poetry amenable to reimagination; and at the very least, is there a chance that in the manner of "aesthetic practitioners" such as Stevens, Borges, or Rilke, bureaucratic praxis might reflect critically on its presuppositional foundations, with a view toward consciously engaging its inherent ontological limitations? This is not to fatuously suggest that the contemplative attitude of the poet, painter, or writer is adaptable to the vicissitudes of the street. However, it is to suggest that the present structure of bureaucracy is neither inevitable nor eternal; and it is also to suggest that even when it does not see itself as such, an act of bureaucratic praxis is no less poetic than writing prose or dabbing paint on a canvas. There is no reason that bureaucratic practitioners in at least some circles could not engage in the sort of critical enterprise undertaken by the psychiatrists and psychologists who participated with Heidegger in the Zollikon Seminars. Even so, bureaucratic policing cannot remotely be expected to vault itself beyond the logic and practice of problematization. To do so would require that modern bureaucracy become its antithesis. For this decisive reason, let me suggest that the entire topic of "reforming" bureaucratic praxis, whether in the field of policing or anywhere else, is ultimately a subsidiary question of philosophical anthropology and political ontology. For if it is true that ontology informs and animates everyday social praxis, then it follows that substantively changing praxis demands nothing less than a reimagining of its presuppositional foundations.

This is why I shall make no pretense in these concluding pages of offering specific recommendations aimed at "reforming" bureaucratic policing. No degree of reform in the ordinary sense of the word will bring bureaucratic policing any closer to engaging the lived actuality of the crises and predicaments to which officers bear witness. However much official police transactions might be carried out with greater compassion, patience, or perspicacity, the animating ontology of bureaucratic problematization will endure unchanged, and hence the human beings encountered by bureaucrats will continue to be approached as "subjects" available for the manipulations of praxis. Whatever their noble intentions, attempts to reform bureaucratic praxis that leave this ontology unexamined and intact cannot go beyond the formulation of bromides and transitory innovations that may salve certain limited ideological and political concerns, but will leave unanswered the deeper question of how to reimagine the bureaucratic approach to human predicaments.

I can well anticipate the objection that in forbearing (or less generously, neglecting) to offer concrete recommendations for reform, I have constructed an analysis that is at best impractical, and at worst fatalistic. Perhaps at some level, it would have been convincing for me to repeat the sorts of familiar mantras that fill the final pages of so many books on policing: the police should be better trained and better educated; they should be more patient and compassionate; they should have keen ethical faculties that prevent them from lapsing into blind obedience, cruelty, and corruption; they should be representative of and more attuned to the demographic complexities of the communities they serve, and so forth. But to be frank, it is hardly necessary to engage in the kind of sustained philosophical critique that I have presented here in order to acknowledge the relative merit of these and other altogether reasonable means for improving the quality of bureaucratic policing. Yet, while I support efforts to reform the institution and practices of late-modern policing, I am even more strongly committed to showing how such efforts can only go so far by virtue of their present ontological horizon.

At this immediate juncture, as I write these words, there are people in crisis who urgently need the services of the police. The responding officers, bound as they are by the conditions of the present, will *make of these moments what they will*—a making that by now I hope the reader might agree with me is an act of poetic creation. Such are the imperfections and inherently tragic limitations of praxis, which as Hegel (1991:21–22) reminds us, is destined always to have to "jump here!" If there is any point to describing the irresolvable tensions of our immediate circumstances without the naïve pretense of their being soon changed, it lies in the hopeful gesture of trying to create the grounds for imagining otherwise. Hence, far from being a futile exercise, my hope in showing the fundamental inseparability of praxis and ontology is to remind theorists and practitioners alike of the historical and volitional contingencies that shape institutions such as policing. At the same time, neither as a veteran of policing nor as a social philosopher can I rationally presume that the daily unfolding of the bureaucratic paradox as I have described it here constitutes a state of affairs that is remotely amenable to rapid change. This is as much a statement about the epistemic and social structure of modernity as it is an assessment of the practical possibilities of police reform. Indeed, although I have made police-citizen encounters the nominal topic of this book, I am ultimately less interested in policing per se than in its complicity in and exemplification of various crises endemic to modern society.

Policing in its present form came into being as the result of world-historical changes definitive of modernity. In its existence as the peculiar institution charged with controlling the anonymous urban social space created by the rapid expansion of civil society, policing both enforces and perpetuates the dialectics to which it can trace its genealogy (compare Hegel, 1991:259–70). Policing is a response necessitated by the essential impersonality of modern social relations, yet it is itself bound by the same ontological precepts that gave rise to the society it is mandated to serve. As such, the abiding public demand for "personal service" and other reforms aimed at transcending the cold logic of bureaucratic action taken *sine ira ac studio* only serves to force the police into the same untenable strictures more generally characteristic of self-estranged modernity: "From a formal standpoint, everything is *outwardly* the reverse of what it is *for itself;* and, again, it is not in truth what it is for itself, but something else that it wants to be. . . ." (Hegel, 1977:317, emphasis original).

With this general critique in mind, it is worth revisiting the paradigm of reform exemplified by Paul Weiss's admirable call for police officers to act with constant, empathetic attunement to the complexities of human presence (see chapter 2). To repeat my earlier argument, the fateful limitation of such an ethical mandate is its ontological incommensurability with modern bureaucratic praxis. Even when bureaucratic organizations train and expect their agents to act empathetically, such institutionalized ethical precepts are never permitted to rise to a level where they will fundamentally subvert the logic of problematization. Furthermore, the actual risk of any such subversion is minimal, because as soon as empathy is reified and routinized as a formal expectation, its original intention and moral impulse are lost; and the ensuing behavior is reduced to an ironic gesture.[2] I do *not* at all mean to say that individual bureaucrats are incapable of acting with authentic concern and compassion; however, when they do so, their approach is ultimately attributable to an intentional stance that transcends the bureaucratic mandate. This impasse in the structure of methodic praxis is a further manifestation of the bureaucratic paradox, and may be defined as an *aporia of responsibility.*

THE APORIA OF RESPONSIBILITY

There is nothing new about the general conflict between holistic and bureaucratic or technical comportments toward people in crisis and need. Hegel (1991:332–34) already recognized in the early nineteenth century that the political and legal order particular to civil society (*bürgerliche Gesellschaft*) could not be secured with the type of arbitrary, irrational power exemplified by the medieval knight-errant. It is no accident that for Hegel, the antithesis of the knight-errant is the modern bureaucrat. Though the knight acts in a discretionary manner ultimately inspired by his own subjective purposes, the bureaucratic civil servant acts purely out of strict necessity, motivated neither by genuine duty nor right, and subsuming his individual will under the fulfillment of an official mandate that is a predetermined end in itself (Hegel, 1991:333). In calling attention to this radical distinction, Hegel substantially anticipates Weber's analysis of modern bureaucracy as a goal-driven form of administration undertaken *sine ira ac studio.* Further anticipating Weber, Hegel discerns that one of the ambivalent effects of bureaucratic administration is its reduction of ethical responsibility to the standards of formalized duty and "a job well done"

(Hegel, 1991:333). The implications of this logic taken to its extreme require no comment in light of modern history, including not least of all the terror of the French Revolution, which Hegel traces to the nihilistic reduction of value to contentless utility (1977:355–63). Less spectacularly, Hegel saw that modern bureaucratic administration by its nature entails a range of ethical quandaries, for which he proposed education and training as a "spiritual counterweight" (1991:335). He appreciated "the immediate and personal character" of that moment when bureaucratic intentions become actualized in the lives of citizens, and correctly argued that its outcome is driven as much by subjective feeling and sentiments as by formal content (Hegel, 1991:334).

In realizing how the administrative structure and logic of modern bureaucracy clash headlong with the emotional and moral complexities of citizens' lives, Hegel identifies a point of enduring conflict between the individual and the modern state. Even more important, he recognizes the origins of the crisis that develops when bureaucratic administration assumes roles previously filled by the organic institutions of family and community, which are continually subverted by the expansion of civil society (see Hegel, 1991:219–39). To a substantive degree, this is the same civilizational and practical milieu in which the police today find themselves encountering their fellow human beings (see Habermas, 1987b:305–12, and Foucault, 1997:409–17). The police officer imagined as a community problem solver or guardian-technocrat exemplifies the ideal of the expert functionary, who acts solely on the basis of "objective considerations" to substitute administrative authority for eroding social institutions and relations dependent on tradition, custom, and other "irrational presuppositions" (see Weber, 1978:975). As the demand for administrative artifice continues to expand apace with the disintegration of social relations created by the inordinate pressures of civil society, the police step into the breach, responding to the urgent and endless need to fix what we have destroyed (compare Hegel, 1991:220–39).[3]

Present-day policing operates within the deeply intimate realm of individual predicaments, yet does so according to a logic that demands the efficient imposition of abstract meanings at precisely those moments where they will never suffice. The poetry of policing is thus always destined to come up short. What ensues is an aporia of responsibility, driven by the irresolvable conflict between official praxis and the realization of its manifest insufficiency. The bureaucratic paradox exists because, however fleetingly or imperfectly, we are able to distinguish human presence as it holistically is from human presence as we abstractly treat it for the instrumental purpose of "solving problems." In taking the measure of the tragic flaws and limitations of bureaucratic praxis, we are ultimately judging its unresponsive quality in the actual *face* of individual existence. Whether at its best or worst, the act of responding is a poetic creation that emerges out of the *recognition* of one's fellow human beings. We also speak of a response as something that is *given* to the other person. It is in this entwinement of recognition and giving that the act of response reveals its elemental grounding in a relationship that is at once both ontological and ethical. As such, response always already implicates responsibility. But that is not all: the economy of response and responsibility defies circumscription by any formal principle or rule (see Derrida, 1995:3–11). Duty alone may suffice within a limited economy of official response; however, to act in genuine acknowledgment of the other person is to be open to the limitless possibilities of human encounter, and to be awestruck by the obligation that comes with participating in every such moment. It is here that poetry either fails or succeeds.

POSTSCRIPT

Imagining Otherwise

ROSE

On a December morning, I responded to an elementary school to deal with what the dispatcher described as an "out of control" eight-year-old girl. The school called police because "Rose" had become physically violent. Among other things, she had reportedly removed her jeans and tried to strangle herself with them. When I arrived at the school, the principal was waiting outside, and accompanied me across the campus to Rose's classroom. The principal explained that Rose was in a class for children diagnosed with severe behavioral and mental disorders. I asked the principal if a parent had been contacted and notified of Rose's current situation. She said that Rose's mother had been called, and had reluctantly agreed to come to the school, although only after being told that the police had also been summoned.

When we arrived at the classroom, the principal and I paused at the door. I explained to her that before I actually contacted Rose, I wanted to know more about her. "Do you have her packet?" I asked, seeking to understand bureaucratically what I would be facing in this encounter. The principal handed me a detailed report, which summarized Rose's diagnosed problems, followed by an intricate plan for "managing" her behavior. The report noted that Rose was unfocused, distracted, and given to extreme outbursts of anger. Although she was only eight years old, she was already taking antidepressants, instructions for the daily administration of which were also listed in the report. Rose's entire existence had effectively been distilled down to a neat grid and summary of risks, to be treated with correspondingly meticulous attention to minimizing liabilities and harms. As if to forestall my inquiring into why I had been called, the principal pointed out that one of the stipulations in the official "response plan" for Rose dictated that police be contacted if she became physically violent.

Upon entering the classroom, the principal, now accompanied by two teach-ers, led me to a secure "time-out" room, into which Rose had been locked. The room was essentially a small, padded cell, with cushioned walls and a carpeted floor, and inner dimensions of perhaps no more than eight by six feet. It was lit by recessed fluorescent fixtures, whose muted light only served further to flatten the already drab colors of the walls and carpet. The room had no win-dows, except for a small view port in the heavy, metal door. The door itself was secured with an electric lock, which was operated by a switch on the outside wall. I was struck by how little the room differed from a police station holding cell for prisoners.

One of the teachers opened the door to the room and let me in. Rose was sitting on the floor, with her back pressed up against the farthest wall. She was completely silent, with a gaze that seemed more lost and sad than angry. I sat down cross-legged on the floor beside her, and introduced myself. One of the teachers stood in the doorway, presumably, I surmised, to serve as an official witness in fulfillment of the school's liability regulations. I asked Rose why she was so upset. She explained to me that one of the teachers had tried to take away her necklace. I explained to Rose that the teacher was concerned that she would hurt herself. Rose looked at me placidly, but was obviously dissatisfied with my answer. I asked Rose if she wanted to hurt herself. She shook her head slowly, indicating that she did not.

As we spoke, another teacher appeared at the door of the "time-out" room, and came inside. She was carrying a small paper pill cup and a foil packet of fruit juice, of the kind that children carry in their school lunches. The teacher leaned over and held out the pill cup and juice. "Here, honey," she said to Rose, "take your pill." In silence, Rose dutifully took the pill cup and packet of juice. She pierced the packet with its accompanying little straw, and swallowed the pill. I found this ritual utterly astonishing.

As I sat watching Rose, I noticed how chilly the room was. Rose was not wearing her pants, which one of the teachers had taken from her after she had tried to wrap them around her neck. "Aren't you cold?" I asked Rose. She said that she was. I had the teacher retrieve Rose's jeans. She put them back on, and promised me that she would be a "good girl." "I think she'll be fine now," said the principal. "She was much worse before you showed up," added one of the teachers. I stood up, and exited the "time-out" room. I stopped to chat with the principal. We discussed Rose's home life. The principal said that there was no evidence of anything that would rise to the legal standards of child abuse or neglect. "Her mother just doesn't want to deal with her," explained the principal. There was no problem. I walked back to my patrol car, and drove away.

Of the many striking aspects of this encounter, three bear particular mention: first, all of the people whom I met at the school that day seemed to care deeply about Rose and obviously felt bad for her. Their compassion and professionalism are indubitable; yet, in the end, they accomplished little. This is because, to note the second striking aspect of the encounter, all of the efforts ostensibly intended to assist Rose became consumed in the process of their own rituals of self-perpetuation and self-legitimation. Nowhere is this better exemplified than in "the surveillance of surveillance," in which the bureaucratic agent of the school watched over me, the bureaucratic agent of the criminal justice system, who, ironically, had been summoned precisely because the school could not physically touch Rose. Not trusting its own agents, or, at the very least, wishing to place the liability for "handling" Rose on other shoulders, the school followed the logic expressed in Bittner's notion of "calling the cops."

In the third striking aspect of this encounter, once I arrived at the school and approached Rose, I found that there was, in fact, "no problem," at least insofar as the police bureaucracy was concerned. She was made the subject of problematization, but no problem could be found: she had not committed a crime; and even if she had, she was too young to be held culpable. She was not suicidal. Finally, although the indifference demonstrated by Rose's mother was contemptible, it was not criminal.

At the age of eight, Rose had already begun to undergo an ontological transformation, and had already been approached many times as an "object" that the criminal justice system and other bureaucratic networks will increasingly subject to processes of surveillance, measurement, prediction, and control. The effects and results of these various operations will be gauged, in turn, by academic research. Moreover, the bureaucratic practitioners and their academic interpreters will likely never recognize, let alone question, the ontological presuppositions they unknowingly share. As this dialectic advances, the practical objectifications of Rose will attain a level of further abstraction by becoming research data. This "objectification of objectification" will eventually be reinscribed in subsequent social praxis, in the form of new policies and procedures that the research will recommend for "handling" or "managing" Rose and children like her. All of the people who encounter Rose—police officers, social workers, teachers, mental health professionals, and others—for whom she is an object to be approached deftly with their confident, technical expertise, will interpret her presence in terms of what they *know* she *really* is. And so on. All the while, Rose will grow older. Barring an essential transformation of her circumstances, it seems all but inevitable that she will have more encounters with the police; and, it may fairly be surmised, a "problem" will eventually be found. The challenge facing all who would be a part of this process is to imagine otherwise.

NOTES

Introduction

1. See chapter 3 for a complete discussion of the poetic aspect of ordinary life.

2. To anticipate what I will discuss in chapter 1, the reader should construe "intentional" in the full phenomenological sense of the word.

3. For other examples, see David Jones (1986), Wayne Morrison (1995), Richard Quinney (2000), and Bruce Arrigo and Christopher Williams (2006).

4. For several related critiques of bureaucratic praxis, see Laurence Tribe (1972), Mark Sagoff (1981, 1986), and John Gillroy and Maurice Wade (1992).

5. For additional remarks on Heidegger's relevance for criminology, see Richard Quinney (2000:97 and 102) and Wayne Morrison (1995:349–52).

6. The term *Dasein* literally means "here-being," or "there-being" (*Da* + *Sein*). Although in normal German usage *Dasein* refers to existence in general, Heidegger uses the word specifically to refer to the kind of existence unique to human beings. For Heidegger, human being is the only kind of being whose very existence is intrinsically meaningful to itself. In this regard, he saw in the word *Dasein* a term that precisely expresses the condition of human being as a mode of existence that always already grasps the fact of its "being-here," or "being-there." More about the concept of *Dasein* follows below in chapter 1.

7. Compare Gabriel Marcel's notion of a "metasociological" perspective (2001:I, 197), which takes up existential foundations of human action that are otherwise overlooked by mainstream sociology. From this perspective, ordinary social dynamics come to be seen as a "particular expression of the mystery of being" (2001:I, 197).

8. Compare Kenneth Stikkers's comments (1980:3) in his introduction to Max Scheler's *Problems of a Sociology of Knowledge.* Stikkers is critical of descriptive sociology that purports to be phenomenological when, in fact, it fails to engage phenomenology with rigor, and thereby results in a hodgepodge of "subjective biases and prejudices." "In general," remarks Stikkers, "these misguided efforts lack any sort of reductive method—which is the heart of any genuine phenomenology—for leading to legitimate phenomenological insights into essences and separating these insights from unfounded assertions. All this has been to the dismay of the more empirical, scientific sociologists—and rightly so—and to the chagrin and detriment of legitimate and more rigorous phenomenology" (p. 3).

9. See Hans-Georg Gadamer's characterization of philosophical hermeneutics in *Truth and Method,* namely, that it is not "a methodology of the human sciences, but an attempt to understand what the human sciences truly are, beyond their method-

ological self-consciousness, and what connects them with the totality of our experience of world" (Gadamer, 1989:xxiii).

Chapter 1: Approaching Human Beings as Problems

1. Readers interested in a more thorough overview of phenomenology may wish to begin with any one of several core works, including Husserl (1960) and (1970), Zaner and Ihde (1973), Spiegelberg (1982), Moran (2000), and Solomon (2001).

2. For a detailed, accessible explanation of the concept of "lifeworld," see Husserl (1970:103–89).

3. The abbreviated discussion of intentionality presented here passes over long-standing debates in philosophy about this extremely complicated idea. The concept of intentionality dates back to medieval philosophy, though its incorporation into the phenomenological tradition is usually identified with the work of Brentano. For further general discussion of intentionality, see Heidegger (1982a), Spiegelberg (1982), and Moran (2000).

4. On this point, it is helpful to consider Husserl's concept of the "horizon-structure" of experience and its relation to the potential knowledge (*Mitwissen*) and fore-knowledge (*Vorwissen*) that shapes its meaning to consciousness: "For us the world is always a world in which cognition in the most diverse ways has already done its work. Thus it is not open to doubt that there is no experience, in the simple and primary sense of an experience of things, which, grasping a thing for the first time and bringing cognition to bear on it, does not already 'know' more about the thing than is in this cognition alone" (Husserl, 1973:32).

5. See Heidegger (1996, esp. pp. 107–22) for a sustained discussion of his concept of being-in-the-world; and compare Merleau-Ponty (1948). Merleau-Ponty's concept of "incarnated spirit" finds a lucid summation on p. 148: " . . . *nous ne sommes pas esprit et corps, conscience en face du monde, mais esprit incarné, être-au-monde.*" ["We are not spirit and body, conscience facing the world, but incarnated spirit, being-in-the-world," emphasis in original.]

6. For an overview of the concept of the *epoché*, see Husserl (1982:xix, 5–7, 33–34, and esp. 51). See, also, Husserl (1970:121–47). For further helpful comments, see Moran (2000:146–52).

7. For further elaboration of the intersecting historical development of criminology and modern social administration, see Johnston and Shearing (2003), Garland (2001 and 1985), Duguid (2000), Nelken (1994), Rose (1990), Cohen (1985), and Foucault (1980b).

8. Hegel's *Philosophy of Right* (1820/1991) stands as the decisive, inaugural analysis of the relationship among the modern state, civil society, and civic/juridical administration. In his *Critique of Hegel's Philosophy of Right* (1843/1970), Marx regarded bureaucracy as the objectification of the spirit of the modern state, and considered how bureaucratic praxis becomes a "hierarchy of knowledge" (p. 47). Marx also lays a key part of the foundation for subsequent critiques of instrumental rationality by

drawing attention to the equivalence of bureaucracy's formal ends with its content (pp. 43–48). Nietzsche's critiques of modernity in *Untimely Meditations* (1873–76/1997), *Will to Power* (1901/1967), *Thus Spake Zarathustra* (1883–85/1974), *The Gay Science* (1887/1974), and *Beyond Good and Evil* (1886/1989) touch varyingly on the rationalization of sociopolitical and ethical life, and were especially important in the development of Weber's theories of disenchantment. For discussion of bureaucracy and the Frankfurt School, see Arato and Gebhardt (1982) and Marcuse (1964).

9. On the general relation between modernization and bureaucratization, see Habermas (1987b). For further consideration of Weber's analysis of bureaucracy, the reader may wish to consult Schluchter (1981), Scaff (1988), and Horowitz and Maley (1994).

10. See Berger and Luckmann (1966), Habermas (1984, 1987a, 1987b), and Giddens (1990).

11. On this point, see Bauman (1990) and MacIntyre (1977).

12. Given Nietzsche's influence on Weber, it is interesting to compare Nietzsche's use of the phrase *sine ira ac studio* (1994:86) within the context of his criticism of philosophical speculation as a potential manifestation of the ascetic ideal: "If we draw up a list of the particular drives and virtues of the philosopher—his drive to doubt, his drive to deny, his drive to prevaricate (his 'ephetic' drive), his drive to analyze, his drive to research, investigate, dare, his drive to compare and counter-balance, his will to neutrality and objectivity, his will to every *sine ira et studio*—: surely we realize that all these ran counter to the primary demands of morality and conscience for the longest period of time?"

13. For Foucault's own conception of his relation to Weber, see the interview reprinted in Baynes, et al. (1987:100–117). The original French text of the interview appears in Perrot (1980). For further analysis of Weber's relation to Foucault, see Susan Hekman's essay in Horowitz and Maley (1994).

14. For key sources on the relation between Heidegger and Foucault, see Dreyfus and Rabinow (1982), Milchman and Rosenberg (2003), and Dreyfus (1989).

15. There is a direct relation between this kind of social interaction and the self-interested interactions of atomistic individuals in the marketplace. The latter finds its most famous summation in Adam Smith's words: "[i]t is not from the benevolence of the butcher, the brewer, or the baker, that we expect our dinner, but from their regard to their own interest. We address ourselves not to their humanity but to their self-love, and never talk to them of our own necessities but of their advantages. Nobody but a beggar chuses to depend chiefly upon the benevolence of his fellow-citizen" (1776/1976:18).

16. As David Carr notes in his English translation of Husserl's *Crisis*, *Sinnesveräusserlichung* literally means "externalization of meaning," "but with the sense of rendering it superficial, separating it from its origin"(Husserl, 1970:44n). The mathematization of the lifeworld is a truly decisive moment, which revolutionizes thinking about the entirety of cosmic and natural order; however, this very quality originates out of an "emptying of meaning."

17. The original German text appears in *Vorträge und Aufsätze* (Heidegger, 2000:25), and reads as follows: "*Ihre Art des Vorstellens stellt der Natur als einem berechenbaren Kräftezusammenhang nach. Die neuzeitliche Physik ist nicht deshalb Experimentalphysik, weil sie Apparaturen zur Befragung der Natur ansetzt, sondern umgekehrt: weil die Physik, und zwar schon als reine Theorie, die Natur daraufhin stellt, sich als einem vorausberechenbaren Zusammenhang von Kräften darzustellen, deshalb wird das Experiment bestellt, nämlich zur Befragung, ob sich die so gestellte Natur und wie sie sich meldet*" [emphasis added]. (compare Ricoeur, 1970:30)

18. The core of Heidegger's description is as follows: "Saying what it is for is not simply naming something, but what is named is understood *as* that *as* which what is in question is to be taken. What is disclosed in understanding, what is understood is always already accessible in such a way that in it its 'as what' can be explicitly delineated. The 'as' constitutes the structure of the explicitness of what is understood; it constitutes the interpretation" (Heidegger, 1996:139–40).

19. Quoted in Habermas (1987a:133); the original passage appears in Heidegger (1982b:28). According to Habermas, "Heidegger's originality consists in delineating the modern dominance of the subject in terms of a history of metaphysics. Descartes stands in the center, as it were, between Protagoras and Nietzsche. He conceives of the subjectivity of self-consciousness as the absolutely certain foundation of representation; being as a whole is thereby transformed into the subjective world of represented objects, and truth is transformed into subjective certitude" (Habermas, 1987a:134).

20. This idea of speculation should be understood in a literal sense: on the basis of its supposed self-certainty, the subject becomes the mirror in which the world and self are reflected. This paradoxical relationship lies at the center of Foucault's analysis of the modern subject, and is precisely what he sees illustrated in Diego Velázquez's painting *Las Meninas,* a provocative reading of which opens *The Order of Things* (1970). Habermas sees a similar connection between Cartesian metaphysics and the speculative quality of knowledge: "In modernity, therefore, religious life, state, and society as well as science, morality, and art are transformed into just so many embodiments of the principle of subjectivity. Its structure is grasped as such in philosophy, namely, as abstract subjectivity in Descartes' *cogito ergo sum* and in the form of absolute self-consciousness in Kant. It is the structure of a self-relating, knowing subject, which bends back upon itself as object, in order to grasp itself as in a mirror image—literally in a speculative way" (Habermas, 1987a:18). Habermas goes on to note the significance of Foucault's reading of *Las Meninas* (p. 259). For further discussion, see Dreyfus and Rabinow (1982:26–32).

21. See note 4, p. 202.

22. For further elaboration of this point, see Heidegger, 1982a:169–70; 1996, and 2001, and also Kockelmans (1972). See especially p. 9, where Kockelmans explains the concept of the "ecstatic" nature of human being: "[e]k-sistent man is essentially a worldly reality that 'gives meaning.' As *lumen naturale* man originates meaning in

everything he does—in every act, in his concern for his fellow men and things, in his work, thought and games" (p. 9).

23. To fully understand Schutz's argument, it is essential to construe time and space in a primordial, existential sense, rather than in the abstract sense of mathematized space-time.

24. Compare Aristotle's distinction in the *Metaphysics* (Book A, 980a25–981b1) between mere sensation (*aiesthesis*) and experience (*empereia*).

Chapter 2: The Common Roots of Bureaucratic Policing and Mainstream Social Science

1. Status comprises social status (race, class, etc.) and situational status (neighbor, stranger, witness, suspect, victim, etc.) (Black and Riess, 1967:8–9).

2. Conversely, officers frequently question the motives of friendly and polite citizens, whom they suspect of trying to curry favor.

3. Compare Heidegger's notion of "idle talk" (*Gerede*) in *Being and Time*.

4. It is worth noting that Reiss's research was based upon intricately detailed observation forms (reproduced in Black, 1980 and McCall, 1978), which use classificatory schemata that bear more than a passing resemblance to police incident report forms.

5. See, also, Skolnick (1966), Wilson (1968), Westley (1970), Sykes and Brent (1983), Bittner (1990), and Waddington (1999).

6. Though his topic is not policing, Katz's *Seductions of Crime* (1988) takes a broadly phenomenological approach worth mentioning here. Katz believes that whatever background factors and events precede a crime, none of them explains completely or adequately that singular moment when a human being commits a criminal act (1988:4). Seduction, compulsion—the indeterminate "push and pull" of human existence—constitute a foreground for action that defies the kind of rational reduction and circumscription attempted by mainstream criminology (Katz, 1988:4). By focusing on the "foreground" of human action and the "ontological validity of passion" (1988:8), Katz presents an experiential interpretation of crime, which preserves (and indeed amplifies!) the capacity for moral revulsion, while nonetheless striving for a more fundamental understanding of crime's "authentic attractions" (1988:8).

7. Quoted in Werthman and Piliavin (1966:75). The original source is David Matza, "The Selection of Deviants," unpublished manuscript, no date, p. 32. Werthman and Piliavin continue: "both [the police officer and sociologist] must classify individuals by searching for the particular actors that best fit a set of social or legal categories, and both are typically forced to use indicators of the categories of persons they are looking for because true referents rarely exist. In brief, then, patrolmen are forced to operate like social scientists. In order to locate 'suspicious persons' they must use indicators, each with a specific but by no means perfect probability of leading them either to the discovery or prevention of a crime" (p. 75).

Chapter 3: The Approach of a Phenomenological Aesthetics of Encounter

1. Consistent with this argument, Heidegger (2001:101) notes how the word "method" (*Methode*) carries the meaning of being a "way toward" something. As he points out (2001:101), the word "method" derives from the Greek *methodos*, which combines *meta* ("among," "with," "beside," "after," "from here to there," "toward something") with *hodos* ("way").

2. On this point, it is essential to consider Husserl's analysis (1970) of the Galilean "mathematization of nature" (p. 23). Husserl argues that despite all that technology and science claim to have accomplished, the world itself remains what is always has been; and the manipulation of that world ultimately amounts to "[n]othing but *prediction* extended to infinity" (1970:51, italics original).

3. See Dostoyevsky (1880/1958). My description of Lise is a composite of material from Book 2, chapter 3, "Devout Peasant Women" (1958:49–57); Book 2, chapter 4, "A Lady of Little Faith" (1958:57–65); and especially from Book 11, chapter 3, "The Little She-Devil" (1958:680–87).

4. This line is also used by Martin Heidegger as the title for his essay, "Poetically Man Dwells . . ." (1971b:213–29). The German text is entitled "*Dichterisch wohnet der Mensch*," and appears in *Vorträge und Aufsätze* (Heidegger, 2000). The full text of the poem may be found in Hölderlin's *Sämtliche Gedichte*, Bd. 1 (Hamburg: Athenäum Verlag, 1970), pp. 462–64. For a dual English-German text, see *Hölderlin: Selected Verse*, ed. Michael Hamburger (London: Anvil Press, 1986), pp. 245–48.

5. See Proust (1981:50–51). The passage reads in part: "But when from a long-distant past nothing subsists, after the people are dead, after the things are broken and scattered, taste and smell alone, more fragile but more enduring, more unsubstantial, more persistent, more faithful, remain poised a long time, like souls, remembering, waiting, hoping, amid the ruins of all the rest; and bear unflinchingly, in the tiny and almost impalpable drop of their essence, the vast structure of recollection [*l'edifice immense du souvenir*]." In describing memory using the metaphor of a building, Proust engages the same theme of dwelling that Bachelard, Heidegger, and Hölderlin invoke in their work. Original French text published as *A la recherche du temps perdu*, vol. 1, *Du cote de chez Swann* (Paris: Gallimard, 1954), pp. 68–69.

6. Examples of such research include Charlesworth (2000), Ihde (1976, 1986), Kersten (1997), Psathas (1995), and Zaner (1981, 1988). In addition to such studies, my approach of a phenomenological aesthetics of encounter also draws upon the strong tradition within anthropology and ethnography of research and theoretical perspectives that acknowledge a substantial influence by phenomenology and hermeneutics, notably the work of Clifford (1986, 1988), Crapanzano (1992), Denzin (1997, 2001), Douglas (1985), Dwyer (1982), Geertz (1980, 1983), Marcus and Fischer (1986), Rabinowitz (1977), Tedlock and Mannheim (1995), Van Maanen (1988), and Webster (1982). Much of their respective research undertakes careful consideration

of the philosophical dimensions of fieldwork, and in so doing represents attentively detailed methodological self-reflections of a kind that has yet to develop a sustained presence in mainstream criminology.

7. Compare Tellenbach's similar argument (1967:261) in the opening words of his phenomenological interpretation of Dostoyevsky's portrayal of epilepsy in the character of Prince Myshkin in *The Idiot*: " . . . in the great novels of Dostoyevsky the phenomenon of the human is so fundamentally open to contemplation that the differences of race, religion, nationality and language moves into the realm of chance."

8. My point intentionally draws on Heidegger's concept of *Gelassenheit* ("letting be"). See Heidegger (1966).

9. Joachim Gasquet, *Cézanne*, quoted by Merleau-Ponty (1964a:159). Compare Jauss's comments (1989:217–18): "The poetic word distinguishes itself from merely informative or goal-oriented utterance to the degree that it can free itself from the intention of its producer, and, at the same time, *from the pragmatic limits of the specific speech context*" (emphasis mine).

Chapter 4: Domestic Violence Encounters: The Eye of the Painter and the Eye of the Police

1. In developing the analysis of the gaze that follows here, and in using it to interpret my encounter with Melissa, I benefited substantially from suggestions and comments from Jack Katz.

2. Obviously, this description does not apply to cases in which police officers have a prior substantive familiarity with someone as the result of previous encounters. Interactions with such "regulars" can assume a personal dimension, which, however insignificantly, begins to dissolve the anonymity of the encounter. On this point, see Natanson (1986) and Bittner (1990:30–62).

3. The policy manuals for the majority of North American police departments usually include a continuum that dictates standards for the use of force according to a progressive scale of proportionate escalation and de-escalation. Although their intermediary steps vary substantially, virtually all continua begin with "officer presence" or "verbal persuasion" and end with deadly force.

4. The term "grounding concepts" as I use it here is essentially identical to Heidegger's notion of *Grundbegriffe*, which Stambaugh translates as "fundamental concepts." According to Heidegger (1996:8), "[f]undamental concepts [*Grundbegriffe*] are determinations in which the area of knowledge underlying all the thematic objects of a science attains an understanding that precedes and guides all positive investigation."

5. For two intricately detailed (and opposing) analyses of the problem of the mirror, see the exchange between de Duve and Elkins (1998).

6. For further discussion of this point, see Hanson, 1977; Boime, 1996; and Herbert, 1996. Compare Clark, 1984 and de Duve, 1998.

7. To be sure, more positive characterizations have also been offered: one contemporary critic, Paul Alexis, described the barmaid as "a beautiful girl, truly alive, truly modern, truly 'Folies-Bergère. . . . '" (Quoted in Clark, 1984:239)

8. On this point, compare Heidegger's concept of *Gelassenheit* (1966).

9. However politically desirable or socially or morally necessary it might be to assist the victim of a crime, this is not the formal, primary concern of the modern state's criminal justice system, inasmuch as the "real" victim of crime is held to be the state itself, rather than the individual person. In light of this point, it might therefore be argued that subsuming the significance of the victim's predicament, both practically and symbolically, within the legal and administrative needs of the state, is altogether logical, and explains in substantial measure why a bureaucratic institution such as the police acts as it does at the operational level. Following this line of thought, it is helpful to compare Foucault's analysis (1977:13) of the logic of modern executions, which are intended to punish an abstract "juridical subject."

10. In a similar vein, people with extensive criminal histories may view their own victimization with greater equanimity than the average citizen. To note one example, I recall a young man who had spent much of his time as a teenager breaking into cars and stealing them. When he filed a police report to document an incident in which someone had broken into *his* car, he volunteered with a wry smile, "oh well, I deserve it; I guess it's bad karma."

11. The term *schwankendes* also connotes the idea of wavering, oscillation, or indecision. *Gleichgewicht* literally means "same weight." It can be used to express either physical or mental balance, as well as concepts such as a strategic or political balance of power. In his translation of Klee's *Notebooks* (1961), Manheim renders *schwankendes Gleichgewicht* as "oscillating balance." "Unstable Equilibrium" is also the title of one of Klee's watercolors. As with *Senecio*, it was painted in 1922. See Klee (1961:389–91), Jaffé (1972:25), and Kudielka (2002:82–85).

12. Together with the vast body of artwork that he created, Klee's prolific intellectual reflections on the nature of art form a legacy that has resonated widely in phenomenological circles. See, especially, Merleau-Ponty's essay, "Eye and Mind" (1964a), Grohmann (1967), Young (2001), Pöggeler (2002), and Kudielka and Riley (2002). Phenomenological interest in Klee's work is substantially motivated by the self-conscious, intellectually refined approach that Klee took toward the act of painting. For Klee, the painter's canvas is not merely a passive, inert space that receives paint, but a "responsive" surface (Greenberg, 1961:195).

13. The poetic quality of Klee's work is no accident. His own accomplishments as a poet are well respected; furthermore, his close friendship with Rilke is also widely reckoned to have had a manifest influence upon his art. See, also, Merleau-Ponty, 1964a:181 and 1996:55–61.

14. Compare Klee's use elsewhere of an "infinity sign" in *Small Room in Venice* (1933, cat. no. 447).

Chapter 5: The Policing of Childhood:
Encounters with Juveniles

1. Abstraction becomes violent when it results in the effacement or obliteration of the being that it represents. The idea of "the violence of abstraction" finds a general approximation in Hegel's concept of laceration (*Zerrissenheit*), which describes the tearing or uprooting of human beings from the actuality of their individual, cultural, and historical nature. See Hegel, (1807/1977:294); and compare Marcuse's concepts of "the mutilated whole" and *déchirement ontologique* ("ontological laceration") (1960:xi).

2. Friedrich Nietzsche, *Complete Works* (18 vols.), ed. Oscar Levy, vol. 5, *Thoughts Out of Season*, trans. Adrian Collins (New York: Russell and Russell, 1964), pp. 136–37, translation modified. The original German text reads, *so wild, so verschlossen, so farblos, so hoffnungslos ist alles* (Nietzsche, 1966:312).

3. The fairly recent advent of patrol car computers has led to the development of the practice among arrestees of craning their necks from the back seat to glean information about themselves from the screen. People who are frequently contacted by the police have learned that what appears on the screen often shapes the outcome of their contacts with officers.

4. Bakhtin is keenly aware of the phenomenological implications of his analysis. See 1984:270, and compare Bakhtin's *Toward a Philosophy of the Act* (Austin: University of Texas Press, 1993). For two examples of phenomenological readings of Dostoyevsky's work, see Silverman (1985) and Tellenbach (1970).

5. Dostoyevsky's use of the term a "certain percentage" is an intentional allusion to Adolphe Quetelet's social statistics and their promulgation in mid-nineteenth-century Russia through the writings of A. Wagner (see Dostoyevsky, 1991:636n; and Murav, 1992:55–59). The passage may therefore be read as a conscious attempt by Dostoyevsky to articulate two conflicting interpretive registers for analyzing social conditions, which, considered with respect to the present book, closely approximate my distinction between co-presence and intersubjectivity (see Jackson, 1974 and Murav, 1992:55–59).

6. There are several definitive English-language studies of Musil's work in general, and of *The Man Without Qualities* in particular: see Peters (1978), Luft (1980), Hickman (1984), Payne (1988), and Rogowski (1994).

7. The complete German sentence reads, *Sie schenkt ihm den Augenblick des Seins, des Spanungsgleichgewichtes zwischen innen und außen, zwischen Zerpreßtwerden und Zerfliegen.* There is a marked similarity between Musil's idea of a tense or suspended balance (*Spanungsgleichgewichtes*) and Klee's concept of "unstable equilibrium" (*schwankendes Gleichgewicht*), which I discussed in the second half of chapter 4.

Chapter 6: The Poetry of Policing: Encounters from the Drug War

1. The qualification is significant. Under United States constitutional law, an officer initiating a social contact has no more authority than an ordinary citizen. Hence, if a person chooses to walk away, the officer is legally powerless to continue the encounter. Still, it doubtless remains true that virtually any initiation of contact by a police officer involves an unspoken degree of coercion or intimidation, even if unintended. When new officers learn how to initiate social contacts, they are taught to "manage" their presence in a way that conveys the voluntary nature of the encounter. This is usually presented less as an ethical concern than as a practical matter of learning to avoid actions the courts will view as unlawful seizures.

2. Of course, police officers also make social contacts for purely personal reasons having nothing at all to do with the discharge of bureaucratically mandated duties. Social contacts of this kind are not immediately relevant to my discussion, because they are not undertaken with the goal of fulfilling officially recognized legal or organizational objectives.

3. For a general overview of Rilke's relation to phenomenology, see Kaufmann (1980) and Holthusen (1980). Heidegger's essay "What Are Poets For?" (1971a:89–142) probably remains the most influential phenomenologically oriented reading of Rilke. See, also, Heidegger's use of Rilke to illuminate the limitations of modern epistemological presuppositions (1982a).

4. See Rilke's *Letters on Cézanne* (1985).

5. Stevens actually uses the term "decreation," which he takes from Simone Weil's *La Pensateur et La Grâce* (Stevens, 1997:750).

6. For critical analysis of the poem, see Baird (1968), Hines (1975:138–212), and Bloom (1977:167–218).

7. See Stevens's earlier work, "A High-Toned Old Christian Woman," in which he wrote, "Poetry is the supreme fiction, madame" (Stevens, 1997:47).

8. Brogan (1986) and Parker (1983), in turn, have specifically applied Derrida's analysis of metaphor to Stevens's poetry.

9. Stevens's idea of the "celestial ennui of apartments" invites a close comparison with Rilke's description of a house in *The Notebooks of Malte Laurids Brigge*, which Heidegger quotes at length in *The Basic Problems of Phenomenology* (1982:171–73) as an example of a poetic disclosure of being-in-the-world. Stevens had a keen interest in the relation between spatiality and modernity and its manifestation in the nature of modern dwellings. The significance for Stevens of the "celestial ennui of apartments" becomes even clearer in light of his comments upon the alienating quality of modern urban life: "The way we live and the way we work alike cast us out on reality. If fifty private homes were to be built in New York this year, it would be a phenomenon. We no longer live in homes but in housing projects and this is so whether the project is literally a project or a club, a dormitory, a camp or an apartment in River House" (Stevens, 1997:653).

10. For another phenomenologically oriented treatment of this theme, compare Stevens's "Thirteen Ways of Looking at a Blackbird" (1997:74–76).

Chapter 7: Encountering the Drama of Mental and Emotional Crisis

1. "Cocked and locked" refers to a gun that is loaded and has a live round of ammunition in the firing chamber.

2. Here the process of bureaucratic problematization combined with self-interest in avoiding what my colleagues and I perceived as a needless risk of injury. It is worth noting that all of the officers involved in the encounter with Philip were seasoned veterans, a fact doubtless reflected in our collective disinclination to provoke a hostile confrontation or resort to physical force.

3. Krysinski (1989) draws important parallels between Pirandello's and the work of Musil, Bakhtin, and Dostoyevsky. It is further worth noting Pirandello's formative influence upon the development of French existential drama, for which Sartre gave him direct credit (see Bishop, 1967). There is also a direct connection between Pirandello and Gabriel Marcel, in the form of commentaries that Marcel wrote on Pirandello's plays. See Marcel (1984).

4. Pirandello's biographers make much of the fact that he refused to have his wife institutionalized, but instead kept her at home. See Cambon (1967:2), Oliver (1979:40), and Esslin (1991:263–64).

5. Other English renditions of the title include, *Right You Are (If You Think So)*, (DiGaetani, 1991); *It Is So (If You Think So)* (Paolucci, 1974); *That's the Way Things Are—If They Seem That Way to You* (Oliver, 1979); *Right You Are If You Think You Are;* and *Thus It Is (If It Seems So to You)* (Matthaei, 1973). Bassanese (1997:46) offers helpful observations about the meaning of the play's title, remarking that the first part suggests a firm sense of truth, which the second part immediately places in doubt or contingency by establishing the contingency of this "truth" upon the mind that holds it do be so. In its apparent intentions and obvious effect, Pirandello's use of parentheses to set off the second half of the title is strongly suggestive of the phenomenological notion of bracketing.

6. For an especially detailed and helpful synopsis of the play, see Oliver (1979:22–46).

7. There are some marked similarities between Pirandello's complete description of Signor Ponza and Lombrosian characterizations of atavistic criminals: Signor Ponza "is a short, dark, thickset man of almost threatening appearance, dressed all in black. He has black, thick hair on a low forehead, and a black moustache. He continually makes fists of his hands and speaks with a force that borders on violence. From time to time he wipes the sweat from his face with a black-edged handkerchief. When he speaks, his eyes are hard, fixed, and sinister" (Pirandello 2000:16).

8. Marcel regarded his plays as more important than his philosophical writings, largely because he thought they offered a more authentic and realistic portrayal of the human condition (Schilpp and Hahn, 1984:xv, and MacKinnon, in Schilpp and Hahn, 1984:573–80). In fact, he maintained that his philosophical work could not be understood properly apart from his dramatic writing (see, for example, 1973b:230). Marcel (1965:15) says of his orientation toward his characters: "But the real reason why I have always taken such pains to make my characters as like as possible to ourselves, to make them live in the same world and share the same experiences, is because by so doing what may be called the metaphysical design became more clear to me, and because I felt that by substituting symbols or intellectual puppets or even legendary figures for the creatures of flesh and blood whose fate I was trying to determine, I would weaken or betray that design."

9. See Belay (1980:3)—"*Elle [sa pensée] vise à dégager des essences, à retrouver l'universel dans le singulier. Elle adopte spontanément le méthode phénoménologique.*"

10. "*Drame et métaphysique sont deux formes d'une même activité, deux moments de la même elucidation de l'existence.*"

11. "*Mieux vaudrait encore voir dans la Méditation un effort pour élucider une certaine situation fondamentale qui dans le drame et présentée dans sa complexité brute et en dernière analyse inextricable. Le Monde cassé n'est pas non plus une 'pièce à problème'; ce serait bien plutôt un mystère*" (Marcel, 1933:8–9). Compare Paul Ricoeur's remarks to Marcel: "Everything in your work comes from drama and everything leads to it as well, especially the analysis of those experiences you have called 'ontological,' insofar as these experiences have a dramatic character" (Marcel, 1973b:230).

12. "*[U]n mystère c'est un problème qui empiète sur ses proposes données, qui les envahit et se dépasse par la même comme simple problème*" (Marcel, 1933:267).

13. These phenomena are also common effects of psychotropic medications. In my encounter with Robert, part of the bureaucratically defined "problem" was that in leaving the hospital, he had stopped receiving and taking his prescribed medications. This is a frequent situation in police encounters with people diagnosed with psychiatric disorders, who are often described by officers or medical personnel as "being off their meds."

14. Compare Marcel's comments (1965:21), written in the context of explaining the meaning of *The Votive Candle:* "We are infinitely more than we are aware of wishing to be and sometimes, strange to say, the apparently most conscious and clear-headed are, in fact, most ignorant of their inner selves."

15. "*Mais c'est quelqu'un qui ne s'efface jamais . . . quis vous empêche d'exister.*"

16. This dialogue is especially interesting in light of Marcel's discussion elsewhere of the moral quandaries facing a doctor who must tell a patient that he is mortally ill. See Marcel (1973b:91–93).

Chapter 8: Policing Death:
The Problematization of Mortality

1. See Eliade, 1959:185–87; Sudnow, 1967; Giddens, 1991:161–62; and Walter, 1996.

2. It is interesting to note the tensions that can occur between emergency medical personnel and police officers, which arise out of their diverging official interests at death scenes. Police officers often voice frustration that paramedics have "contaminated" or "screwed up" a crime scene in the frenzied activity of trying to save a life. As a practical matter, of course, there is often little that can be done to avoid the disturbing or destruction of forensic evidence on a body, or in the immediate area around it.

3. In other instances, where death has just occurred (for example, in "CPR in progress" calls) I have frequently seen paramedics prolong lifesaving efforts beyond what is clinically warranted, in order to give watching loved ones a feeling that "something is being done" to save a life that is already lost. This practice is especially common when the death is wholly unexpected, or virtually any time when it involves a baby or child. Beyond the comfort that it offers to family members, clinically superfluous resuscitation efforts also provide an unofficially recognized though invaluable opportunity for emergency medical crews to gain "real life" practice in skills such as airway intubation, defibrillation, and intravenous drug administration. Considerations that are far less pragmatic also arise: in some situations, lifesavers become emotionally invested in their actions, which can cause arguments in the field about when to terminate resuscitation efforts.

4. Officers' first question to their colleagues upon entering a death scene is rarely, "Does it look bad?" but, "Does it stink?" Relief will often be expressed that a body has been found shortly after death, before it has had time to decompose and begin emitting the horrific odor of putrefaction.

5. The symbolic significance and ironic value of the card game take on added meaning when the reader learns later in the story that Ivan Ilych himself had a fondness for playing cards.

6. This humor has its unwritten limits, which are rarely transgressed. Nowhere is this more apparent than at scenes involving the death of an infant or preadolescent child, or what officers regard as the "death of an innocent." For example, the death of a sixteen-year-old girl, who had been a passenger in a car that collided head-on with another vehicle, was viewed as an absolute tragedy that was clearly off-limits as a topic of jokes. On the other hand, another traffic collision involving the death of an adult male, who was driving alone, and was killed when he sped out of control and completely demolished his sports car when it left the roadway, was not similarly immune from humor. Unlike the girl, the man was regarded by officers at the scene as a "smart ass" who had paid the ultimate price for his arrogance and poor judgment. Another example of this sentiment, which further shows that youth by itself does not necessarily suffice as a guarantee of immunity from macabre jokes,

was the death of a fourteen-year-old boy, who was shot while trying to break into a drug dealer's house. Some officers saw this incident as worthy of wry comments and ironic humor, because the boy, who had been heavily involved in gang activity, was deemed in a number of circles to have gotten his just deserts.

7. My attitude, which is fairly typical for a veteran officer, can prove extremely dangerous. In another situation, I responded to a reported suicide by gunshot, in which a woman called police after her husband had shot himself in the head with a pistol. Upon making a tactical entry to the house, two colleagues and I found the man lying on a sofa with a large pool of blood beneath his head. More blood, along with fragments of scalp and hair, were spattered across the wall behind him. The man still had the pistol in his hand. Presuming the man to be dead, I drew near for a closer look, and was startled when the man suddenly gave a loud, guttural snort. I glanced back and forth for a moment between the man's face and the gun, and then quickly snatched the gun from his hand. The subsequent investigation determined that the man had flinched at the moment he pulled the trigger, which caused the bullet to enter between his scalp and cranium, where it followed a trajectory across the top of his head that severed numerous blood vessels but never actually penetrated his skull. The man suffered a major scalp laceration, though was otherwise uninjured. I have often recounted this incident to new officers as a cautionary tale about the potentially fatal danger of prejudging situations, and of taking appearances at face value.

8. The practice of covering dead bodies to avoid looking at them or to avoid their unsettling "gaze" is often portrayed in popular representations of policing. However, in operational reality, covering bodies has become increasingly discouraged in recent years, because sheets or blankets can contaminate a body with fibers, and otherwise destroy delicate forensic evidence. Emergency medical crews, who previously covered people after declaring them dead, have now been widely trained not to do so. The more common practice now is to surround a body with a tarpaulin barricade.

Chapter 9: Policing and the Poetics of Everyday Life

1. Compare this to the gaze of Manet's barmaid, which we are unable to meet, regardless of our position vis-à-vis the canvas.

2. To continue my appeal to Hegel's critique of self-alienated spirit, it could well be said that the studiously performative quality of community policing and similar ideological fictions of police reform closely mirror the tragicomic spectacle of *Lui* in *Rameau's Nephew*, which Hegel memorably cites in the *Phenomenology of Spirit* (1977:318).

3. The growth of privatized policing and other similar developments in the neoliberal governance of risk and insecurity adds a complex dimension to this situation that is crucial to note, although I cannot give it due consideration here.

BIBLIOGRAPHY

Arato, Andrew, and Eike Gebhart, eds. *The Essential Frankfurt School Reader*. New York: Continuum, 1982.

Aristotle. *Complete Works of Aristotle: The Revised Oxford Translation*. Edited by Jonathan Barnes. 2 vols. Bollingen Series. Princeton, N.J.: Princeton University Press, 1984.

Armstrong, Carol. "Counter, Mirror, Maid: Some Infra-thin Notes on *A Bar at the Folies-Bergère*." In *12 Views of Manet's Bar*. Edited by Bradford G. Collins. 25–46. Princeton, N.J.: Princeton University Press, 1996.

Arrigo, Bruce, and Christopher Williams, eds. *Philosophy, Crime, and Criminology*. Champaign: University of Illinois Press, 2006.

Bachelard, Gaston. *La psychanalyse du feu*. Paris: Éditions Gallimard, 1949.

———. *La poétique de l'espace*. 4ième ed. Paris: Presses Universitaires de France, 1964.

———. *l'air et les songes: essai sur l'imagination du mouvement*. Paris: Librairie José Corti, 1990.

———. *The Poetics of Space*. Translated by Maria Jolas. Boston: Beacon Press, 1994.

Baird, James. *The Dome and the Rock: Structure in the Poetry of Wallace Stevens*. Baltimore: Johns Hopkins University Press, 1968.

Bakhtin, Mikhail. *Problems of Dostoevsky's Poetics*. Edited and translated by Caryl Emerson. Minneapolis: University of Minnesota Press, 1984.

———. *Art and Answerability: Early Essays by M.M. Bakhtin*. Edited by Michael Holmquist and Vadim Liapunov. Austin: University of Texas Press, 1990.

———. *Toward a Philosophy of the Act*. Translated by Vadim Liapunov. Edited by Vadim Liapunov and Michael Holquist. Austin: University of Texas Press, 1993.

Banton, Michael. *The Policeman in the Community*. London: Tavistock, 1964.

Bassanese, Fiora. *Understanding Luigi Pirandello*. Columbia: University of South Carolina Press, 1997.

Bassnett-McGuire, Susan. *Luigi Pirandello*. London: Macmillan, 1983.

Bataille, Georges. *Manet*. New York: Skira, 1955.

Baudelaire, Charles. *The Painter of Modern Life and Other Essays*. Translated and edited by Jonathan Mayne. London: Phaidon Press, 1964.

Bauman, Zygmunt. *Modernity and the Holocaust*. Ithaca, N.Y.: Cornell University Press, 1989.

———. "Effacing the Face: On the Social Management of Moral Proximity." *Theory, Culture & Society* 7 (1990): 5–38.

Baumann, Bedrich. "G. H. Mead and L. Pirandello: Some Parallels Between the Theoretical & Artistic Representation of the Social Role Concept." *Social Research* 34 (1967): 563–607.

Baynes, Kenneth. "Questions of Method: An Interview with Michel Foucault." In *After Philosophy: End or Transformation?* Edited by Kenneth Baynes, James Bohman, and Thomas McCarthy. 100–117. Cambridge, Mass.: MIT Press, 1987.

Belay, Marcel. *La Mort dans le Théatre de Gabriel Marcel.* Paris: Librairie Philosophique J. Vrin, 1980.

Benjamin, Walter. *Illuminations.* Edited by Hannah Arendt. New York: Schocken Books, 1968.

Berger, Peter. "The Problem of Multiple Realities: Alfred Schutz and Robert Musil." In *Phenomenology and Social Reality: Essays in Memory of Alfred Schutz.* Edited by Maurice Natanson. 213–33. The Hague: Martinus Nijhoff, 1970.

Berger, Peter, and Thomas Luckmann. *The Social Construction of Reality: A Treatise in the Sociology of Knowledge.* New York: Doubleday, 1966.

Bernstein, George. "Pirandello: The Sicilian Experience." In *A Companion to Pirandello Studies.* Edited by John L. DiGaetani. Westport, Conn.: Greenwood Press, 1991.

Bernstein, Jay. *The Fate of Art: Aesthetic Alienation from Kant to Derrida and Adorno.* University Park: Pennsylvania State University Press, 1992.

Bianchi, Herman. *Position and Subject Matter of Criminology: Inquiry Concerning Theoretical Criminology.* Amsterdam: North Holland Publishing Co, 1956. Reprinted by Xerox University Microfilms, Ann Arbor, Mich., 1975.

Bien, Joseph, ed. *Phenomenology and the Social Sciences: A Dialogue.* The Hague: Martinus Nijhof, 1978.

Bishop, Thomas. "Pirandello's Influence on French Drama." In *Pirandello: A Collection of Critical Essays.* Edited by Glauco Cambon. 43–56. Englewood Cliffs, N.J.: Prentice-Hall, 1967.

Bittner, Egon. "The Police on Skid Row: A Study of Peacekeeping." *American Sociological Review* 32:5 (1967a): 699–715.

———. "Police Discretion in Emergency Apprehension of Mentally Ill Persons." *Social Problems* 14:3 (1967b): 278–92.

———. "Police Research and Police Work." In *The Police Yearbook, 1973.* Gaithersburg, Md.: International Association of Chiefs of Police, 1973.

———. "Florence Nightingale in Pursuit of Willie Sutton: A Theory of the Police." In *The Potential for Reform of the Criminal Justice System.* Edited by Herbert Jacob. Thousand Oaks, Calif.: Sage, 1974.

———. *The Functions of the Police in Modern Society.* Cambridge, Mass.: Oelgeschlager, Gunn and Hain, 1980.

———. *Aspects of Police Work.* Boston: Northeastern University Press, 1990.

Black, Donald. *The Manners and Customs of the Police.* New York: Academic Press, 1980.

Black, Donald, and Albert Reiss. *Patterns of Behavior in Police and Citizen Transactions.*

Studies in Crime and Law Enforcement in Major Metropolitan Areas. Volume 2. Washington, D.C.: United States Government Printing Office, 1967.

Bloom, Harold. *Wallace Stevens: The Poems of Our Climate*. Ithaca, N.Y.: Cornell University Press, 1977.

———, ed. *Leo Tolstoy*. New York: Chelsea House, 1986.

Boime, Albert. "Manet's *A Bar at the Folies-Bergère* as an Allegory of Nostalgia." In *12 Views of Manet's Bar*. Edited by Bradford G. Collins. 47–70. Princeton, N.J.: Princeton University Press, 1996.

Bordua, David. *The Police: Six Sociological Essays*. New York: Wiley, 1966.

Borges, Jorge-Luis. *Collected Fictions*. Translated by Andrew Hurley. London: Penguin Books, 1998.

Braithwaite, John. *Crime, Shame, and Reintegration*. Cambridge, Eng.: Cambridge University Press, 1989.

———. "The New Regulatory State and the Transformation of Criminology." In *Criminology and Social Theory*. Edited by David Garland and Richard Sparks. 47–69. Oxford, Eng.: Clarendon Press, 2000.

Brewer, Neil, and Carlene Wilson. *Psychology and Policing*. Hillsdale, N.J.: Lawrence Erlbaum, 1995.

Brodsky, Patricia. *Rainer Maria Rilke*. Boston: Twayne, 1988.

Brogan, Jacqueline. *Stevens and Simile: A Theory of Language*. Princeton, N.J.: Princeton University Press, 1986.

Brombert, Beth. *Edouard Manet: Rebel in a Frock Coat*. New York: Little Brown, 1996.

Brown, William. "It Means Something: The Ghosts of War." In *Storytelling Sociology: Narrative as Sociology*. Edited by Ronald J. Berger and Richard Quinney. 245–63. Boulder, Colo.: Lynne Rienner, 2005.

Buber, Martin. *I and Thou*. Translated by Ronald G. Smith. Edinburgh: T & T Clark, 1958.

Burke, Kenneth. *Grammar of Motives*. New York: Prentice-Hall, 1945.

———. *Permanence and Change: An Anatomy of Purpose*. Berkeley: University of California Press, 1954.

Burnett, David. "Klee as Senecio: Self-Portraits 1908–1922." *Art International* 21:6 (1977): 12–18.

Cachin, Françoise. *Manet: The Influence of the Modern*. New York: Harry Abrams, 1995.

Cambon, Glauco, ed. *Pirandello: A Collection of Critical Essays*. Englewood Cliffs, N.J.: Prentice-Hall, 1967.

Cassirer, Ernst. *The Philosophy of the Enlightenment*. Translated by Fritz C. A. Koelln and James P. Pettegrove. Princeton, N.J.: Princeton University Press, 1951.

Certeau, Michel de. *The Practice of Everyday Life*. Translated by Steven Rendall. Berkeley: University of California Press, 1984.

Charlesworth, Simon. *A Phenomenology of Working Class Experience*. Cambridge, Eng.: Cambridge University Press, 2000.

Chekhov, Anton. *The Essential Tales of Chekhov.* Edited by Richard Ford. Hopewell, N.J.: Ecco Press, 1998.

———. *Early Short Stories, 1883–1888.* Edited by Shelby Foote. Translated by Constance Garnet. New York: Modern Library, 1999a.

———. *Later Short Stories, 1888–1903.* Edited by Shelby Foote. Translated by Constance Garnet. New York: Modern Library, 1999b.

Chenu, Joseph. *Le théâtre de Gabriel Marcel et sa signification métaphysique.* Paris: Editions Montaigne, 1948.

Chrétien, Jean-Louis. *The Call and the Response.* Translated by Anne Davenport. New York: Fordham University Press, 2004.

Christian, Reginald. *Tolstoy: A Critical Introduction.* Cambridge, Eng.: Cambridge University Press, 1969.

Christie, Nils. *Crime Control as Industry: Towards Gulags, Western Style.* 3rd rev. ed. London: Routledge, 2000.

Chudakov, Aleksandr. *Chekhov's Poetics.* Translated by Edwina Cruise and Donald Dragt. Ann Arbor, Mich.: Ardis, 1983.

———. "Dr. Chekhov: A Biographical Essay (29 January 1860–15 July 1904)." In *The Cambridge Companion to Chekhov.* Edited by Vera Gottlieb and Paul Allain. 3–16. Cambridge, Eng.: Cambridge University Press, 2000.

Cicourel, Aaron. *The Social Organization of Juvenile Justice.* New York: Wiley, 1968.

Clark, Timothy J. *The Painting of Modern Life: Paris in the Art of Manet and His Followers.* Princeton: Princeton University Press, 1984.

Clifford, James. *Writing Culture: the Poetics and Politics of Ethnography.* Berkeley: University of California Press, 1986.

———. *The Predicament of Culture: Twentieth-Century Ethnography.* Cambridge, Mass.: Harvard University Press, 1988.

Clyman, Toby, ed. *A Chekhov Companion.* Westport, Conn.: Greenwood Press, 1985.

Cohen, Stanley. *Visions of Control.* New York: Polity Press, 1985.

Collins, Bradford, ed. *12 Views of Manet's Bar.* Princeton, N.J.: Princeton University Press, 1996.

Costa, Gustavo. "Pirandello and Philosophy." In *A Companion to Pirandello Studies.* Edited by John L. DiGaetani. 3–16. Westport, Conn.: Greenwood Press, 1991.

Crapanzano, Vincent. *Hermes' Dilemma & Hamlet's Desire: On the Epistemology of Interpretation.* Cambridge, Mass.: Harvard University Press, 1992.

Croce, Benedetto. *Aesthetic As Science of Expression and General Linguistic.* Translated by Douglas Ainslie. New York: Noonday Press, 1922.

Cumming, Elaine, Ian Cumming, and Laura Edell. "Policeman as Philosopher, Guide and Friend." *Social Problems* 12 (1965): 276–86.

Davignon, Rene. *Le mal chez Gabriel Marcel.* Montréal: Éditions Bellarmin, 1985.

Denzin, Norman. *Interpretive Ethnography: Ethnographic Practices for the 21st Century.* Thousand Oaks, Calif.: Sage, 1997.

———. *Interpretive Interactionism.* 2nd edition. Thousand Oaks, Calif.: Sage, 2001.

Derrida, Jacques. "White Mythology: Metaphor in the Text of Philosophy." *New Literary History* 6 (1975): 5–74.

———. *On the Name.* Translated by David Wood, John P. Leavey Jr., and Ian McLeod. Stanford, Calif.: Stanford University Press, 1995.

DiGaetani, John, ed. *A Companion to Pirandello Studies.* New York: Greenwood Press, 1991.

Dostoyevsky, Fyodor. *The Brothers Karamazov.* Translated by David Magarshack. London: Penguin Classics, 1958.

———. *Crime and Punishment.* Translated by David McDuff. London: Penguin Classics, 1991.

Douglas, Jack. *Understanding Everyday Life.* Chicago: Aldine Publishing, 1970.

———. *Creative Interviewing.* Beverly Hills, Calif.: Sage, 1985.

Douglas, Jack, and John Johnson. *Existential Sociology.* Cambridge, Eng.: Cambridge University Press, 1977.

Downes, David, and Paul Rock. *Understanding Deviance: A Guide to the Sociology of Crime and Rule Breaking.* Oxford, Eng.: Oxford University Press, 2003.

Dreyfus, Hubert. "On the Ordering of Things: Being and Power in Heidegger and Foucault." *Southern Journal of Philosophy* 28 (1989): 83–96.

Dreyfus, Hubert, and Paul Rabinow. *Michel Foucault: Beyond Structuralism and Hermeneutics.* 2nd edition. Chicago: University of Chicago Press, 1983.

Düchting, Hajo. *Edouard Manet: Images of Parisian Life.* Munich: Prestel, 1995.

Dufrenne, Mikel. *The Phenomenology of Aesthetic Experience.* Translated by Edward Casey. Evanston, Ill.: Northwestern University Press, 1973.

Duguid, Stephen. *Can Prisons Work? The Prisoner as Object and Subject in Modern Corrections.* Toronto: University of Toronto Press, 2000.

Duve, Thierry de. "How Manet's A Bar at the Folies-Bergère Is Constructed." *Critical Inquiry* 25 (1998): 136–68 and 181–89.

———. "On Incarnation: Sylvia Blocher's 'l'announce amoureuse' and Edouard Manet's 'A Bar at the Folies-Bergère.'" In *Time and the Image.* Edited by Carolyn Gill. 100–121. Manchester, Eng.: Manchester University Press, 2000.

Dwyer, Kevin. *Moroccan Dialogues: Anthropology in Question.* Baltimore: Johns Hopkins University Press, 1982.

Eagleton, Terry. *Sweet Violence: The Idea of the Tragic.* Oxford, Eng.: Blackwell, 2003.

Eeckhout, Bart. "Of Pears, Oxen, and Mediterranean Landscapes: Three Stevensian Ways of (Un)Painting the Thing Itself." *Wallace Stevens Journal* 23:1 (1999): 3–26.

Eliade, Mircea. *The Sacred and the Profane: The Nature of Religion.* Translated by Willard Trask. New York: Harcourt, 1987.

Elkins, James. "Critical Response." *Critical Inquiry* 25 (1998): 169–80.

Ericson, Richard. *Reproducing Order: A Study of Police Patrol Work.* Toronto: University of Toronto Press, 1982.

Esslin, Martin. "A Hole Torn in a Paper Sky: Pirandello and Modern Drama." In *A

Companion to Pirandello Studies. Edited by John DiGaetani. New York: Greenwood Press, 1991.

Ferrell, Jeff, Wayne Morrison, and Keith Hayward, eds. *Cultural Criminology Unleashed.* London: Cavendish, 2004.

Flam, Jack. "Looking into the Abyss: The Poetics of Manet's 'A Bar at the Folies-Bergère.'" In *12 Views of Manet's Bar.* Edited by Bradford G. Collins. 164–88. Princeton, N.J.: Princeton University Press, 1996.

Foucault, Michel. *The Order of Things: An Archaeology of the Human Sciences.* New York: Random House, 1970.

———. *Discipline and Punish: The Birth of the Prison.* Translated by Alan Sheridan. New York: Random House, 1977.

———. *The History of Sexuality. Volume 1: An Introduction.* Translated by Robert Hurley. New York: Vintage, 1980a.

———. *Power/Knowledge: Selected Interviews and Other Writings, 1972–1977.* New York: Pantheon, 1980b.

———. "Questions of Method: An Interview with Michel Foucault." In *After Philosophy: End or Transformation?* Edited by K. Baynes, J. Bohman, and T. McCarthy. 100–117. Cambridge, Mass.: MIT Press, 1987.

———. *The Hermeneutics of the Subject: Lectures at the College de France 1981–1982.* Edited by Frédéric Gros. Translated by Graham Burchell. New York: Picador, 2005.

Gadamer, Hans-Georg. *Philosophical Hermeneutics.* Translated by David Linge. Berkeley: University of California Press, 1976.

———. *Reason in the Age of Science.* Translated by Frederick G. Lawrence. Cambridge, Mass.: MIT Press, 1981.

———. *The Relevance of the Beautiful and Other Essays.* Edited by Robert Bernasconi. Cambridge, Eng.: Cambridge University Press, 1986.

———. *Truth and Method.* 2nd revised edition. Translated by Joel Weinsheimer and Donald G. Marshall. New York: Crossroad, 1989.

———. *Heidegger's Ways.* Translated by John W. Stanley. Albany: State University of New York Press, 1994.

Garfinkel, Harold. *Studies in Ethnomethodology.* Englewood Cliffs, N.J.: Prentice-Hall, 1967.

———. "The Origin of the Term 'Ethnomethodology.'" In *Proceedings of the Purdue Symposium on Ethnomethodology.* Edited by R. Hill and K. Crittenden. 5–11. Lafayette, Ind.: Purdue University Press, 1968.

Garland, David. *Punishment & Welfare: A History of Penal Strategies.* Aldershot, Eng.: Gower Publishing Company, 1985.

———. *The Culture of Control: Crime and Social Order in Contemporary Society.* Oxford, Eng.: Oxford University Press, 2001.

Garland, David, and Richard Sparks, eds. *Criminology and Social Theory.* London: Oxford University Press, 2000.

Gasquet, Joachim. *Cézanne.* Translated by Christopher Pemberton. London: Thames and Hudson, 1991.

Geertz, Clifford. "Blurred Genres." *American Scholar* 49:2 (1980): 165–79.

———. *Local Knowledge: Further Essays in Interpretive Ethnography*. New York: Basic Books, 1983.

Gellner, Ernest. "Ethnomethodology: the Re-enchantment Industry or the Californian Way of Subjectivity." *Philosophy of the Social Sciences* 5 (1975): 431–50.

Giddens, Anthony. *The Consequences of Modernity*. Stanford, Calif.: Stanford University Press, 1990.

———. *Modernity and Self-Identity: Self and Society in the Late Modern Age*. Stanford, Calif.: Stanford University Press, 1991.

Gillroy, John, and Maurice Wade, eds. *The Moral Dimensions of Public Policy Choice*. Pittsburgh: University of Pittsburgh Press, 1992.

Goethe, Johann Wolfgang von. *Maximen und Reflexionen: A Selection*. Edited and translated by R. H. Stephenson. Glasgow: Scottish Papers in Germanic Studies, 1986.

Goffman, Erving. *Encounters: Two Studies in the Sociology of Interaction*. Indianapolis, Ind.: Bobbs-Merrill, 1961.

———. *Interaction Ritual: Essays on Face-to-Face Behavior*. New York: Pantheon, 1967.

———. *Frame Analysis: An Essay on the Organization of Experience*. Cambridge, Mass.: Harvard University Press, 1974.

Goldstein, Herman. *Policing a Free Society*. Cambridge, Mass.: Ballinger Publishing, 1977.

Greenberg, Clement. *Art and Culture: Critical Essays*. Boston: Beacon Press, 1961.

Greenwood, Edward. *Tolstoy: The Comprehensive Vision*. New York: St. Martin's Press, 1975.

Grohmann, Will. *Paul Klee*. New York: Harry Abrams, 1967.

Gurwitsch, Aron. *Human Encounters in the Social World*. Pittsburgh: Duquesne University Press, 1979.

Habermas, Jürgen. *Legitimation Crisis*. Translated by Thomas McCarthy. Boston: Beacon Press, 1975.

———. *The Theory of Communicative Action*. Volume 1, *Reason and the Rationalization of Society*. Boston: Beacon Press, 1984.

———. *The Philosophical Discourses of Modernity: Twelve Lectures*. Translated by F. Lawrence. Cambridge, Mass.: MIT Press, 1987a.

———. *The Theory of Communicative Action*. Volume 2, *Lifeworld and System: A Critique of Functionalist Reason*. Boston: Beacon Press, 1987b.

Hahn, Beverly. *Chekhov: A Study of the Major Stories and Plays*. Cambridge, Eng.: Cambridge University Press, 1977.

Hall, Douglas. *Klee*. London: Phaidon Press, 1992.

Hanley, Katherine. *Dramatic Approaches to Creative Fidelity: A Study in the Theater of Gabriel Marcel (1889–1973)*. Lanham, Md.: University Press of America, 1987.

Hanson, Anne. *Manet and the Modern Tradition*. New Haven, Conn.: Yale University Press, 1977.

Hegel, Georg W. F. *Phenomenology of Spirit*. Translated by A. V. Miller. Oxford, Eng.: Oxford University Press, 1977.

————. *Elements of the Philosophy of Right*. Translated by H. B. Nisbet. Cambridge, Eng.: Cambridge University Press, 1991.

Heidegger, Martin. *Discourse on Thinking: A Translation of Gelassenheit*. Translated by John M. Anderson and E. Hans Freund. New York: Harper and Row, 1966.

————. *Poetry, Language, Thought*. Translated by Albert Hofstadter. New York: Harper and Row, 1971a.

————."The Origin of the Work of Art." In *Poetry, Language, Thought*. Translated by Albert Hofstadter. New York: Harper and Row, 1971b.

————. *The Basic Problems of Phenomenology*. Translated by Albert Hofstadter. Bloomington: Indiana University Press, 1982a.

————. *Nietzsche*. Volume 4, *Nihilism*. Translated by Frank Capuzzi. New York: Harper and Row, 1982b.

————. "The Question Concerning Technology." In *Basic Writings*, edited by David F. Krell. 307–41. New York: HarperCollins, 1993.

————. *Being and Time*. Translated by Joan Stambaugh. Albany: State University of New York Press, 1996.

————. *Vorträge und Aufsätze*. Frankfurt: Vittorio Klostermann, 2000.

————. *Zollikon Seminars: Protocols—Conversations—Letters*. Edited by Medard Boss. Translated by Franz Mayr and Richard Askay. Evanston, Ill.: Northwestern University Press, 2001.

Hekman, Susan. "Max Weber and Post-Positivist Social Theory." In *The Barbarism of Reason: Max Weber and the Twilight of Enlightenment*. Edited by Asher Horowitz and Terry Malley. 267–86. Toronto: University of Toronto Press, 1994.

Herbert, James. "Privilege and Illusion of the Real." In *12 Views of Manet's Bar*. Edited by Bradford G. Collins. 214–32. Princeton, N.J.: Princeton University Press, 1996.

Herbert, Steve. *Policing Space: Territoriality and the Los Angeles Police Department*. Minneapolis: University of Minnesota Press, 1997.

Herz, Denise. "Improving Police Encounters with Juveniles: Does Training Make a Difference?" *Justice Research and Policy* 3:2 (2001): 57–77.

Hickman, Hannah. *Robert Musil and the Culture of Vienna*. London: Croon Helm, 1984.

Hines, Thomas. *The Later Poetry of Wallace Stevens: Phenomenological Parallels with Husserl and Heidegger*. Lewisburg, Pa.: Bucknell University Press, 1975.

Hogg, Russell. "Crime, Criminology, and Government." In *The New Criminology Revisited*. Edited by Paul Walton and Jock Young. New York: St. Martin's Press, 1998.

Hogg, Russell, and Kerry Carrington, eds. *Critical Criminology: Issues, Debates, Challenges*. Cullompton, Eng.: Willan Publishing, 2002.

Holdaway, Simon, ed. *The British Police*. Thousand Oaks, Calif.: Sage, 1979.

————. "Discovering Structure: Studies of the British Police Occupational Culture." In *Police Research: Some Future Prospects*. Edited by Molly Weatheritt. Aldershot, Eng.: Avebury, 1989.

Hölderlin, Friedrich. *Sämtliche Gedichte.* Band 1. Hamburg: Athenäum Verlag, 1970.

———. *Hölderlin: Selected Verse.* Edited by Michael Hamburger. London: Anvil Press, 1986.

Holthusen, Hans. "The Poet and the Lion of Toledo." In *Rilke: The Alchemy of Alienation.* Edited by Frank Baron, Ernst Dick, and Warren Maurer. 29–46. Lawrence: Regents Press of Kansas, 1980.

Horkheimer, Max, and Theodor Adorno. *Dialectic of Enlightenment.* Translated by John Cumming. New York: Continuum, 1994.

Horowitz, Asher, and Terry Maley, eds. *The Barbarism of Reason: Max Weber and the Twilight of Enlightenment.* Toronto: University of Toronto Press, 1994.

Husserl, Edmund. *Cartesian Meditations: An Introduction to Phenomenology.* The Hague: Martinus Nijhoff, 1960.

———. *The Crisis of European Sciences and Transcendental Phenomenology: An Introduction to Phenomenological Philosophy.* Translated by David Carr. Evanston, Ill.: Northwestern University Press, 1970.

———. *Experience and Judgment: Investigations in a Genealogy of Logic.* Revised and edited by Ludwig Landgrebe. Translated by James S. Churchill and Karl Ameriks. Evanston, Ill.: Northwestern University Press, 1973.

———. *Ideas Pertaining to a Pure Phenomenology and to a Phenomenological Philosophy, First Book, General Introduction to a Pure Phenomenology.* Translated by F. Kersten. The Hague: Martinus Nijhoff, 1982.

Ihde, Don. *Experimental Phenomenology: An Introduction.* New York: Putnam, 1977.

Ingarden, Roman. *Ontology of the Work of Art.* Translated by Raymond Meyer. Athens: Ohio University Press, 1989.

Jackson, Robert, ed. *Twentieth Century Interpretations of Crime and Punishment: A Collection of Critical Essays.* Englewood Cliffs, N.J.: Prentice-Hall, 1974.

Jardí, Enric. *Paul Klee.* New York: Rizzoli International, 1990.

Jauss, Hans. *Aesthetic Experience and Literary Hermeneutics.* Minneapolis: University of Minnesota Press, 1982.

Jayne, Richard. *The Symbolism of Space and Motion in the Works of Rainer Maria Rilke.* Frankfurt: Athenäum Verlag, 1972.

Johnston, Les, and Clifford Shearing. *Governing Security: Explorations in Policing and Justice.* London: Routledge, 2003.

Jones, David. *History of Criminology: A Philosophical Perspective.* Westport, Conn.: Greenwood Press, 1986.

Jonsson, Stefan. *Subject Without Nation: Robert Musil and the History of Modern Identity.* Durham, N.C.: Duke University Press, 2000.

Jordan, Jim. *Paul Klee and Cubism.* Princeton, N.J.: Princeton University Press, 1984.

Kaelin, Eugene. *Art and Existence: A Phenomenological Aesthetics.* Lewisburg, Pa.: Bucknell University Press, 1970.

Kant, Immanuel. *Critique of Judgment.* Translated by J. H. Bernard. London: Macmillan, 1931.

Katz, Jack. *Seductions of Crime: Moral and Sensual Attractions in Doing Evil*. New York: Basic Books, 1988.

Kaufmann, Fritz. "Art and Phenomenology." In *Essays in Phenomenology*. Edited by Maurice Natanson. 144–56. The Hague: Martinus Nijhoff, 1966.

Kearney, Richard. *Poetics of Imagining: Modern to Post-Modern*. New York: Fordham University Press, 1998.

Kermode, Frank. "Dwelling Poetically in Connecticut." In *Wallace Stevens: A Celebration*. Edited by Frank Doggett and Robert Buttel. 256–73. Princeton, N.J.: Princeton University Press, 1980.

Klee, Paul. *The Thinking Eye: The Notebooks of Paul Klee*. Edited by Jürg Spiller. Translated by Ralph Manheim. New York: G. Wittenborn, 1961.

———. *The Diaries of Paul Klee, 1898–1918*. Berkeley: University of California Press, 1964.

———. *On Modern Art*. Translated by Paul Findlay. London: Faber & Faber, 1966.

Kockelmans, Joseph, ed. *On Heidegger and Language*. Evanston, Ill.: Northwestern University Press, 1972.

Krysinski, Wladimir. *La paradigme inquiet: Pirandello et la champ de la modernité*. Montreal: Les Éditions du Préambule, 1989.

Kudielka, Robert, and Bridget Riley. *Paul Klee: The Nature of Creation, Works 1914–1940*. London: Hayward Gallery, 2002.

Lakoff, George, and Mark Johnson. *Metaphors We Live By*. Chicago: University of Chicago Press, 1980.

Landsberg, Paul-Louis. "The Experience of Death." In *Essays in Phenomenology*. Edited by Maurice Natanson. 193–231. The Hague: Martinus Nijhoff, 1966.

Latour, Bruno. *We Have Never Been Modern*. Translated by Catherine Porter. Cambridge, Mass.: Harvard University Press, 1993.

Lazaron, Hilda. *Gabriel Marcel the Dramatist*. Gerrards Cross, Eng.: Colin Smythe, 1978.

Leo, Richard. "Police Scholarship for the Future: Resisting the Pull of the Policy Audience." *Law and Society Review* 30:4 (1996): 865–79.

Leppman, Wolfgang. *Rilke: A Life*. Translated by Russell Stockman. New York: Fromm International, 1984.

Lévi-Strauss, Claude. *The Raw and the Cooked*. Translated by John and Doreen Weightman. Chicago: University of Chicago Press, 1983.

Levinas, Emmanuel. *Totality and Infinity*. Translated by Alphonso Lingis. The Hague: Martinus Nijhoff, 1979.

———. *Entre Nous: On Thinking-of-the-Other*. Translated by Michael Smit and Barbara Harshav. New York: Columbia University Press, 1998.

Lieberman, Brian. "Ethical Issues in the Use of Confidential Informants for Narcotics Operations." *The Police Chief* 74:6 (2007): 62–66.

Lindgren, Sven-Åke. "Social Constructionism and Criminology: Traditions, Problems and Possibilities." *Journal of Scandinavian Studies in Criminology and Crime Prevention* 6:1 (2005): 4–22.

Loader, Ian. "Policing, Recognition, and Belonging." *Annals of the AAPSS* 605 (2006): 202–21.

Luft, David. *Robert Musil and the Crisis of European Culture*. Berkeley: University of California Press, 1980.

Luhmann, Niklas. *Essays on Self-Reference*. New York: Columbia University Press, 1990.

MacIntyre, Alasdair. "Utilitarianism and Cost-Benefit Analysis: An Essay on the Relevance of Moral Philosophy to Bureaucratic Theory." In *Values in the Electric Power Industry*. Edited by Kenneth Sayre. 217–37. Notre Dame, Ind. Notre Dame University Press, 1977.

MacKinnon, Donald. "Drama and Memory." In *The Philosophy of Gabriel Marcel*. Edited by Paul Schilpp and Lewis Hahn. 573–80. The Library of Living Philosophers, vol. XVII. La Salle, Ill.: Open Court, 1984.

McCall, George. *Observing the Law: Field Methods in the Study of Crime and the Criminal Justice System*. New York: Free Press, 1978.

Maguire, Mike, Rod Morgan, and Robert Reiner, eds. *The Oxford Handbook of Criminology*. 3rd edition. London: Oxford University Press, 2002.

Mandel, Siegfried. *Rainer Maria Rilke: The Poetic Instinct*. Carbondale, Ill.: Southern Illinois University Press, 1965.

Manning, Peter. *Police Work: The Social Organization of Policing*. Cambridge, Mass.: MIT Press, 1977.

———. *Symbolic Communication: Signifying Calls and the Police Response*. Cambridge, Mass.: MIT Press, 1988.

———. *Policing Contingencies*. Chicago: University of Chicago Press, 2003.

Marcel, Gabriel. *Le monde cassé (Piece en quatre actes) suivi de "Position et approaches concrètes du mystère ontologique."* Paris: Desclée de Brouwer, 1933.

———. *La Chapelle Ardente* (Piece en trois acts). Paris: La Table Rond, 1950.

———. *Homo Viator: Introduction to a Metaphysic of Hope*. Chicago: Henry Regnery, 1951.

———. *Man Against Mass Society*. Chicago: Henry Regnery, 1952.

———. *l'homme problématique*. Paris: Editions Montaigne, 1955.

———. *The Existential Background of Human Dignity*. Cambridge, Mass.: Harvard University Press, 1963.

———. *Three Plays*. New York: Hill and Wang, 1965.

———. *Searchings*. New York: Newman Press, 1967.

———. *Cinq pieces majeures*. Paris: Plon, 1973a.

———. *Tragic Wisdom and Beyond*. Translated by Stephen Jolin and Peter McCormick. Evanston, Ill: Northwestern University Press, 1973b.

———. *Il Problema Pirandelliano*. Padova, It.: Edizioni CEDAM, 1984.

———. *Gabriel Marcel's Perspectives on "The Broken World."* Translated by Katharine Rose Hanley. Milwaukee: Marquette University Press, 1998.

———. *The Mystery of Being*. 2 volumes. Volume I: *Reflection and Mystery*. Translated by G. S. Fraser. South Bend, Ind.: St. Augustine's Press, 2001.

———. *Awakenings: A Translation of Marcel's Autobiography, "En chemin, vers quel éveil?"* Translated by Peter S. Rogers. Milwaukee: Marquette University Press, 2002a.

———. *Creative Fidelity.* Translated by Robert Rosthal. New York: Fordham University Press, 2002b.

Marcus, George, and Michael Fischer. *Anthropology as Cultural Critique: An Experimental Moment in the Human Sciences.* Chicago: University of Chicago Press, 1986.

Marcuse, Herbert. *Reason and Revolution: Hegel and the Rise of Social Theory.* Boston: Beacon Press, 1960.

———. *One Dimensional Man: Studies in the Ideology of Advanced Industrial Society.* Boston: Beacon Press, 1964.

Marx, Karl. *Critique of Hegel's "Philosophy of Right."* Translated by Annette Jolin and Joseph O'Malley. Cambridge, Eng.: Cambridge University Press, 1970.

Matthaei, Renate. *Luigi Pirandello.* Translated by Simon and Erika Young. New York: Frederick Ungar, 1973.

Matza, David. *Becoming Deviant.* Englewood Cliffs, N.J.: Prentice-Hall, 1969.

Mauner, George. *Manet, Peintre-Philosophe: A Study of the Painter's Themes.* University Park: Pennsylvania State University Press, 1975.

May, Charles. "Chekhov and the Modern Short Story." In *A Chekhov Companion.* Edited by Toby W. Clyman. 147–63. Westport, Conn.: Greenwood Press, 1985.

Mead, George H. *Mind, Self and Society: From the Standpoint of a Social Behaviorist.* Chicago: University of Chicago Press, 1934.

Menzies, Robert. "Psychiatrists in Blue: Police Apprehension of Mental Disorder and Dangerousness." *Criminology* 25 (1987): 429–53.

Merleau-Ponty, Maurice. *Sens et non-sens.* Paris: Nagel, 1948.

———. "Le Philosophe et la Sociologie." *Cahiers Internationaux de Sociologie* 10 (1951): 50–69.

———. *Phenomenology of Perception.* Translated by Colin Smith. London: Routledge, 1962.

———. *The Primacy of Perception.* Translated by James Edie. Evanston, Ill.: Northwestern University Press, 1964a.

———. *Sense and Non-Sense.* Translated by Hubert L. Dreyfus and Patricia A. Dreyfus. Evanston, Ill.: Northwestern University Press, 1964b.

———. *The Prose of the World.* Translated by John O'Neill. Evanston, Ill.: Northwestern University Press, 1973.

———. *Phenomenology, Language and Sociology: Selected Essays of Maurice Merleau-Ponty.* Edited by John O'Neill. London: Heinemann Educational, 1974.

———. *Notes des cours au Collège de France, 1958–1959 et 1960–1961.* Paris: Gallimard, 1996.

Michael, Jerome, and Mortimer Alder. *Crime, Law, and Social Science.* Montclair, N.J.: Patterson Smith, 1933/1971.

Milchman, Alan, and Alan Rosenberg, eds. *Foucault and Heidegger: Critical Encounters.* Minneapolis: University of Minnesota Press, 2003.

Moestrup, Jørn. *The Structural Patterns of Pirandello's Work*. Odense, Den.: Odense University Press, 1972.

Moran, Dermot. *Introduction to Phenomenology*. London: Routledge, 2000.

Morrison, Wayne. *Theoretical Criminology: From Modernity to Post-Modernism*. London: Cavendish Publishing, 1995.

Muir, William. *Police: Streetcorner Politicians*. Chicago: University of Chicago Press, 1977.

Murav, Harriet. *Holy Foolishness: Dostoevsky's Novels & the Politics of Cultural Critique*. Stanford, Calif.: Stanford University Press, 1992.

Musheno, Michael. "Interrogating Richard Leo's Claims about Police Scholarship." *Law and Society Review* 31:2 (1997): 389–91.

Musil, Robert. *Der Mann ohne Eigenschaften*. Hamburg: E. Rowohlt, 1952.

———. *Selected Writings*. Edited by Burton Pike. New York: Continuum, 1986.

———. *The Man Without Qualities*. 2 volumes. Translated by Sophie Wilkins and Burton Pike. New York: Vintage, 1995.

Natanson, Maurice. *Literature, Philosophy, and the Social Sciences: Essays in Existentialism and Phenomenology*. The Hague: Martinus Nijhoff, 1962.

———, ed. *Essays in Phenomenology*. The Hague: Martinus Nijhoff, 1966.

———, ed. *Phenomenology and Social Reality: Essays in Memory of Alfred Schutz*. The Hague: Martinus Nijhoff, 1970.

———, ed. *Phenomenology and the Social Sciences*. 2 volumes. Evanston, Ill.: Northwestern University Press, 1973.

———. *Phenomenology, Role, and Reason: Essays on the Coherence and Deformation of Social Reality*. Springfield, Ill.: Charles C. Thomas, 1974.

———. *Anonymity: A Study in the Philosophy of Alfred Schutz*. Bloomington: Indiana University Press, 1986.

———. *The Erotic Bird: Phenomenology in Literature*. Princeton, N.J.: Princeton University Press, 1998.

Naylor, Paul. "'The Idea of It': Wallace Stevens and Edmund Husserl." *Wallace Stevens Journal* 12:1 (1988): 44–55.

Nelken, David, ed. *The Futures of Criminology*. Thousand Oaks, Calif.: Sage, 1994.

Neyroud, Peter, and Alan Beckley. *Policing, Ethics and Human Rights*. Portland, Ore.: Willan Publishing, 2001.

Nietzsche, Friedrich. *Thus Spake Zarathustra*. Translated by Thomas Common. New York: Heritage Press, 1962.

———. *Werke*. Band I. Darmstadt, Ger.: Wissenschaftliche Buchgesellschaft, 1966.

———. *The Will to Power*. Translated by Walter Kaufmann and R. J. Hollingdale. New York: Random House, 1967.

———. *Also sprach Zarathustra*. Kritische Gesamtausgabe, Abteilung 6, Band 1. Berlin: Walter de Gruyter, 1968.

———. *The Gay Science*. Translated by Walter Kaufmann. New York: Vintage, 1974.

———. *Beyond Good and Evil*. Translated by Walter Kaufmann. New York: Vintage, 1989.

————. *On the Genealogy of Morality*. Translated by Carol Diethe. Cambridge, Eng.: Cambridge University Press, 1994.

————. *Untimely Meditations*. Edited by Daniel Breazeale. Translated by R. J. Hollingdale. Cambridge, Eng.: Cambridge University Press, 1997.

Offord, Derek. "The Causes of Crime and the Meaning of Law: *Crime and Punishment* and Contemporary Radical Thought." In *New Essays on Dostoyevsky*. Edited by Malcolm Jones and Garth Terry. 41–66. Cambridge, Eng.: Cambridge University Press, 1983.

Oliver, Roger. *Dreams of Passion: The Theater of Luigi Pirandello*. New York: New York University Press, 1979.

O'Malley, John. *The Fellowship of Being: An Essay on the Concept of Person in the Philosophy of Gabriel Marcel*. The Hague: Martinus Nijhoff, 1966.

O'Neill, John. *The Poverty of Postmodernism*. London: Routledge, 1995.

Paolucci, Anne. *Pirandello's Theater: The Recovery of the Modern Stage for Dramatic Art*. Carbondale: Southern Illinois University Press, 1974.

Paperman, Patricia. "Surveillance Underground: The Uniform as an Interaction Device." *Ethnography* 4:3 (2003): 397–419.

Parker, Patricia. "The Motive for Metaphor: Stevens and Derrida." *Wallace Stevens Journal* 7:3 (1983): 76–88.

Payne, Philip. *Robert Musil's "The Man Without Qualities": A Critical Study*. Cambridge, Eng.: Cambridge University Press, 1988.

Perrot, Michelle. *L'impossible prison: recherches sur le système pénitentiaire aux XIXe siècle*. Paris: Editions du Seuil, 1980.

Peters, Frederick. *Robert Musil, Master of the Hovering Life*. New York: Columbia University Press, 1978.

Peters, Heinz. *Rainer Maria Rilke: Masks and the Man*. Seattle: University of Washington Press, 1960.

Piliavin, Ivan, and Scott Briar. "Police Encounters With Juveniles." *American Journal of Sociology* 70:2 (1964): 206–14.

Pirandello, Luigi. *Così è (se vi pare)*. In *Maschere Nude*. Verona: Arnaldo Mondadori, 1953.

————. *Three Major Plays*. Translated by Carl R. Mueller. Hanover, N.H.: Smith and Kraus, 2000.

Plant, Margaret. *Paul Klee: Figures and Faces*. London: Thames and Hudson, 1978.

Pöggeler, Otto. *Bild und Technik: Heidegger, Klee, und die Moderne Kunst*. Munich: Fink, 2002.

Presdee, Mike. *Cultural Criminology and the Carnival of Crime*. London: Routledge, 2002.

Price, R., and B. Price. "Should the Police Officer Know What's Happening?" In *The Police in Society*. Edited by Emilio Viano and Jeffrey H. Reiman. 167–72. Lexington, Mass.: Lexington Books, 1975.

Prini, Pietro. "A Methodology of the Unverifiable." In *The Philosophy of Gabriel Marcel*.

Edited by Paul Schilpp and Lewis Hahn. 205–39. The Library of Living Philosophers, vol. XVII. La Salle, Ill.: Open Court, 1984.

Proust, Marcel. *À la recherche du temps perdu.* Volume 1, *Du cote de chez Swann.* Paris: Gallimard, 1954.

———. *Remembrance of Things Past.* Translated by C. K. Scott Moncrieff and Terence Kilmartin. Volume 1, *Swann's Way and Within a Budding Grove.* New York: Random House, 1981.

Punch, Maurice. *Policing the Inner City: A Study of Amsterdam's Warmoesstraat.* London: Macmillan, 1979.

Quinney, Richard. *Criminology: Analysis and Critique of Crime in America.* Boston: Little, Brown, 1975.

———. *Bearing Witness to Crime and Social Justice.* Albany: State University of New York Press, 2000.

Rabinowitz, Peter. "Truth in Fiction: A Reexamination of Audiences." *Critical Inquiry* 4 (1977): 121–41.

Rader, Dean. "Wallace Stevens, Octavio Paz, and the Poetry of Social Engagement." *Wallace Stevens Journal* 21:2 (1997): 175–94.

Ragusa, Olga. *Luigi Pirandello: An Approach to His Theatre.* Edinburgh: Edinburgh University Press, 1980.

Rayfield, Donald. *Understanding Chekhov: A Critical Study of Chekhov's Prose and Drama.* Madison: University of Wisconsin Press, 1999.

Reiman, Jeffrey. *Critical Moral Liberalism: Theory and Practice.* London: Rowman & Littlefield, 1997.

Reiss, Albert. "Stuff and Nonsense about Social Surveys and Observations." In *Institutions and the Person: Papers Presented to Everett C. Hughes.* Edited by Howard S. Becker et al. 351–67. Chicago: Aldine Publishing Company, 1968.

———. *The Police and the Public.* New Haven, Conn.: Yale University Press, 1971a.

———. "Systematic Observation of Natural Social Phenomena." In *Sociological Methodology.* Edited by Herbert Costner. San Francisco: Jossey-Bass, 1971b.

Reiss, Albert, and David Bordua. "Environment and Organization: A Perspective on the Police." In *The Police: Six Sociological Essays.* New York: Wiley, 1966.

Ricoeur, Paul. *The Symbolism of Evil.* Boston: Beacon Press, 1967.

———. *Freud and Philosophy: An Essay on Interpretation.* Translated by Denis Savage. New Haven, Conn.: Yale University Press, 1970.

———. *The Conflict of Interpretations: Essays in Hermeneutics.* Edited by Don Idhe. Evanston, Ill.: Northwestern University Press, 1974.

———. *The Rule of Metaphor: Multi-disciplinary Studies of the Creation of Meaning in Language.* Toronto: University of Toronto Press, 1977.

———. *Hermeneutics and the Human Sciences.* Cambridge, Eng.: Cambridge University Press, 1981.

———. "Gabriel Marcel and Phenomenology." In *The Philosophy of Gabriel Marcel.* Edited by Paul A. Schilpp and Lewis E. Hahn. 471–94. The Library of Living Philosophers, vol. 17. La Salle, Ill.: Open Court, 1984.

———. *From Text to Action: Essays in Hermeneutics*. Evanston, Ill: Northwestern University Press, 1991.

Riddel, Joseph. *The Clairvoyant Eye: The Poetry and Poetics of Wallace Stevens*. Baton Rouge: Louisiana State University Press, 1965.

Rieff, Philip. *The Triumph of the Therapeutic: Uses of Faith After Freud*. New York: Harper & Row, 1966.

Rilke, Rainer Maria. *Duino Elegies and The Sonnets to Orpheus*. Translated by A. Poulin Jr. Boston: Houghton Mifflin, 1975.

———. *New Poems*. Translated by Edward Snow. New York: North Point Press, 1907/1984.

———. *Letters on Cézanne*. Edited by Clara Rilke. Translated by Joel Agee. New York: Fromm International, 1985.

———. *New Poems: the Other Part*. Translated by Edward Snow. New York: North Point Press, 1908/1987.

———. *New Poems*. Revised bilingual edition. Translated by Edward Snow. New York: North Point Press, 2001.

Rock, Paul. *Deviant Behaviour*. London: Hutchinson & Co., 1973.

Rorty, Amélie. *The Many Faces of Evil: Historical Perspectives*. London: Routledge, 2001.

Rose, Niklas. *Governing the Soul: The Shaping of the Private Self*. London: Routledge, 1990.

Ross, Novelene. *Manet's Bar at the Folies-Bergère and the Myths of Popular Illustration*. Ann Arbor, Mich.: UMI Research Press, 1982.

Rowgowski, Christian. *Distinguished Outsider: Robert Musil and His Critics*. Columbia, S.C.: Camden House, 1994.

Rubin, James. *Manet's Silence and the Poetics of Bouquets*. London: Reaktion Books, 1994.

———. *Impressionism*. London: Phaidon Press, 1999.

Rubinstein, Jonathan. *City Police*. New York: Farrar, Straus and Giroux, 1973.

Ryan, Judith. *Rilke, Modernism, and Poetic Tradition*. Cambridge, Eng.: Cambridge University Press, 1999.

Ryan, Lawrence. "Neue Gedichte—New Poems." In *A Companion to the Works of Rainer Maria Rilke*. Edited by Erika Metzger and Michael Metzger. 128–53. Suffolk, Eng.: Camden House, 2001.

Sacks, Harvey. "Notes on Police Assessment of Moral Character." In *Studies in Social Interaction*. Edited by David Sudnow. 280–333. New York: Free Press, 1972.

Sagoff, Mark. "At the Shrine of Our Lady of Fatima or Why Political Questions Are Not All Economic." *Arizona Law Review* 23 (1981): 1283–98.

———. "The Principles of Federal Pollution Control Law." *Minnesota Law Review* 71 (1986): 55–68.

Sampson, Theodore. *A Cure of the Mind: The Poetics of Wallace Stevens*. Montreal: Black Rose Books, 2000.

Sartre, Jean-Paul. *Being and Nothingness: An Essay on Phenomenological Ontology.* Translated by Hazel Barnes. New York: Washington Square Press, 1966.

Scaff, Lawrence. *Fleeing the Iron Cage: Culture, Politics, and Modernity in the Thought of Max Weber.* Berkeley: University of California Press, 1988.

Scheler, Max. *Problems of a Sociology of Knowledge.* Translated by Manfred S. Frings. Edited by Kenneth W. Stikkers. London: Routledge & Kegan Paul, 1980.

———. *Ressentiment.* Translated by Lewis B. Coser and William W. Holdheim. Milwaukee: Marquette University Press, 1994.

Schilpp, Paul, and Lewis Hahn, eds. *The Philosophy of Gabriel Marcel.* The Library of Living Philosophers, vol. XVII. La Salle, Ill.: Open Court, 1984.

Schluchter, Wolfgang. *The Rise of Western Rationalism.* Berkeley: University of California Press, 1980.

Schutz, Alfred. *The Problem of Social Reality.* Collected Papers, volume 1. Edited by Maurice Natanson. The Hague: Martinus Nijhoff, 1962.

———. *On Phenomenology and Social Relations.* Edited by Helmut Wagner. Chicago: University of Chicago Press, 1970.

———. *Studies in Social Theory.* Collected Papers, volume 2. Edited by Arvid Broderson. The Hague: Martinus Nijhoff, 1971.

———. *The Phenomenology of the Social World.* Evanston, Ill.: Northwestern University Press, 1997.

Schutz, Alfred, and Thomas Luckmann. *The Structures of the Lifeworld.* 2 volumes. Translated by Richard M. Zaner and H. Tristram Engelhardt. Evanston, Ill.: Northwestern University Press, 1973/1989 [vol. 2].

Schwarz, Egon, ed. *Rainer Maria Rilke: Prose and Poetry.* New York: Continuum, 1984.

Shapiro, Gary, and Alan Sica, eds. *Hermeneutics: Questions and Prospects.* Amherst: University of Massachusetts Press, 1984.

Shaw, Priscilla. *Rilke, Valéry, and Yeats: The Domain of the Self.* New Brunswick, N.J.: Rutgers University Press, 1964.

Shearing, Clifford, and Peter Stenning. *Private Policing.* Newbury Park, Calif.: Sage Publications, 1987.

Sherman, Lawrence. "The Use and Usefulness of Criminology, 1751–2005: Enlightened Justice and Its Failures." *Annals of the AAPSS* 600 (2005): 115–35.

Silverman, Hugh. "The Self in Question." In *Phenomenology in Practice and Theory.* Edited by William S. Hamrick. 153–60. The Hague: Martinus Nijhoff, 1985.

Simmel, Georg. *On Individuality and Social Forms.* Edited by Donald N. Levine. Chicago: University of Chicago Press, 1971.

———. *Philosophy of Money.* 2nd edition. Edited by David Frisby. Translated by Tom Bottomore and David Frisby. London: Routledge, 1990.

Simmons, Ernest. *Introduction to Tolstoy's Writings.* Chicago: University of Chicago Press, 1968.

Sinicropi, Giovanni. "The Metaphysical Dimension and Pirandello's Theatre." *Modern Drama* 20:4 (1977): 353–80.

Skogan, Wesley. *Disorder and Decline: Crime and the Spiral of Decay in American Neighborhoods*. New York: Free Press, 1990.

Skolnick, Jerome. *Justice Without Trial: Law Enforcement in Democratic Society*. New York: Wiley, 1966.

Smith, Adam. *An Inquiry into the Nature and Causes of The Wealth of Nations*. Edited by Edwin Cannan. Chicago: University of Chicago Press, 1976.

Solomon, Robert, ed. *Phenomenology and Existentialism*. Lanham, Md.: Rowman & Littlefield, 2001.

Sophocles. *Antigone*. In *Sophocles II*. Edited and translated by Hugh Lloyd-Jones. Loeb Classical Library, volume 21. Cambridge, Mass.: Harvard University Press, 1994.

Speirs, Logan. *Tolstoy and Chekhov*. Cambridge, Eng.: Cambridge University Press, 1971.

Spiegelberg, Herbert. *The Phenomenological Movement: A Historical Introduction*. 3rd revised edition. The Hague: Martinus Nijhoff, 1982.

Steiner, George. *Tolstoy or Dostoevsky: An Essay in the Old Criticism*. New York: Alfred J. Knopf, 1959.

Stern, Joseph P. " 'Reality' in *Der Man ohne Eigenschaften*." In *Musil in Focus*. Edited by Lothar Huber and John J. White. 74–84. London: Institute for Germanic Studies, 1982.

Stevens, Wallace. *Collected Poetry and Prose*. Edited by Frank Kermode and Joan Richardson. New York: Library of America, 1997.

Straus, Erwin, and Richard Griffith, eds. *Aesthesis and Aesthetics: The Fourth Lexington Conference on Pure and Applied Phenomenology*. Pittsburgh: Duquesne University Press, 1970.

Strauss, Walter. "Rilke and Ponge: 'l'Objet c'est la Poétique.'" In *Rilke: The Alchemy of Alienation*. Edited by Frank Baron, Ernst Dick, and Warren Maurer. 63–94. Lawrence: Regents Press of Kansas, 1980.

Sudnow, David. *Passing On*. Englewood Cliffs, N.J.: Prentice-Hall, 1967.

———. *Studies in Social Interaction*. New York: Free Press, 1972.

Swaaningen, René van. *Critical Criminology: Visions from Europe*. London: Sage, 1997.

Sykes, Richard, and Edward Brent. *Policing: A Social Behaviorist Perspective*. New Brunswick, N.J.: Rutgers University Press, 1983.

Sykes, Richard, and John Clark. "A Theory of Deference Exchange in Police-Civilian Encounters." *American Journal of Sociology* 81 (1975): 584–600.

Taylor, Ian, Paul Walton, and Jock Young. *The New Criminology: For a Social Theory of Deviance*. London: Routledge & Kegan Paul, 1973.

Tedlock, Dennis, and Bruce Manheim, eds. *The Dialogic Emergence of Culture*. Champaign: University of Illinois Press, 1995.

Tellenbach, Hubertus. "Dostoyevsky's Prince Myshkin: Epilepsy Portrayed." In *Aesthesis and Aesthetics: The Fourth Lexington Conference on Pure and Applied Phenomenology*. Edited by Erwin Straus and Richard Griffith. Pittsburgh: Duquesne University Press, 1967.

Terry v. Ohio, 392 U.S. 1 (1968).

Theunissen, Michael. *The Other: Studies in the Social Ontology of Husserl, Heidegger, Sartre, and Buber.* Translated by Christopher Macann. Cambridge, Mass.: MIT Press, 1984.

Tiryakian, Edward. "Sociology and Existential Phenomenology." In *Phenomenology and the Social Sciences.* Volume 1. Edited by Maurice Natanson. 187–222. Evanston, Ill.: Northwestern University Press, 1973.

Toch, Hans, and J. Douglas Grant. *Police as Problem Solvers.* New York: Plenum Press, 1991.

Tolstoy, Leo. *Short Fiction.* Edited and translated by Michael R. Katz. New York: W.W. Norton, 1991.

Tribe, Laurence. "Policy Science: Analysis or Ideology?" *Philosophy and Public Affairs* 2 (1972): 66–110.

Trojanowicz, Robert, and Samuel Dixon. *Criminal Justice and the Community.* Englewood Cliffs, N.J.: Prentice-Hall, 1974.

Turner, Bryan, ed. *Theories of Modernity and Postmodernity.* London: Sage, 1990.

Van Maanen, John. "On Watching the Watchers." In *Policing: A View from the Street.* Edited by Peter K. Manning and John Van Maanen. 309–59. Santa Monica, Calif.: Goodyear Publishing, 1978.

———. *Tales of the Field: On Writing Ethnography.* Chicago: University of Chicago Press, 1988.

Vendler, Helen. *Wallace Stevens: Words Chosen Out of Desire.* Knoxville: University of Tennessee Press, 1984.

Verdi, Richard. *Klee and Nature.* London: A. Zwemmer, 1984.

Viano, Emilio, and Jeffrey Reiman, eds. *The Police in Society.* Proceedings of the First National Symposium on the Humanities and the Police. Lexington, Mass.: Lexington Books, 1975.

Vivante, Leone. *Essays on Art and Ontology.* Translated by Arturo Vivante. Salt Lake City: University of Utah Press, 1980.

Waddington, P. A. J. *Policing Citizens: Authenticity and Rights.* London: UCL Press, 1999.

Walter, Tony. *The Eclipse of Eternity: A Sociology of the Afterlife.* London: Macmillan, 1996.

Walton, Paul, and Jock Young, eds. *The New Criminology Revisited.* New York: St. Martin's Press, 1998.

Walzer, Michael. *Just and Unjust Wars: A Moral Argument with Historical Illustrations.* 4th edition. New York: Basic Books, 2006.

Wasiolek, Edward. *Tolstoy's Major Fiction.* Chicago: University of Chicago Press, 1978.

Weber, Max. *From Max Weber: Essays in Sociology.* Translated by H. Gerth and C. Wright Mills. Oxford, Eng.: Oxford University Press, 1946.

———. *On Law in Economy and Society.* Edited by Max. Rheinstein. Translated by Edward Shils and Max Rheinstein. New York: Simon and Schuster, 1954.

———. *The Protestant Ethic and the Spirit of Capitalism.* Translated by Talcott Parsons. New York: Scribner, 1958.

———. *Economy and Society.* 2 volumes. Edited by Guenther Roth and Claus Wittich. Berkeley: University of California Press, 1978.

Websdale, Neil. *Policing the Poor: From Slave Plantation to Public Housing.* Boston: Northeastern University Press, 2001.

Webster, Steven. "Dialogue and Fiction in Ethnography." *Dialectical Anthropology* 7 (1982): 91–114.

Weiss, Paul. "The Policeman: His Nature and Duties." In *The Police in Society.* Edited by Emilio Viano and Jeffrey Reiman. 25–31. Lexington, Mass.: Lexington Books, 1975.

Wellek, René. *Dostoevsky: A Collection of Critical Essays.* Englewood Cliffs, N.J.: Prentice-Hall, 1962.

Welty, Eudora. "Reality in Chekhov's Stories." In *Chekhov and Our Age: Responses to Chekhov by American Writers and Scholars.* Edited by James McConkey. 103–24. Ithaca, N.Y.: Center for International Studies and The Council of the Creative and Performing Arts, Cornell University, 1984.

Wender, Jonathan. "Phenomenology, Cultural Criminology and the Return to Astonishment." In *Cultural Criminology Unleashed.* 49–60. Edited by Jeff Ferrell, Keith Hayward, Wayne Morrison, and Mike Presdee. London: Routledge/Glasshouse, 2004.

Werckmeister, Otto. *The Making of Paul Klee's Career.* Chicago: University of Chicago Press, 1989.

Werthman, Carl, and Irving Piliavin. "Gang Members and the Police." In *The Police: Six Sociological Essays.* Edited by David Bordua. 56–98. New York: Wiley, 1966.

Westley, William. *Violence and the Police: A Sociological Study of Law, Custom, and Morality.* Cambridge, Mass.: MIT Press, 1970.

Wharton, Christine, and James Leonard. "Wallace Stevens as Phenomenologist." *Texas Studies in Literature and Language* 26 (1984): 331–61.

Wilson, Carlene, and Helen Braithwaite. "Police Patrolling, Resistance, and Conflict Resolution." In *Psychology and Policing.* Edited by N. Brewer and C. Wilson. 5–29. Hillsdale, N.J.: Lawrence Erlbaum, 1995.

Wilson, Christopher. *Cop Knowledge: Police Power and Cultural Narrative in Twentieth-Century America.* Chicago: University of Chicago Press, 2000.

Wilson, James Q. *Varieties of Police Behavior: The Management of Law and Order in Eight Communities.* Cambridge, Mass.: Harvard University Press, 1968.

Wilson, James Q., and George Kelling. "Broken Windows: The Police and Neighborhood Safety." *Atlantic Monthly* 127:3 (1982): 29–38.

Wood, Frank. *Rainer Maria Rilke: The Ring of Forms.* New York: Octagon Books, 1970.

Woods, Roy. *Rilke Through a Glass Darkly: Poetry of R. M. Rilke and Its English Translations.* Trier, Ger.: Wissenschaftlicher Verlag, 1996.

Young, Julian. *Heidegger's Philosophy of Art*. Cambridge, Eng.: Cambridge University Press, 2001.

Zaner, Richard. "*Eidos* and Science." In *Phenomenology and the Social Sciences: A Dialogue*. Edited by Joseph Bien. 1–19. The Hague: Martinus Nijhoff, 1978.

———. *The Context of Self: A Phenomenological Inquiry Using Medicine As A Clue*. Athens: Ohio University Press, 1981.

———. *Conversations on the Edge: Narratives of Ethics and Illness*. Washington, D.C.: Georgetown University Press, 2004.

Zaner, Richard, and Don Ihde. *Phenomenology and Existentialism*. New York: Putnam, 1973.

Ziarek, Krzysztof. *Inflected Language: Toward a Hermeneutics of Nearness*. Albany: State University of New York Press, 1994.

INDEX

JONATHAN M. WENDER is a former police sergeant
and is now a lecturer at the University of Washington in
the Department of Sociology and the Law, Societies, and
Justice Program.

The University of Illinois Press
is a founding member of the
Association of American University Presses.

Composed in 9.75/13.5 Scala
by Celia Shapland
at the University of Illinois Press
Manufactured by Thomson-Shore, Inc.

University of Illinois Press
1325 South Oak Street
Champaign, IL 61820-6903
www.press.uillinois.edu